# — Before the —
# SECOND COMING

# — Before the —
# SECOND COMING

RICHARD BRUNSON

CFI
An imprint of Cedar Fort, Inc.
Springville, Utah

Paperback ISBN 13: 978-1-4621-4948-3
eBook ISBN 13: 978-1-4621-4949-0

Published by CFI, an imprint of Cedar Fort, Inc.
2373 W. 700 S., Suite 100, Springville, UT 84663
Distributed by Cedar Fort, Inc., www.cedarfort.com

Library of Congress Control Number: 2025935306

Cover design by Shawnda Craig

Edited and Typeset by Liz Kazandzhy

Printed in the United States of America

10 9 8 7 6 5 4 3 2 1

Printed on acid-free paper

*This book is dedicated to my grandfather, Robert O. Brunson (1931–2012), and was written with him in mind.*

# Contents

## Part II: Understanding the Second Coming through Types and Shadows

# Preface

There is no easy way to say it. Some of the events leading up to the Second Coming are unpleasant to contemplate, let alone experience. However, because the purpose of this book is to place each of the various "signs of the times" in their correct chronological order, I was left with no choice but to discuss several of these unpleasant future events, and some in great detail.

Therefore, when reading this book, I would advise you of two things. First, we must not let our fear become stronger than our faith. We are told by the Lord that "if ye are prepared ye shall not fear" (Doctrine and Covenants 38:30). Second, it is only the events discussed early on in this book (chapters 1 through 4) that may bring fear and apprehension to you as you read. If you're feeling discouraged at any time during these first few chapters, I would advise you to continue reading through to chapter 5 and beyond. Chapter 5 of this work deals with the council of Adam-ondi-Ahman, which is a major turning point in the winding-up scenes of this temporal earth and marks a significant shift from bitter to sweet for those who seek after righteousness. The majority of events that occur after this council at Adam-ondi-Ahman (chapters 5–12) should bring nothing but comfort and joy to faithful Latter-day Saints.

# Part I

---

## The Signs of the Times

# 1
# Stakes of Zion

We know of many events that must occur before the Second Coming. But which of them will happen first? And which of them will happen last? One of the more difficult tasks when studying the Second Coming is determining the correct order in which these "signs of the times" are to occur. However, if we are able to place these future events in their proper order, we will be better prepared for what lies immediately ahead of us.

The purpose of this book is to give the reader a frame of reference regarding the timing of the Second Coming. While it is true that "no man knoweth" the day or hour of the Second Coming (Doctrine and Covenants 49:7), the Lord has nevertheless given us many signs to help us recognize when his coming is nigh: "And unto you it shall be given to know the signs of the times, and the signs of the coming of the Son of Man" (Doctrine and Covenants 68:11).

This book will place each of these "signs of the times" in chronological order so that we may look for them as they are happening. We will begin with the first sign that has yet to be fulfilled and work our way through each of the future signs that we as members of The Church of Jesus Christ of Latter-day Saints can expect to see before the Second Coming.

## Determining the First Sign

When the Apostle John was banished to the Isle of Patmos, the Lord revealed to him the entire 7,000-year period of the earth's existence. In the vision, John saw a scroll sealed with seven seals. The scroll represented the earth, and each seal represented one thousand years of the earth's temporal existence (see Doctrine and Covenants 77:6–7). When the first seal was opened, John saw the first thousand years of the earth's history; when the second seal was opened, he saw the second thousand years, and so on until all seven seals had been opened and shown to John.

We are currently living in the sixth seal. In other words, we are nearing the end of the earth's sixth thousand-year history.[1] Having this information allows us to study each event that is to occur at the end of the sixth seal and the beginning of the seventh seal—all of which must come to pass before the Second Coming (see Doctrine and Covenants 77:12–13).

In addition to John the Revelator, the prophet Nephi was also shown in vision many of these same future events. Nephi's record, however, contains the first half of this latter-day vision, while John's record focuses more on the second half (see 1 Nephi 14:18–30). It is therefore in Nephi's record where we begin our study.

## Upon All the Face of the Earth

After Nephi was shown in vision the events leading up to our day, including the discovery of America and the Restoration of the gospel (see 1 Nephi 13), his record states, "I beheld that the church of the Lamb, who were the saints of God, were also upon all the face of the earth" (1 Nephi 14:12).

As far as we can tell, this is the time period in which we are currently living. Much like Nephi, many of us have had the privilege of witnessing firsthand the gospel message being spread "upon all the face of the earth" (1 Nephi 14:12). Remarkably, however, as much membership growth as our Church has experienced to date, all signs

---

1. When this sixth thousand-year history comes to an end, the final thousand-year period known as the Millennium will begin (see Doctrine and Covenants 77:12).

seem to indicate that there is still more to come. For example, the Prophet Joseph Smith stated, "The Standard of Truth has been erected; no unhallowed hand can stop the work from progressing; persecutions may rage, mobs may combine, armies may assemble, calumny may defame, but the truth of God will go forth boldly, nobly, and independent, till it has penetrated every continent, visited every clime, swept every country, and sounded in every ear."[2]

Elder Bruce R. McConkie stated in 1978:

> There are nations today to whom we have not gone. . . . But you can rest assured that we will fulfill the requirement of taking the gospel to those nations before the Second Coming of the Son of Man. . . .
>
> I have no hesitancy whatever in saying that before the Lord comes, in all those nations we will have congregations that are stable, secure, devoted, and sound. We will have stakes of Zion. We will have people who have progressed in spiritual things to the point where they have received all of the blessings of the house of the Lord. That is the destiny.[3]

Of course, as the gospel message continues to spread throughout the earth in the latter days, Satan and his forces of evil will also continue to gain momentum in their efforts as well. Nephi wrote, "And it came to pass that I looked and beheld the whore of all the earth, and she sat upon many waters; and she had dominion over all the earth, among all nations, kindreds, tongues, and people" (1 Nephi 14:11). At this point in his vision, Nephi was then shown something that all Latter-day Saints living in our day should be cognizant of. We read, "I beheld that the great mother of abominations did gather together multitudes upon the face of all the earth, among all the nations of the Gentiles, to fight against the Lamb of God" (1 Nephi 14:13).

---

2. *History of the Church*, 4:540. The Prophet Joseph Smith said on a second occasion that this Church will eventually "fill the world" (Wilford Woodruff, in Conference Report, Apr.1898, 57). Similarly, Wilford Woodruff said that "there is no ear but what has to be penetrated with the sound of the Gospel of Christ" (*Journal of Discourses*, 10:16).

3. Bruce R. McConkie, "All Are Alike Unto God" (Brigham Young University devotional, Aug. 18, 1978), 2, speeches.byu.edu. See also Bruce R. McConkie, "New Revelation On Priesthood," in *Priesthood* (Deseret Book, 1981), 126–137; Doctrine and Covenants 65:2.

What will this fight entail? Where and how will it be fought? And who will prevail? The answer to these questions and more will be the subject matter of our next chapter.

# 2
# Persecution

As it turns out, Nephi was not the only prophet who was shown this upcoming conflict between Satan's followers and the followers of Christ. Indeed, many modern-day prophets were also shown this particular time period in vision, and as we shall see, they described this conflict not as a fight or war but rather as a period of bitter persecution.

For example, Elder Heber C. Kimball tells of an occasion when he and Brigham Young were together pondering the restored gospel when the heavens were opened unto them. He stated, "The glory of God shone upon us, and we saw the gathering of the saints . . . and many more things connected with that great event, such as the sufferings and persecutions that would come upon the people of God."[1]

Later in his life, when Elder Kimball was living in Salt Lake City, Utah, he expounded further on this heavenly vision and gave more details.[2] He said:

---

1. Orson F. Whitney, *Life of Heber C. Kimball* (Bookcraft, 1945), 19.
2. That Heber C. Kimball is referencing this same vision is an assumption made by this author.

> An army of Elders will be sent to the four quarters of the earth to search out the righteous and warn the wicked of what is coming. All kinds of religions will be started and miracles performed that will deceive the very elect if that were possible. Our sons and daughters must live pure lives so as to be prepared for what is coming.
>
> After a while the Gentiles will gather by the thousands to this place, and Salt Lake City will be classed among the wicked cities of the world. A spirit of speculation and extravagance will take possession of the Saints, and the results will be financial bondage.
>
> Persecution comes next and all true Latter-day Saints will be tested to the limit. Many will apostatize and others will be still not knowing what to do. . . .
>
> The Saints will be put to tests that will try the integrity of the best of them. The pressure will become so great that the more righteous among them will cry unto the Lord day and night until deliverance comes.[3]

This Heber C. Kimball prophecy provides us with a wealth of information. Among other things, it speaks of a day when missionaries will be sent to the "four quarters of the earth," a time period which could very well be describing our day. It also reveals that toward the later end of this period of missionary work, we will experience some economic turmoil of sorts, which will result in financial bondage, and we will also be subject to some persecution.

Of this future persecution, Elder Orson Pratt said that there will come a time when the Gentiles will "persecute [God's] servants and his people all the day long."[4] Joseph Smith prophesied that prior to Zion being built, then "will persecution rage more and more, for the iniquities of men shall be revealed, and those who are not built upon the rock will seek to overthrow this church."[5]

While we are not told how long this persecution will last, Elder Heber C. Kimball did reveal that the Saints will "cry unto the Lord day and night until deliverance comes."[6] This phrase suggests that the faith and patience of all of us will be tried and tested to the limit.

---

3. "Prophecy of Heber C. Kimball," *Deseret News,* May 23, 1931, 3.

4. *Journal of Discourses*, 20:146.

5. Joseph Smith, "Letter VIII," *Messenger and Advocate*, Oct. 2, 1835, 199.

6. "Prophecy of Heber C. Kimball," 3.

Elder Orson Pratt went so far as to say that the Lord may bring us into "greater tribulation than that which we have hitherto had."[7] President J. Reuben Clark agreed, saying, "We of this Church will . . . have more sacrifices to make and more persecutions to endure than we have yet known, heavy as our sacrifices and grievous as our persecutions of the past have been."[8]

These last two statements are impressive when we consider the many persecutions that the early Saints endured.

## The Purpose of Persecution

Why then, would God allow this persecution? What good can possibly come from having us endure such hardship? President Brigham Young explains: "I know that those who have been in our past troubles—those who have been in the midst of death and destitution can bear testimony that they never enjoyed so much of the Spirit of the Lord at any other time in their lives."[9]

Hugh Nibley gave us the following insight regarding persecution: "In every dispensation of the gospel, the Lord has insisted on segregating his covenant people from the rest of the world: if they were not ready to 'come out of her, my people' willingly, he saw to it that the world was more than willing to persecute and expel them."[10] He also stated, "'Happy is the man whom God correcteth!' If the Lord still loves the Saints, He will treat them as before and give them some very rough times indeed to bring them to their senses."[11]

As Brother Nibley explains, those who endure this persecution will have great cause to rejoice; for as the Lord said during the Sermon on the Mount, "Blessed are ye, when men shall revile you, and persecute you, and shall say all manner of evil against you falsely, for my sake. Rejoice, and be exceeding glad: for great is your reward in

---

7. *Journal of Discourses*, 17:303.
8. Conference Report, Apr. 1944, 116.
9. *Journal of Discourses*, 5:337–38.
10. Hugh Nibley, *Approaching Zion*, ed. Don E. Norton (Deseret Book and FARMS, 1991), 341.
11. Nibley, *Approaching Zion*, 369.

heaven: for so persecuted they the prophets which were before you" (Matthew 5:11–12).

Elder Bruce R. McConkie added, "When the saints suffer persecution for righteousness' sake, they stand in the place and stead of Christ and are receiving what the ungodly would heap upon the Son of God were he personally present."[12]

In anticipation of this period of persecution, President Jeffery R. Holland gave us these words of reassurance:

> With admiration and encouragement for everyone who will need to remain steadfast in these latter days, I say to all and especially the youth of the Church that if you haven't already, you will one day find yourself called upon to defend your faith or perhaps even endure some personal abuse simply because you are a member of The Church of Jesus Christ of Latter-day Saints.[13]

> When you struggle, when you are rejected, when you are spit upon and cast out and made a hiss and a byword, you are standing with the best life this world has ever known, the only pure life ever lived. You have reason to stand tall and be grateful that the Living Son of the Living God knows all about your sorrows and afflictions.[14]

In order to understand the purpose of this future persecution, it must be remembered that the Lord needs a group of worthy Saints to assist in building up Zion, and as the Lord said in the Doctrine and Covenants, "Zion cannot be built up unless it is by the principles of the law of the celestial kingdom; otherwise I cannot receive her unto myself. *And my people must needs be chastened until they learn obedience*, if it must needs be, by the things which they suffer" (Doctrine and Covenants 105:5–6; emphasis added).

This persecution phase will do two things. First, it will help us learn obedience and rely on the Lord. This will strengthen those who

---

12. Bruce R. McConkie, *Doctrinal New Testament Commentary* (Bookcraft, 1973), 2:530.
13. Jeffrey R. Holland, "The Cost—and Blessings—of Discipleship," *Ensign*, May 2014, 6.
14. Jeffrey R. Holland, "Missionary Work and the Atonement," *Ensign*, Mar. 2001, 15.

desire to live a celestial law and help them build up Zion. Second, it will separate out from the righteous the less faithful members of the Church who secretly desire to follow after worldly things.[15] This is important because the Lord cannot allow half-committed people to dwell in Zion; it is reserved exclusively for the pure in heart (see Doctrine and Covenants 97:21). Elder McConkie taught us the following: “Persecution is the tool of Satan to harass, hinder, and destroy, if possible, the cause of righteousness. The spiritually weak, the lukewarm disciples, those who have not given themselves wholly to the Cause of Christ are purged from the Church by persecution.”[16]

## The Constitution to Hang by a Thread

What will be the cause of this future persecution? If we were to use world history as our guide, we would discover that the worst cases of religious persecutions—whether among Christians or otherwise—is usually inflicted upon the believers by a wicked government.

For example, the ancient Israelites were put in bondage by the pharaoh of Egypt. The early Christians suffered bitter persecutions at the hand of the Roman Empire. The Jews, during World War II, were placed in concentration camps by Nazi Germany. The Saints of this dispensation suffered terribly under the Extermination Order, signed into effect by Missouri governor Lilburn Boggs, which called for the extermination and expulsion of all Latter-day Saints from the state of Missouri.

These are just a few examples of the abuses that have been inflicted upon a religious people by wicked governments throughout history. With this in mind, is it inconceivable to think that the prophesied persecutions of our day will come at the hands of a corrupt United States government?

While we cannot say for sure, it is certainly a possibility. Joseph Smith once prophesied that “the time would come when the

---

15. An example of how persecution separates out the less faithful while at the same time strengthens the humble followers of God is found in Alma 1:19–28.

16. Bruce R. McConkie, *Doctrinal New Testament Commentary*, 2:63.

Constitution . . . would hang by a brittle thread,"[17] and it is not a stretch of the imagination to believe that our future persecutions would come as a result of this event. Brigham Young stated that "mobs . . . will increase until the whole [United States] government becomes a mob."[18] And President J. Reuben Clark shared, "I say unto you with all the soberness I can, that we stand in danger of losing our liberties, and that once lost . . . we of this Church will, in order to keep the Church going forward, have more sacrifices to make and more persecutions to endure than we have yet known."[19]

## Armed with the Power of God

While we are unsure where the source of this persecution will ultimately come from, one thing we do know for certain is that those who choose to remain on the Lord's side during this persecution phase will be given great power from God to endure their hardships and will make it through with a strengthened desire to build Zion. As Nephi shared in his vision, "I, Nephi, beheld the power of the Lamb of God, that it descended upon the saints of the church of the Lamb, and upon the covenant people of the Lord, who were scattered upon all the face of the earth; *and they were armed with righteousness and with the power of God in great glory*" (1 Nephi 14:14; emphasis added).

President Russell M. Nelson said of this verse, "We live in the day that 'our forefathers have awaited with anxious expectation.' We have front-row seats to witness live what the prophet Nephi saw only in vision. . . . You, my brothers and sisters, are among those men, women, and children whom Nephi saw. Think of that!"[20]

If we continue to live faithfully, we will continue to see God's power being poured down upon our heads, which will help us bear our trials with patience. And with this increase of faith in the Lord,

---

17. James Burgess Journal, 1818–1904, Church Archives, vol. 1—found among loose sermons, as quoted in D. Michael Stewart, "What Do We Know About the Purported Statement of Joseph Smith That the Constitution Would Hang by a Thread and That the Elders Would Save It?," *Ensign*, June 1976, 65.

18. *Journal of Discourses*, 9:5.

19. Conference Report, Apr. 1944, 116.

20. Russell M. Nelson, "Hear Him," *Ensign*, May 2020, 88.

we as members of the Church will move one step closer to building up Zion.

Before we are allowed to build this Zion, however, there is much that needs to occur. Nephi went on to tell us of one thing that must happen first: "And it came to pass that I beheld that the wrath of God was poured out upon that great and abominable church" (1 Nephi 14:15).

As we shall see in the upcoming chapters, this wrath of God will be manifest by a worldwide destruction of nations.

# 3
# The Times of the Gentiles

Before we can fully comprehend what happens after the persecution stage discussed in the previous chapter, we must first understand what is meant by the phrase "times of the Gentiles" (Doctrine and Covenants 45:25).

During the Savior's ministry on earth, the gospel message went almost exclusively to the literal descendants of the house of Israel (see Matthew 10:5–6; 15:24). However, after Jesus was crucified and after the Jews had rejected the gospel message, Peter was told in vision that the new priority was to send the gospel message not to the Jews but to the Gentiles (see Acts 10:9–16).[1] This opened a new era in the Lord's missionary program, and the "times of the Gentiles" officially began.[2]

The important thing to keep in mind as we discuss the events of the last days is that the Lord has not yet reversed this command given to Peter. This means that we are still living during the times of the Gentiles. In other words, to this day we are instructed to take the

---

1. See also *Teachings of the Prophet Joseph Smith*, sel. Joseph Fielding Smith (1976), 15.

2. The times of the Gentiles was renewed again in the latter days in connection with the Restoration of the gospel (see Doctrine and Covenants 45:28).

gospel message "first unto the Gentiles and secondly unto the Jews" (Doctrine and Covenants 107:33). It is for this reason that Elder Orson Pratt said, "We have sought diligently, therefore, to perform our mission to the Gentiles. We have not gone to the house of Israel, because that was not the commandment. We were commanded of the Lord our God, to preach to, the Gentiles first."[3]

We are told that all Gentiles who become converted to the Lord's Church, during the times of the Gentiles or otherwise, will be adopted into the house of Israel. Joseph Smith taught that "the effect of the Holy Ghost upon a Gentile, is to purge out the old blood, and make him actually of the seed of Abraham."[4] However, while the Church will see many Gentile converts during this time period, we are told that the majority of the Gentiles will reject the gospel message and continue to sin against God.

Either by and by, or perhaps at a fixed point in time, we are told that "the times of the Gentiles [will] be fulfilled" (Doctrine and Covenants 45:25). In other words, there will come a time when missionary work will be re-prioritized and the gospel message will be taken from the Gentiles and offered instead to the literal descendants of the house of Israel (see Doctrine and Covenants 133:8; Romans 8:25–27; Luke 21:21). In this way, "the last shall be first, and the first shall be last" (1 Nephi 13:42). Elder Orson Pratt explained:

> Having established his kingdom, [God] offers it first to these Gentile nations, if they will receive it; and when they shall account themselves unworthy of the kingdom, unworthy of eternal life, unworthy of the message which God has sent to them, and shall persecute his servants and his people all the day long, and shall close up their sanctuaries, their Churches, their chapels, their meetinghouses, and their places of worship against this message, and when it can no longer find place among them . . . the servants of God will . . . confine no longer their mission to the Gentiles; but they will receive a commission from the Almighty to go to the

---

3. *Journal of Discourses*, 20:146.

4. *Teachings of the Prophet Joseph Smith*, 149.

> scattered remnants of the House of Israel, wherever they may be located.[5]

## Missionaries Called Home

The method the Lord will use to take the gospel message from among the Gentile nations will be to literally bring his missionaries home. This was made clear by Elder Heber C. Kimball who taught that once the times of the Gentiles are fulfilled, "our Elders from far and near will be called home, or in other words the gospel will be taken from the Gentiles and later on carried to the Jews."[6]

Elder Orson Pratt also declared:

> When God has called out the righteous, when the warning voice has been sufficiently proclaimed among these Gentile nations, and the Lord says "It is enough," he will also say to his servants—"O, ye, my servants, come home, come out from the midst of these Gentile nations, where you have labored and borne testimony for so long a period; come out from among them, for they are not worthy; they do not receive the message that I have sent forth, they do not repent of their sins; come out from their midst, their times are fulfilled . . . " What then? Then the word of the Lord will be—"O, ye, my servants, I have a new commission for you. Instead of going forth to convert the Gentile nations, go unto the remnants of the house of Israel that are scattered in the four quarters of the earth. Go and proclaim to them that the times of their dispersion are accomplished; that the times of the Gentiles are fulfilled."[7]

As we shall soon see, the scattered Israelites that Elder Pratt is referring to here will include the Jews, the Lamanites, and the lost

---

5. *Journal of Discourses*, 20:146. See also *Journal of Discourses*, 18:177.

6. *Deseret News*, May 23, 1931.

7. *Journal of Discourses*, 18:64. Elder Orson Pratt on a second occasion said that when the times of the Gentiles are fulfilled, "the Lord will, after a while, designate by revelation, and say unto his servants, 'It is enough. You have been faithful in laboring in my vineyard, for the last time.'" *Journal of Discourses*, 20:146.

ten tribes.[8] It should also be noted that while the Lord's missionary efforts will shift to the house of Israel at this time, their conversions will come by and by.

Each of these Israelite conversions will be discussed as they occur in our story, but first, we are told that before the house of Israel is converted at large, there will be terrible destructions among many of the Gentile nations who rejected the gospel message.

## Destruction of Gentile Nations

We are told that the times of the Gentiles will come to an end once the Gentiles nations have sufficiently ignored the missionaries' call to repentance. Once this occurs, the Lord Himself will begin to preach repentance to these nations, but rather than doing so by the testimonies of His missionaries, he will begin preaching sermons in the form of natural disasters. In section 88 of the Doctrine and Covenants, the Lord has instructed his missionaries:

> Go forth among the Gentiles for the last time. . . .
>
> Verily, I say unto you . . . continue in the vineyard until the mouth of the Lord shall call them [home]. . . .
>
> For after your testimony cometh the testimony of earthquakes. . . .
>
> And also cometh the testimony of the voice of thunderings, and the voice of lightnings, and the voice of tempests, and the voice of the waves of the sea heaving themselves beyond their bounds.
>
> And all things shall be in commotion; and surely, men's hearts shall fail them; for fear shall come upon all people. (Doctrine and Covenants 88:84–85, 89–91; see also 90:7–11)

Perhaps this was the time period the Lord had in mind when He said:

> For if I, who am a man, do lift up my voice and call upon you to repent, and ye hate me, what will ye say when the day cometh when the thunders shall utter their voices from the ends of the earth,

8. At this point in our story, the whereabouts of the lost ten tribes will still be unknown to the world, and the fulness of the gospel will not be offered to them until they have made their return. The details of their return and conversion will be discussed in chapters 7 and 8.

> speaking to the ears of all that live, saying—Repent, and prepare for the great day of the Lord?
>
> Yea, and again, when the lightnings shall streak forth from the east unto the west, and shall utter forth their voices unto all that live, and make the ears of all tingle that hear, saying these words—Repent ye, for the great day of the Lord is come? (Doctrine and Covenants 43:21–22)

President Wilford Woodruff spoke of many of these future natural disasters when he said:

> By-and-by the Elders of Israel will be taken from those nations where they are now preaching, and there will be another set of Missionaries sent amongst the people; there will be the voice of lightning, the noise of war, and of all those judgments which have been enumerated and prophesied of since the beginning of time, and they will go forth among the nations until the land is cleansed from the abominations that now reign upon the face of the earth.[9]

As alluded to here by President Woodruff, in addition to natural disasters, we are told that terrible wars will also arise at this time, along with famines, plagues, scourges, and other forms of destruction. Each of these forms of destruction will be discussed in more detail hereafter.

## Doctrine and Covenants Section 45

Perhaps the best place to learn about this timeline is found in section 45 of the Doctrine and Covenants. Here the Lord repeats a conversation He had with His original disciples upon the Mount of Olives at Jerusalem during His mortal ministry. He states, "And this I have told you concerning [the future destruction of] Jerusalem [by the Romans in AD 70]; and when that day shall come, shall a remnant [of the Jews] be scattered among all nations; But they shall be gathered again; but they shall remain [scattered] *until the times of the Gentiles be fulfilled*" (Doctrine and Covenants 45:24–25; emphasis added).

---

9. *Journal of Discourses,* 10:16.

An important takeaway from these verses is that the Jews and other branches of the house of Israel are to remain scattered until the times of the Gentiles are fulfilled. The Lord continued:

> And in that day [once the times of the Gentiles are fulfilled] shall be heard of wars and rumors of wars, and the whole earth shall be in commotion, and men's hearts shall fail them, and they shall say that Christ delayeth his coming until the end of the earth. . . .
>
> And there shall be men standing in that generation, that shall not pass until they shall see an overflowing scourge; for a desolating sickness shall cover the land. . . .
>
> And there shall be earthquakes also in divers places, and many desolations; yet men will harden their hearts against me, and they will take up the sword, one against another, and they will kill one another. (Doctrine and Covenants 45:26, 31, 33)

The Lord in these verses speaks of several forms of destruction that will occur once the times of the Gentiles are fulfilled. These include wars and rumors of wars (verse 26), an overflowing scourge (verse 31), a sickness that shall cover the land (verse 31), earthquakes (verse 33), desolations (verse 33), and last but not least, men who will be determined to take up the sword to kill one another (verse 33). We are told that these various destructions will take so many lives during this time period that those who remain will wonder if there will be anyone on earth left alive by the time the Lord makes His return (verse 26).

The Lord concluded this sermon as follows: "And now, when I the Lord had spoken these words unto my disciples, they were troubled. And I said unto them: Be not troubled, for, when all these things shall come to pass, ye may know that the promises which have been made unto you shall be fulfilled" (Doctrine and Covenants 45:34–35).

The "promises" that the Lord is referring to here include the promise to gather the house of Israel to the lands of their inheritance (see 1 Nephi 10:5–7; 19:13–16; 3 Nephi 20:29). And as we shall see in later chapters, for some branches of the house of Israel, these promises also include the opportunity to partake in the building up of Zion, the New Jerusalem (see 3 Nephi 20:21–22).

## Nephi's Account

In addition to the Lord, there have been many prophets who have also given us valuable commentary on these future events. One of these prophets was Nephi. After Nephi described the period of persecution that the Saints must endure (see 1 Nephi 14:13), he described the period of destruction that follows once the times of the Gentiles are fulfilled: "And it came to pass that I beheld that the wrath of God was poured out upon that great and abominable church, insomuch that there were wars and rumors of wars among all the nations and kindreds of the earth" (1 Nephi 14:15).

After Nephi saw this future destruction, his angelic guide spoke unto him, saying, "And when the day cometh that the wrath of God is poured out upon the mother of harlots, which is the great and abominable church of all the earth, whose founder is the devil, then, at that day, the work of the Father shall commence, in preparing the way for the fulfilling of his covenants, which he hath made to his people who are of the house of Israel" (1 Nephi 14:17).

Thus, after the period of persecution has passed, the times of the Gentiles will be fulfilled, which will bring with it a period of devastating destruction. After this destruction, the Lord will fulfill His promises by once again bringing the fulness of the gospel to the house of Israel, which will result in a great spiritual and physical gathering and eventually the building up of Zion.

## By Way of Comparison

It is important to understand that these future natural disasters will be much worse and will occur at a much more accelerated rate than at the present. Many Latter-day Saints have simply assumed that because we have witnessed natural disasters occurring more frequently in our lifetimes, we must be living in the time period spoken of in these passages.

While it's clear that we have seen a large increase in natural disasters over the past century or so, we will no doubt find that they will pale in comparison to the natural disasters that will occur once the times of the Gentiles are fulfilled. President Brigham Young taught:

Do you think there is calamity abroad now among the people? Not much. All we have yet heard and all we have experienced is scarcely a preface to the sermon that is going to be preached. When the testimony of the Elders ceases to be given, and the Lord says to them, "Come home; I will now preach my own sermons to the nations of the earth," all you now know can scarcely be called a preface to the sermon that will be preached with fire and sword, tempests, earthquakes, hail, rain, thunders and lightnings, and fearful destruction. . . . You will hear of magnificent cities, now idolized by the people, sinking in the earth, entombing the inhabitants. The sea will heave itself beyond its bounds, engulfing mighty cities. Famine will spread over the nations. . . . You may think that the little you hear of now is grievous; yet the faithful of God's people will see days that will cause them to close their eyes because of the sorrow that will come upon the wicked nations.[10]

10. *Journal of Discourses*, 8:123. See also *Journal of Discourses*, 18:38.

# 4

# What of the United States?

While we are told that these prophesied destructions will affect many Gentile nations worldwide, there is one nation in particular that has been singled out by the prophets: the United States of America. The Prophet Joseph Smith stated, "I am prepared to say by the authority of Jesus Christ, that not many years shall pass away before the United States shall present such a scene of bloodshed as has not a parallel in the history of our nation; pestilence, hail, famine, and earthquake will sweep the wicked of this generation from off the face of the land."[1]

President Wilford Woodruff added: "The American nation will be broken in pieces like a potter's vessel, and will be cast down to hell if it does not repent—and this, because of murders, whoredoms, wickedness and all manner of abominations, for the Lord has spoken it."[2]

Looking back at the history of North and South America, it is very apparent that the Lord views these lands as sacred. So sacred, in fact, that the Lord either destroyed or nearly destroyed several civilizations

---

1. *Teachings of the Prophet Joseph Smith,* sel. Joseph Fielding Smith (1976), 17.
2. Matthias F. Cowley, *Wilford Woodruff: History of His Life and Labors* (Bookcraft, 1964), 500.

who lived on these lands because of wickedness. This includes the Antediluvians—or those who were destroyed at the time of the Flood (see Genesis 7)[3]—the Jaredites (see Ether 15:29–32), the Nephites (see Mormon 6), the Lamanites (see 1 Nephi 13:14), and others.[4]

Many of these civilizations were taught the gospel and were ultimately destroyed because of their refusal to keep the commandments. When we compare these civilizations to other civilizations who were living in other parts of the world during these same time periods, we find out just how serious God is about having the inhabitants of this land keep His commandments. In the words of Hugh Nibley, "Egypt, Greece, India, China, the unchanging East have all paid the price of survival with endless suffering, yet their civilizations are still in place. But it is a different story in the New World, where great civilizations have arisen and collapsed for reasons that students are still wholly at a loss to explain. They just disappeared, and nobody knows why. And I think that is a warning."[5]

A warning it is indeed. We are the next to live on this great land. Those who think that we as Americans can live on this land and break God's commandments without facing the same consequences that previous civilizations faced have failed to learn from history.

Sadly, several Book of Mormon prophets "foresaw that we would take the same dangerous path as their people did."[6] One such prophet was Mormon, who warned, "O ye Gentiles, how can ye stand before the power of God, except ye shall repent and turn from your evil ways? Know ye not that ye are in the hands of God? Know ye not that he hath all power, and at his great command the earth shall be rolled

3. According to Elder Orson Pratt, "It was on this land Noah built his ark, which was blown by the winds of Heaven away to the east, and landed on [Mount] Ararat." *Journal of Discourses*, 12:338.

4. This also includes other ancient civilizations in North and South America, such as the Aztec Empire and to some extent the Inca Empire and the American Indians. For clarification, it is of this author's opinion that the Jaredites were among the Olmec civilization and that the Nephites and Lamanites were among the Maya civilization.

5. Hugh Nibley, *Approaching Zion*, ed. Don E. Norton (Deseret Book and FARMS, 1991), 416.

6. Douglas E. Brinley, *America's Hope: Why Every Other Civilization Has Failed and What You Can Do to Save This One* (Deseret Book, 2005), 31.

together as a scroll? Therefore, repent ye, and humble yourselves before him, *lest he shall come out in justice against you*" (Mormon 5:22–24; emphasis added).

Moroni was another Book of Mormon prophet to see our day (see Mormon 8:35). On several occasions, Moroni felt compelled to warn us about the destructions that are at our door. For example, he told us :

> [The Lord] had sworn in his wrath . . . that whoso should possess this land of promise . . . should serve him, the true and only God, or they should be swept off when the fulness of his wrath should come upon them . . .
>
> And the fulness of his wrath cometh upon them when they are ripened in iniquity.
>
> For behold, this is a land which is choice above all other lands; wherefore he that doth possess it shall serve God or shall be swept off; for it is the everlasting decree of God.
>
> *And this cometh unto you, O ye Gentiles*, that ye may know the decrees of God—that ye may repent, and not continue in your iniquities . . . *that ye may not bring down the fulness of the wrath of God upon you as the inhabitants of the land have hitherto done.* (Ether 2:8–11; emphasis added)

On a second occasion, Moroni warned us again, saying, "O ye Gentiles, it is wisdom in God that these things should be shown unto you, that thereby ye may repent of your sins . . . *or wo be unto it*" (Ether 8:23–24; emphasis added).

On a third occasion, Moroni warned us yet again: "Behold, I speak unto you as if ye were present, and yet ye are not. But behold, Jesus Christ hath shown you unto me, and I know your doing. . . . *Behold, the sword of vengeance hangeth over you*" (Mormon 8:35, 41; emphasis added).

As Hugh Nibley noted, "It is into our hands that the Book of Mormon has been placed. . . . Plainly it is meant for us, as it reminds us many times; it is the story of what happened to the Nephites—*and we are the Nephites*: 'It must needs be that the riches of the earth are mine to give; but beware of pride, lest ye become as the Nephites of old' (Doctrine and Covenants 38:39)."[7]

With these warnings in mind, we now turn to some of the prophesied destructions that will occur in America if we as a nation do not repent.

## THE REMNANT OF JACOB

When the Lord appeared to the Nephites in the Book of Mormon after His Resurrection, He taught them throughout several chapters (3 Nephi 16, 20, and 21) of a future conflict between the latter-day Gentiles living in America[8] and a group of people the Lord referred to as "a remnant of Jacob" (3 Nephi 21:12)—a group identified in the Book of Mormon as the seed of Lehi, which consists primarily of Lamanite descendants today (see 1 Nephi 13:34; Alma 46:23; 3 Nephi 20:10–16; 3 Nephi 21:3).

The Lord set the stage for these sermons by first explaining to the Nephites what the times of the Gentiles were and what would occur once they are fulfilled (see 3 Nephi 16:10–11; 3 Nephi 20:28–29). Once the Lord established this timeline, He then described the conflict that would occur between these two groups of people after the times of the Gentiles have come to an end:

> And my people who are a remnant of Jacob shall be among the Gentiles, yea, in the midst of them as a lion among the beasts of the forest, as a young lion among the flocks of sheep, who, if he go through both treadeth down and teareth in pieces, and none can deliver.
>
> Their hand shall be lifted up upon their adversaries, and all their enemies shall be cut off.

---

7. Hugh Nibley, *Since Cumorah*, ed. John W. Welch (Deseret Book and FARMS, 1988), 354; emphasis added.

8. The chapter heading of 3 Nephi 21 identifies the Gentiles in this particular context as Americans. It reads, "The Gentiles will be established as a free people in America." Other passages of scripture help to identify the Gentiles in this context as Americans as well, such as 3 Nephi 16:7–8; 3 Nephi 21:4; 3 Nephi 21:27.

> Yea, wo be unto the Gentiles except they repent; for it shall come to pass in that day, saith the Father, that . . . I will cut off the cities of thy land, and throw down all thy strongholds. . . .
>
> So will I destroy thy cities. (3 Nephi 21:12–15, 18)[9]

What these events are describing exactly is largely unknown, and we will likely have to wait for their fulfillment before we can fully understand them.

In any event, the Lord concluded His sermons on this subject by telling the Nephites that after this conflict has ended, many of this remnant of Jacob would thereafter be converted to the gospel of Jesus Christ (see 3 Nephi 21:26) and would assist the Church in building up Zion (see 3 Nephi 21:23–25; 20:22; 16:17–18).

More of this group's conversion and the building up of Zion will be discussed hereafter.

## Natural Disasters

In addition to the conflict mentioned above, other prophesied destructions that will occur in America after the times of the Gentiles have been fulfilled include a series of natural disasters. Many of these natural disasters were described generally in the previous chapter; however, several prophets have given us further insights as to where in particular many of these natural disasters will take place.

For example, President Wilford Woodruff said that once Zion has been built, we will look back at the landscape of America and say, "That was . . . before New York was destroyed by an earthquake; it was before Boston was swept into the sea, by the sea heaving itself beyond its bounds; it was before Albany was destroyed by fire."[10]

What makes this statement interesting is that in the Doctrine and Covenants, the Lord also warned these three cities specifically of destruction if they did not repent. Speaking to Newel K. Whitney, the Lord said:

---

9. See also 3 Nephi 16:13–16; 20:15–20; Mormon 5:22–24; Doctrine and Covenants 87:5–6.

10. *Doctrine and Covenants Student Manual* (2001), 180. After Wilford Woodruff had spoken these words, President Brigham Young said to those in attendance, "What Brother Woodruff has said is revelation and will be fulfilled."

> Go unto the city of New York, also to the city of Albany, and also to the city of Boston, and warn the people of those cities with the sound of the gospel, with a loud voice, of the desolation and utter abolishment which await them if they do reject these things.
>
> For if they do reject these things the hour of their judgment is nigh, and their house shall be left unto them desolate. (Doctrine and Covenants 84:114–15)

Elder Orson Pratt also spoke specifically about New York City:

> The great, powerful and populous city of New York, that may be considered one of the greatest cities of the world, will in a few years become a mass of ruins. The people will wonder while gazing on the ruins that cost hundreds of millions to build, what has become of its inhabitants. Their houses will be there, but they will be left desolate. So saith the Lord God. That will be only a sample of numerous other towns and cities on the face of this continent.[11]

## Warfare in America

Another prophesied destruction to occur in America after the times of the Gentiles have been fulfilled is warfare. Elder Orson Pratt spoke of what this future war would look like:

> What about my own nation—the American nation? . . . [The Civil War] that destroyed the lives of [so many people] was nothing, compared to that which will eventually devastate that country. The time is not very far distant in the future, when the Lord God will lay his hand heavily upon that nation. "How do you know this? inquires one." I know from the revelations which God has given upon this subject.
>
> What then will be the condition of that people, when this great and terrible war shall come? . . . Do you wish me to describe it? I will do so. It will be a war of neighborhood against neighborhood, city against city, town against town, county against county, state against state, and they will go forth destroying and being destroyed and manufacturing will, in a great measure, cease, for a time, among the American nation. Why? Because in these terrible wars, they will not be privileged to manufacture, there will be too

11. *Journal of Discourses*, 12:344; see also *Journal of Discourses*, 20:152.

> much bloodshed—too much mobocracy—too much going forth in bands and destroying and pillaging the land to suffer people to pursue any local vocation with any degree of safety. What will become of millions of the farmers upon that land? They will leave their farms and they will remain uncultivated, and they will flee before the ravaging armies from place to place; and thus will they go forth burning and pillaging the whole country; and that great and powerful nation, now consisting of some forty millions of people, will be wasted away, unless they repent. Now these are predictions you may record. You may let them sink down into your hearts. And if the Lord your God shall permit you to live, you will see my words fulfilled to the very letter.[12]

This future conflict, as described by Elder Pratt, appears to be a war not fought against an outside nation but rather a civil war, where brother fights against brother and city fights against city. Perhaps we can take this to mean that various federal, state, and local governments across the United States will have lost complete control of their constituents or possibly even collapsed entirely by this time, for as Brigham Young prophesied, "the Government of the United States [will] be shivered to pieces."[13]

If our governments have indeed collapsed by this time, it could conceivably be in part because of the prophesied destructions that will one day pass through this country. One thing we can be certain of, however, is that a weakened or collapsed United States government would result in a massive state of anarchy, leaving every person to fend for themself, which seems to be what Elder Orson Pratt is here describing.

## Overflowing Scourge

In addition to natural disasters and guerrilla warfare, the Lord has also revealed that after the times of the Gentiles are fulfilled, humankind would see an "overflowing scourge; for a desolating sickness shall cover the land" (Doctrine and Covenants 45:31). This overflowing scourge seems to be descriptive of a plague of some sort that

---

12. *Journal of Discourses*, 20:151.

13. *Journal of Discourses*, 12:119.

will spread throughout the land. The Lord stated, "For a desolating scourge shall go forth among the inhabitants of the earth, and shall continue to be poured out from time to time, if they repent not, until the earth is empty" (Doctrine and Covenants 5:19).

The Lord also warned:

> I will take vengeance upon the wicked, for they will not repent. . . .
>
> Wherefore, I the Lord God will send forth flies upon the face of the earth, which shall take hold of the inhabitants thereof, and shall eat their flesh, and shall cause maggots to come in upon them;
>
> And their tongues shall be stayed that they shall not utter against me; and their flesh shall fall from off their bones, and their eyes from their sockets; And it shall come to pass that the beast of the forest and the fowls of the air shall devour them up. (Doctrine and Covenants 29:17–19)

The imagery in these verses is very similar to a plague that Charles D. Evans—a Patriarch to the Church living in Springville, Utah, in the 1800s—witnessed in a vision given to him of the last days. In this vision, Elder Evans described this plague as follows: "A purple spot which appeared on the cheek, or on the back of the hand, and which invariably enlarged until it spread over the entire surface of the body, producing certain death. . . . This plague, in grown persons, rotted the eyes in the sockets and consumed the tongue as would a powerful acid. . . . Other plagues followed I forbear to record."[14]

## John Taylor's Vision

Perhaps the best reference we have concerning this overflowing scourge comes to us from President John Taylor, who witnessed the aftermath of this plague in vision. While this excerpt is rather long, and graphic at times, it is extremely valuable to those who desire to learn about this future time period. Here is his account:

> I went to bed as usual at about 7:30 PM. I had been reading a revelation in the French language. My mind was calm, more so than usual if possible, so I composed myself for sleep, but could not. . . .

---

14. *Contributor*, 15:640. This unofficial Latter-day Saint publication was a precursor to the *Improvement Era*.

I was then in a dream, immediately in the city of Salt Lake, and wandering around in the streets and in all parts of the city, and on the doors of the houses I found badges of mourning and I could not find a house but was in mourning. . . .

I seemed to be in their houses with the sick, but saw no funeral procession, nor anything of the kind, but the city looking still and as though the people were praying. And it seemed that they had controlled the disease, but what the disease was I did not learn; it was not made known to me. I then looked over the country, north, east, south, and west, and the same mourning was in every land and in every place.

The next thing I knew I was just this side of Omaha. It seemed though I was above the earth, and looking down upon it. As I passed along upon my way east I saw the road full of people, mostly women, with just what they could carry in bundles on their backs, traveling to the mountains on foot. I wondered how they would get through with such a small pack on their backs. It was remarkable to us that there were so few men among them. It didn't seem to me as though the cars were running, the rails looked rusty and the roads abandoned; and I have no conception of how I traveled as I looked down upon the people.

I continued east by the way of Omaha and Council Bluffs, which were full of disease. There were women everywhere. The state of Illinois and Missouri were in a tumult, men killing one another, women joining the fighting, family against family in the most horrid manner.

I imagined next that I was in Washington and I found desolation there. The White House was empty and the Halls of Congress the same, and everything in ruins. The people seemed to have left the city and left it to take care of itself.

I was in Baltimore. . . . I saw no man except they were dead or dying in the streets and very few women. Those I saw were crazy and in an ugly condition. Everywhere I went I beheld the same sights all over the city; it was terrible beyond description to look upon.

I thought this must be the end; but no, I was seemingly in an instant in the city of Philadelphia. There everything was still. No living soul was there to greet me. It seemed the whole city was without any inhabitants. . . .

Next I found myself in Broadway, in the city of New York, and there it seemed the people had done the best they could to overcome the disease, but in wandering down Broadway I saw the bodies of beautiful women lying, some dead and others in a dying condition, on the sidewalks. . . . Everywhere I went I saw the same scene of horror and destruction and death and rapine.

No carriages, buggies, or cars were running; but death and destruction were everywhere. Then I saw fire start and just at that moment a mighty East wind sprang up and carried the flames over the city and it burned until there was not a single building left standing there, even down to the waters edge. . . .

I supposed this was the end; but it was not. I was given to understand the same horror was being enacted all over the country, east, west, north, and south. Few were left alive, still there were some.

Immediately after I seemed to be standing on the left bank of the Missouri River, opposite the City of Independence, but there was no city. I saw the whole state of Missouri and Illinois and all of Iowa, a complete desert with no living being there. A short distance from the river however, I saw twelve men dressed in temple robes, standing in a square or nearly so (and I understood it represented the Twelve Gates of the New Jerusalem.) Their hands were uplifted in consecration of the ground and laying the corner stone of the temple. I saw myriads of angels hovering over them, and saw also an immense pillar of clouds over them and heard the angels singing the most heavenly music. The words were "Now is established the Kingdom of God and his Christ, which shall never more be thrown down."

I saw people coming from the river and from the desert places a long way off to help build the temple and it seemed that hosts of angels all helped to get material to build with and I saw some of them who wore temple clothes come and build the temple and the city, and all the time I saw the great pillar of clouds hovering over the place . . . the angels were singing the same music I had heard before. "Now is established the Kingdom of God and his Christ, which shall never more be thrown down." . . .

> Then I rolled over in bed and awoke just as the city clock was striking twelve.[15]

The timeline laid out by President Taylor is clear: Zion is to be built after a period of devastating destruction in America.

## Isaiah 3–4

It is also interesting to note that President Taylor's vision seems to closely resemble the events described in Isaiah 3–4. In Isaiah 3, we read of a terrible destruction that is to occur in the Americas.[16] Specifically, Isaiah's record states that "men shall fall by the sword" (Isaiah 3:25), and the land will be left "desolate" (Isaiah 3:26). Isaiah also tells us that this destruction will cause the land to "lament and mourn" (Isaiah 3:26).

Isaiah 4 tells us that when this destruction has passed, "seven women shall take hold of one man" (Isaiah 4:1), which President John Taylor attributed to the destruction in the land that left "so few men among them."[17]

Isaiah 4 then proceeds to describe the building up of Zion that will soon follow this destruction: "When the Lord shall have washed away the filth [by way of destructions] . . . the Lord will create upon every dwelling place of mount Zion, and upon her assemblies, a cloud and smoke by day, and the shining of a flaming fire by night: for upon all the glory shall be a defence" (Isaiah 4:4–5).

---

15. "A Vision, Salt Lake City, Night of Dec 16, 1877," in *Wilford Woodruff's Journal*, ed. Scott G. Kenny (Signature Books, 1985), 4:419 (June 15, 1878).

16. Specifically, Isaiah states this destruction will be in "Zion" (Isaiah 3:16). However, Joseph Smith defined Zion as North and South America. See *Teachings of Joseph Smith*, 362; Andrew F. Ehat and Lyndon W. Cook, *The Words of Joseph Smith* (Bookcraft, 1980), 363–415. Additionally, as we shall see, this destruction will begin first among those members of the Church (Zion) who have not kept the commandments of God as they should have (see Doctrine and Covenants 112:24–26). Both definitions lead us to believe that this destruction mentioned in Isaiah will begin and take place in America.

17. "A Vision, Salt Lake City, Night of Dec 16, 1877," 4:419.

## The Setting in Zion

With this information, we now have an idea of what the scene in America will look like right before Zion is built. Multiple cities and houses spread out across the land will be left desolate and chaos will reign. As we shall soon see, many of these desolate cities will soon be inhabited by the lost ten tribes when they return. Joseph Smith prophesied:

> I am prepared to say by the authority of Jesus Christ, that not many years shall pass away before the United States shall present such a scene of bloodshed as has not a parallel in the history of our nation; pestilence, hail, famine, and earthquake will sweep the wicked of this generation from off the face of the land, *to open and prepare the way for the return of the lost tribes of Israel from the north country.*[18]

This statement by Joseph Smith closely echoes the Lord's promise to the lost ten tribes that when they make their return, they "shall inherit the Gentiles [land], and make the desolate cities to be inhabited" (Isaiah 54:3).[19] More of these details will be discussed hereafter as they occur in our story.

## Jackson County, Missouri

In addition to President Taylor, there have been many other prophets who spoke of this future destruction of Jackson County, Missouri, just prior to Zion being built. For example, Elder Heber C. Kimball said, "The western boundaries of the State of Missouri will be swept so clean of its inhabitants that as President [Brigham] Young tells us, when we return to that place there will not be as much as a yellow dog to wag his tail."[20]

---

18. *Teachings of the Prophet Joseph Smith*, 17; emphasis added.

19. The Lord has also said to the house of Israel on a number of other occasions that they shall "repair the waste cities" (Isaiah 61:4) and "build up the waste places of Zion" (Doctrine and Covenants 101:17–18). In addition, He has said that these desolate "cities shall be inhabited, and the wastes shall be builded" (Ezekiel 36:10). Each of these scriptures fits right into this period of time we have been discussing.

20. *Deseret News*, May 23, 1931.

The term *dog* in the scriptures often refers to a Gentile (see Matthew 15:21–28). What Brigham Young and Heber C. Kimball are saying here is that there will not be any Gentiles in "the State of Missouri" who will be able to prevent the Saints from returning and building up Zion. This information originated from Joseph Smith, who said, "I prophecy that the time shall be when these saints shall ride proudly over the mountains of Missouri and no Gentile dog nor Missouri dog shall dare lift a tongue against them but will lick up the dust from beneath their feet."[21]

The Lord in the Doctrine and Covenants also predicted the cleansing of Jackson County, Missouri, prior to Zion being built. He said, "Behold, the destroyer I have sent forth to destroy and lay waste mine enemies; and not many years hence they shall not be left to pollute mine heritage, and to blaspheme my name upon the lands which I have consecrated for the gathering together of my saints" (Doctrine and Covenants 105:15).

## Who Will Escape?

With this information, it is natural to ask if the Saints living at this time will be able to escape these destructions. The answer is yes, and no. The Lord has made it clear that this destruction will start first among those in the Church who have not kept their covenants:

> Behold, vengeance cometh speedily upon the inhabitants of the earth, a day of wrath, a day of burning, a day of desolation, of weeping, of mourning, and of lamentation; and as a whirlwind it shall come upon all the face of the earth, saith the Lord.
>
> *And upon my house shall it begin,* and from my house shall it go forth, saith the Lord;
>
> *First among those among you, saith the Lord, who have professed to know my name and have not known me, and have blasphemed against me in the midst of my house*, saith the Lord. (Doctrine and Covenants 112:24–26; emphasis added)

---

21. Ehat and Cook, *Words of Joseph Smith*, 418 (grammar corrected). This statement is also helpful in understanding many confusing passages found throughout Isaiah that also use this same imagery (see, for example, Isaiah 49:23).

What about the faithful members of the Church? Will they escape? The Lord Himself answered this question when He asked:

> Vengeance cometh speedily upon the ungodly as the whirlwind; and *who shall escape it?*
>
> The Lord's scourge shall pass over by night and by day, and the report thereof shall vex all people; yea, it shall not be stayed until the Lord come;
>
> For the indignation of the Lord is kindled against their abominations and all their wicked works.
>
> *Nevertheless, Zion shall escape if she observe to do all things whatsoever I have commanded her.*
>
> But if she observe not to do whatsoever I have commanded her, I will visit her according to all her works, with sore affliction, with pestilence, with plague, with sword, with vengeance, with devouring fire.
>
> Nevertheless . . . if she sin no more none of these things shall come upon her. (Doctrine and Covenants 97:22–27; emphasis added)

We must remember:

> Even in war, plagues, and starvation, the Lord can preserve whom He will and leave the rest to die. In the great destructions in the Americas before Christ's visit, though thousands were killed, the more righteous were spared (see 3 Nephi 10:12). Even though there will be martyrs and other exceptions, the Saints of this day have a promise that generally the righteous will be preserved in the tribulations to come (see 1 Nephi 22:16–17; 2 Nephi 30:10; Doctrine and Covenants 97:25–27; 115:6; Moses 7:61–62). To a great extent, the preservation of the righteous is a natural expectation since they follow inspired counsel by which they are led to make choices favorable to their well-being.[22]

Elder Orson Pratt taught that emerging from these destructions, "there will be a remnant who will be spared. It will be those who repent of their sins; it will be those who believe in the Lord Jesus Christ,

22. *Old Testament Student Manual* (2003), 2:270.

and are willing to obey his commandments. . . . These and these only will be spared, for it is the decree of Jehovah."[23]

We should point out that it is not as simple as stating that *all* the righteous Saints will survive, for as Joseph Smith said, "It is a false idea that the Saints will escape all judgments, whilst the wicked suffer; for all flesh is subject to suffer, and 'the righteous shall hardly escape;' still many of the Saints will escape, for the just shall live by faith; yet many of the righteous shall fall a prey to disease, to pestilence, etc., by reason of the weakness of the flesh, and yet be saved in the kingdom of God."[24]

We should remember that the Lord needs righteous people to help build His Zion. While some will likely fall in the midst of these judgments, we know that many righteous Saints will be preserved during these destructions so that they may take part in the building up of Zion.

23. *Journal of Discourses*, 20:152.

24. *History of the Church*, 4:11. See also Doctrine and Covenants 63:34.

# 5

# Adam-ondi-Ahman

As we have just shown, the scene in America will be one of desolation and destruction just prior to Zion being built. Once this destruction period has passed, Joseph Smith revealed what is to immediately follow. He said, "[The destruction] will come as did the cholera; war, fires, and earthquakes; one pestilence after another, *until the Ancient of Days comes.*"[1]

The Ancient of Days, according to Joseph Smith, is a title for "our Father Adam."[2] The phrase "until the Ancient of Days comes" was defined by Joseph Smith as a "council"[3] that will be held by Adam in a valley known as Adam-ondi-Ahman.

This valley of Adam-ondi-Ahman is located in Spring Hill, Missouri, and is where Adam dwelled after he was cast out of the Garden of Eden.[4] It will be here, in this location, that Adam will hold an important conference known as the council at

1. *History of the Church*, 3:390–391; emphasis added.
2. *Teachings of the Prophet Joseph Smith*, sel. Joseph Fielding Smith (1976), 157.
3. *Teachings of the Prophet Joseph Smith*, 157–58.
4. Compare Doctrine and Covenants 117:8 with Doctrine and Covenants 116:1. See also John Taylor, *The Mediation and Atonement* (Deseret Printers and

Adam-ondi-Ahman, and according to Joseph Smith, it will occur immediately following the destruction in America.[5]

## The First Council at Adam-ondi-Ahman

Before we discuss this conference, however, it should be noted that this will actually be the second major conference to be held at this location. The first took place three years before the death of Adam. We learn this from the Doctrine and Covenants, which states, "Three years previous to the death of Adam, he [Adam] called Seth, Enos, Cainan, Mahalaleel, Jared, Enoch, and Methuselah, who were all high priests, with the residue of his posterity who were righteous, into the valley of Adam-ondi-Ahman, and there bestowed upon them his last blessing" (Doctrine and Covenants 107:53).

According to Joseph Smith, this last blessing was given by Adam to his posterity because "[Adam] wanted to bring them into the presence of God."[6] President Ezra Taft Benson, after quoting this statement from Joseph Smith, asked, "How did Adam bring his descendants into the presence of the Lord? The answer: Adam and his descendants entered into the priesthood order of God."[7]

While President Benson states that Adam's descendants "entered into the priesthood order of God" during this council, he does *not* mean that they were ordained to the priesthood at this time. The scripture states that many in attendance were already "high priests" (Doctrine and Covenants 107:53) prior to this meeting, which means they had already been ordained to the priesthood long before this council at Adam-ondi-Ahman.

What then does President Benson mean when he says that Adam's descendants "entered into the priesthood order of God" during this council at Adam-ondi-Ahman? As we shall see, this phrase has

---

Publishers, 1882), 69; Joseph Fielding Smith Jr. and John J. Stewart, *The Life of Joseph Fielding Smith* (Deseret Book, 1972), 340.

5. See *History of the Church*, 3:390–91.

6. *Teachings of the Prophet Joseph Smith*, 159.

7. Ezra Taft Benson, "What I Hope You Will Teach Your Children About the Temple," *Ensign*, Aug. 1985, 8–10.

reference to the "fulness of the priesthood,"[8] which is a separate matter entirely from being ordained to the priesthood.

Receiving the "fulness of the priesthood" is another term for being sealed up unto eternal life. It is the equivalent of having your calling and election made sure. Joseph Smith explained, "Those holding the fulness of the Melchizedek Priesthood are kings and priests of the Most High God."[9] And the Lord in the Doctrine and Covenants tells us exactly what it means to become a king and priest unto God: "They who are priests and kings . . . have received of his fulness, and of his glory. . . . Wherefore, as it is written, they are gods, even the sons of God" (Doctrine and Covenants 76:56–58).

In other words, those holding the fulness of the priesthood will become not servants but "kings and priests [unto] the Most High God."[10] They are assured an inheritance in the highest degree of the celestial kingdom. We are told that those who are fortunate enough to receive the fulness of the priesthood in this life will receive it in the temple. President Joseph Fielding Smith said, "Only in the temple of the Lord can the fulness of the priesthood be received."[11] Similarly, Elder Bruce R. McConkie said, "A temple is also a sanctuary . . . where the fulness of the priesthood is received; and where those who are true and faithful in all things receive the assurance of eternal life in the eternal presence."[12]

---

8. *Teachings of the Prophet Joseph Smith*, 308.
9. *Teachings of the Prophet Joseph Smith*, 322.
10. *Teachings of the Prophet Joseph Smith*, 322.
11. Joseph Fielding Smith, *Doctrines of Salvation*, comp. Bruce R. McConkie (Bookcraft, 1954–56), 3:133.
12. Bruce R. McConkie, *The Millennial Messiah* (Deseret Book, 1982), 273. Joseph Smith revealed that the fulness of the priesthood is an ordinance: "If a man gets a fulness of the priesthood of God he has to get it . . . by keeping all the commandments and obeying all the ordinances of the house of the Lord." *Teachings of the Prophet Joseph Smith,* 308. Joseph Fielding Smith also alluded to this fact when he said, "You cannot receive the fullness of the priesthood and the fullness of eternal reward unless you receive the ordinances of the house of the Lord." Conference Report, Apr. 1970, 58–60; see also Joseph Fielding Smith, *Doctrines of Salvation*, 3:131–134. Furthermore, Elder James, E. Talmage taught that this ordinance was performed in a specific room in the

With this in mind, we can return to the full quote from President Benson, who stated that during the first council at Adam-ondi-Ahman, "Adam and his descendants entered into the priesthood order of God. Today we would say they went to the House of the Lord and received their blessings."[13]

In other words, President Benson is letting us know that Adam's descendants received the fulness of the priesthood during this first council at Adam-ondi-Ahman.

Having received the fulness of the priesthood, those in attendance were then eligible to receive the Second Comforter, which, according to Joseph Smith, consists of a personal appearance from the Savior Jesus Christ.[14] It is one of the greatest blessings one can receive in this life, and it is only given to those who have already received the fulness of the priesthood and proven themselves worthy through their faithfulness to be in Christ's presence.[15]

According to the Doctrine and Covenants, this may have been what happened next to those in attendance. We read that "the Lord appeared unto them" (Doctrine and Covenants 107:54).

It should be noted that entering into the Savior's presence is only one blessing that comes from receiving the Second Comforter. Joseph

---

temple known as the Holy of Holies. See James E. Talmage, *The House of the Lord* (Deseret Book, 1968), 161–62.

13. Ezra Taft Benson, "What I Hope You Will Teach Your Children About the Temple," 8–10.

14. *Teachings of the Prophet Joseph Smith*, 149–151.

15. It should be noted that not everyone who receives the fulness of the priesthood in this life will receive the Second Comforter in this life. Receiving the fulness of the priesthood in this life only *qualifies* you to receive the Second Comforter. In other words, it is possible to receive the fulness of the priesthood and not receive the Second Comforter while in mortality. Joseph Smith taught that those who receive their calling and election have the *privilege* of receiving the Second Comforter (see *Teachings of the Prophet Joseph Smith,* 150); however, they often must continue to live worthy of this sacred experience and wait on the Lord's timing before actually receiving it. See also Bruce R. McConkie, *Doctrinal New Testament Commentary* (Bookcraft, 1973), 3:337–42. Furthermore, it is important to note that seeing Christ on its own does not necessarily mean one has received the Second Comforter. To receive the Second Comforter, Christ must reveal Himself to you *and* reveal to you the mysteries of heaven (see *Teachings of the Prophet Joseph Smith*, 150).

Smith explained, "When any man obtains this [second] Comforter, he will have the personage of Jesus Christ to attend him . . . and the visions of the heavens will be opened unto him, and the Lord will teach him face to face, and he may have a perfect knowledge of the mysteries of the Kingdom of God."[16]

This may have been what happened to our Father Adam at this conference, who, after seeing the Savior, "stood up in the midst of the congregation; and, notwithstanding he was bowed down with age, being full of the Holy Ghost, predicted whatsoever should befall his posterity unto the latest generation" (Doctrine and Covenants 107:56).

These events, according to the Lord, "were all written in the book of Enoch, and are to be testified of in due time" (Doctrine and Covenants 107:57). Of this future record,[17] Elder Bruce R. McConkie wrote:

> When the full account comes to us, we suppose we shall read of the offering of sacrifices in similitude of the sacrifice of the Only Begotten; of the testimonies borne by both men and women; of great doctrinal sermons delivered by the preachers of righteousness who then ministered among them; and of the outpouring of spiritual gifts upon the faithful then assembled. What visions they must have seen; what revelations they must have received; what feelings of rapture must have filled their bosoms as they feasted upon the things of eternity![18]

These are the events that likely took place at the first council at Adam-ondi-Ahman. We have discussed them here because this first council, according to Elder Bruce R. McConkie, is "but a type and a shadow"[19] of the latter-day council that will be held at this same location. By studying one, we can often learn much about the other, and vice versa.

---

16. *Teachings of the Prophet Joseph Smith*, 150.

17. Although several apocryphal texts associated with Enoch have been discovered since the Lord made this statement, none include the events that took place during the first council at Adam-ondi-Ahman. Therefore, "the book of Enoch" referred to by the Lord (Doctrine and Covenants 76:57) has yet to be revealed.

18. Bruce R. McConkie, *The Millennial Messiah*, 580.

19. Bruce R. McConkie, *The Millennial Messiah*, 580.

One such similarity worth noting is the fact that in each case, a city called Zion is built immediately following the council. Since Enoch was in attendance at this first council, perhaps we can conclude that he was given instructions from heaven on how to build a Zion society, for it was not long after this council that he was able to have his city translated.[20]

If this is the case, perhaps we can also conclude that the prophet who will preside over the building of the latter-day Zion will also be given further instructions on how to build the New Jerusalem at the latter-day council at Adam-ondi-Ahman. Whatever the case may be, this future council will no doubt prove to be extremely important to all the Saints living on the earth during that time.

Keeping in mind that this first council was "but a type and a shadow,"[21] we now shift our attention to the second conference, which will take place in this same valley shortly after the destruction in America has passed.

## The Latter-day Council at Adam-ondi-Ahman

Just as Adam was the one to call together his posterity for the first council at Adam-ondi-Ahman, so too will Adam be the one to call his righteous posterity together for this second council. Furthermore, Adam will once again be in attendance and will once again be the presiding officer at this conference. Joseph Smith taught, "Our Father Adam . . . will call his children together and hold a council with them to prepare them for the coming of the Son of Man."[22]

This statement from Joseph Smith also tells us the purpose of this council: to prepare the Saints for the Second Coming of Jesus Christ.

In order to understand how this is to be accomplished, we must first understand some important things about Adam. Joseph Smith tells us, "The Priesthood was first given to Adam; he . . . held the keys

20. Assuming a date of 4,000 BC for the Fall of Adam, the first council of Adam-ondi-Ahman would have been held in 3073 BC and the city of Enoch would have been translated in 2948 BC. See W. Cleon Skousen, *The First 2,000 Years* (Ensign Publishing, 1996), 150, 153.

21. Bruce R. McConkie, *The Millennial Messiah,* 580.

22. *Teachings of the Prophet Joseph Smith,* 157. See also Doctrine and Covenants 116:1.

from generation to generation. He obtained it in the Creation, before the world was formed. . . . The keys have to be brought from heaven whenever the Gospel is sent. When they are revealed from heaven, it is by Adam's authority."[23]

This tells us that Adam was the first to hold the keys of the priesthood. Furthermore, according to another statement made by Joseph Smith, these keys "were first given to him, and by him to others."[24]

Joseph Smith taught that at this second council at Adam-ondi-Ahman, all who have received these priesthood keys on earth "must stand before [Adam] in this grand council."[25] In other words, in addition to preparing the Saints for the Second Coming, a second purpose of this council is to give these keys back to Adam.

President John Taylor tells us that all priesthood key holders will then give an accounting to Adam:

> All who have held the keys of priesthood will then have to give an account to those from whom they received them. . . .
>
> The elders give an account to [stake] presidents of conferences; and presidents of conferences to presidents of [seventy]. Those presidents and the seventies give an account to the twelve apostles; the twelve to the First Presidency; and they to Joseph, from whom they, and the twelve, received their priesthood. . . . Joseph delivers his authority to Peter, who held the keys before him, and delivered them to him; and Peter to Moses and Elias, who endowed him with this authority on the Mount; and they to those from whom they received them [back to Adam]. And thus the world's affairs will be regulated and put right, the restitution of all things be accomplished, and the kingdom of God be ushered in.[26]

Once these keys have all been given back to Adam, the Savior, just as He appeared at the first council, will again appear at this second council. The prophet Daniel saw this sacred scene in vision and wrote, "The Son of man came with the clouds of heaven, and came to the

23. *Teachings of the Prophet Joseph Smith,* 157.

24. *Teachings of the Prophet Joseph Smith,* 158.

25. *Teachings of the Prophet Joseph Smith,* 157.

26. John Taylor, *The Gospel Kingdom* (Bookcraft, 1987), 217.

Ancient of days" (Daniel 7:13).[27] Once Christ makes his appearance, Adam will then turn these keys over to the Savior. Joseph Smith said, "The Son of Man stands before [Adam], and there is given him glory and dominion. Adam delivers up his stewardship to Christ, that which was delivered to him as holding the keys of the universe, but retains his standing as head of the human family."[28]

Once the Savior receives these keys, it will be His prerogative to rule on this earth. The authority to govern will, at this time, be turned over from man to God, and consequently, no longer will Satan have a right to rule over the righteous as the god of this earth.

Satan will, however, still retain "power over his own dominion" (Doctrine and Covenants 1:35), but he will begin to lose his control over the righteous after this council has ended; for, from this point forward, "the Lord shall have power over his saints, and shall reign in their midst" (Doctrine and Covenants 1:36). Of this, Elder Bruce R. McConkie said, "In this present world Lucifer reigns. This is the great day of his power. The kingdoms of men prevail in many ways over the Church and kingdom of God. . . . But Lucifer's day is limited."[29]

President Joseph Fielding Smith explained that Lucifer's reign over the righteous will come to an end at the conference at Adam-ondi-Ahman:

> This council in the valley of Adam-ondi-Ahman is to be of the greatest importance to this world. At that time there will be a transfer of authority from the usurper and impostor, Lucifer, to the rightful King, Jesus Christ. . . .

---

27. It should be noted that this appearance by the Savior will be the first appearance of the Second Coming. Elder Bruce R. McConkie has told us, "Before the Lord Jesus descends openly and publicly in the clouds of glory . . . before he stands on Mount Zion, or sets his feet on Olivet . . . before all flesh shall see him together . . . before all these, there is to be a secret appearance to selected members of His Church. He will come in private to his prophet and to the apostles then living. . . . And it will take place in Davies County, Missouri, at a place called Adam-ondi-Ahman." Bruce R. McConkie, *The Millennial Messiah*, 578–79. See also Bruce R. McConkie, *A New Witness of the Articles of Faith* (Deseret Book, 1985), 640.

28. *Teachings of the Prophet Joseph Smith*, 157.

29. Bruce R. McConkie, *The Millennial Messiah*, 586.

> In this council Christ will take over the reigns of the government, officially, on this earth. . . . Until this grand council is held, Satan shall hold rule in the nations of the earth; but at that time thrones are to be cast down and man's rule shall come to an end—for it is decreed that the Lord shall make an end of all nations (Doctrine and Covenants 87:6).[30]
>
> At this council Christ will be received and acknowledged as the rightful ruler of the earth. Satan will be replaced. Following this event every government in the world, including the United States, will have to become part of the government of God.[31]

This falls right in line with what we have previously discussed, namely, that many Gentile nations and governments, including that of the United States, will either be destroyed, or rendered helpless, just prior to this council (see Doctrine and Covenants 87:6).

This collapse of nations and governments will allow the kingdom of God to become established, first in the Americas and later extended to the entire world.

## Who Will Be in Attendance?

It should be noted that not all the Saints living at this time will be invited to this second council at Adam-ondi-Ahman. In fact, President Joseph Fielding Smith tells us that most Church members will not even know about it: "The Saints cannot know of it—except those who officially shall be called into this council—for it shall precede the coming of Jesus Christ as a thief in the night, unbeknown to all the world."[32]

Which Saints, then, will be in attendance? We have already mentioned above that according to Joseph Smith, all who have held priesthood keys must be present to give an account of their stewardship.[33] Elder Bruce R. McConkie said that this would include "all who have held keys," including "every prophet, apostle, president, bishop, elder

30. Joseph Fielding Smith, *The Way to Perfection* (Zion's Publishing Company, 1940), 291, 290.

31. Joseph Fielding Smith, *Doctrines of Salvation*, 3:13–14.

32. Joseph Fielding Smith, *The Way to Perfection*, 291.

33. *Teachings of the Prophet Joseph Smith,* 157.

or church officer."[34] Furthermore, as we have also mentioned, both the Savior and our Father Adam will be in attendance as well.

From section 27 of the Doctrine and Covenants, we also learn of other prophets who will make an appearance during this council through the veil. This list of prophets includes Moroni, Noah,[35] John the Baptist, Elijah, Abraham, Isaac, Jacob, and Joseph, as well as Peter, James, and John (see Doctrine and Covenants 27:5–13).

In addition to these ancient prophets, there will be other righteous Saints from both sides of the veil who will also be in attendance. The Savior has told us that this group includes "all those whom my Father hath given me out of the world" (Doctrine and Covenants 27:14). According to the Savior, this phrase has reference to all those who will inherit eternal life (see Doctrine and Covenants 17:2). Of this group of people, Elder Bruce R. McConkie asked, "Are they not . . . kings and priests . . . who will live and reign with Christ a thousand years? . . . Truly, it is so."[36]

Here again we find the first council at Adam-ondi-Ahman acting as a type for the second council, for those in attendance will be kings and priests, queens and priestesses, unto God.

When one contemplates just how many righteous Saints this will include, it is soon realized that this latter-day gathering at Adam-ondi-Ahman will indeed involve, as Elder McConkie has said, "a great host of people."[37] In fact, the prophet Daniel tells us that there will be "ten thousand times ten thousand" (Daniel 7:10)—100 million—righteous Saints in attendance. Whether or not this figure of 100 million should be taken literally or not is unknown; however, it is safe to assume that a very large number of righteous Saints will be in

---

34. Bruce R. McConkie, *The Millennial Messiah*, 582. See also Doctrine and Covenants 27:13.

35. Also referred to as Elias. Doctrine and Covenants 27:7 identifies Elias as the angel who appeared to Zacharias. Luke 1:26 identifies this same angel as Gabriel, whom Joseph Smith identified as Noah (see *Teachings of the Prophet Joseph Smith*, 147). We can therefore conclude that the Elias here referred to in Doctrine and Covenants 27:7 is the prophet Noah.

36. Bruce R. McConkie, *The Millennial Messiah*, 585

37. Bruce R. McConkie, *The Millennial Messiah*, 583–84.

attendance, although most of the attendees will be among those from the other side of the veil.

## Additional Events to Take Place

In addition to turning the priesthood keys over to the Savior, there will also be many other events to take place during this council. Perhaps the most sacred event to be held at this conference will be a sacrament meeting, during which those in attendance will partake of the sacrament with our Savior Jesus Christ.

This future sacrament meeting was alluded to by the Lord in the Upper Room, where He, during the Last Supper, said to His Apostles, "I say unto you, I will not drink henceforth of this fruit of the vine, until that day when I drink it new with you in my Father's kingdom" (Matthew 26:29; see also Doctrine and Covenants 27:5).

As this scripture states, Jesus did not partake of the sacrament with His disciples during the Last Supper. For whatever reason, the Lord instead chose to postpone this act until the sacrament meeting at Adam-ondi-Ahman is underway (see Doctrine and Covenants 27:5). Elder Bruce R. McConkie said, "The sacrament is to be administered in a future day, on this earth, when the Lord Jesus is present, and when all the righteous of all ages are present. This, of course, will be a part of the grand council at Adam-ondi-Ahman."[38]

Elder Bruce R. McConkie also told us that this administration of the sacrament is only one of "numerous meetings" to be held during this council: "[Concerning] the great events soon to transpire at Adam-ondi-Ahman . . . we need not suppose that all these things shall happen in one single meeting or at one single hour in time. It is proper to hold numerous meetings at a general conference, some for the instruction of leaders, others for edification of all the saints. In some, business is transacted; others are for worship and spiritual refreshment."[39]

As we have already pointed out, no doubt much of this conference will be focused on instructing the Church leadership in all things pertaining to the building up of Zion.

---

38. Bruce R. McConkie, *The Millennial Messiah*, 587.

39. Bruce R. McConkie, *The Millennial Messiah*, 585.

## Daniel's Vision

It should be noted that the prophet Daniel was actually shown this second council at Adam-ondi-Ahman in vision, along with many other worldwide events which will occur both before and after this important council (see Daniel 7).

In the vision, Daniel was shown "four great beasts" (Daniel 7:3) which included a lion, a bear, a leopard, and a fourth beast that Daniel does not associate with an animal (see Daniel 7:1–7).[40] Most scholars believe that the interpretation of these "four great beasts" aligns very closely with the interpretation of the "great image" (Daniel 2:31) that was shown in a dream to King Nebuchadnezzar and later interpreted by Daniel (see Daniel 2).[41] As the reader will recall, the "great image" in King Nebuchadnezzar's dream contained a head of gold, chest and arms of silver, a belly and thighs of bronze, legs of iron, and feet and toes made of a mixture of iron and clay (see Daniel 2). The "great image" shown to King Nebuchadnezzar represented the Babylonian (gold), Medo-Persian (silver), Macedo-Grecian (bronze), and Roman (iron and clay) empires respectively.[42]

It is important to note that the feet and toes of the "great image" did not just represent the Roman Empire, but they also represented all the kingdoms of the world that would be built from the time of the Roman Empire until the latter days.[43] Elder Orson Pratt made this

---

40. According to an apocryphal vision that Esdras received, the fourth beast that Daniel saw was in the image of an eagle. "This is the interpretation of the vision: the eagle, whom thou sawest come up from the sea, is the kingdom which was seen in the vision of thy brother Daniel." 2 Esdras 13:40–50, *Apocrypha*.

41. According to Keil and Delitzsch, "Almost all commentaries understand that these two great revelations are to be interpreted in the same way." *Commentary on the Old Testament: The Book of the Prophet Daniel* (Hendrickson Publishers, 2011), 245, as quoted in G. Eric Brandt, *The Book of Daniel: Writings and Prophecies* (Independent Publisher, 2018), 163.

42. Daniel said to King Nebuchadnezzar, "Thou art this head of gold (Daniel 2:38).

43. See Brandt, *The Book of Daniel*, 175–81.

clear when he said that the feet and toes also represented "the kingdoms of modern Europe and the Republic of America."[44]

In this same vision, Daniel saw that in the latter days, "the God of heaven [would] set up a kingdom, which shall never be destroyed" (Daniel 2:44). This kingdom was represented by a "stone . . . cut out of the mountain without hands, and that it brake in pieces the iron, the brass, the clay, the silver, and the gold" (Daniel 2:45). The Lord revealed that the stone in Daniel's vision is the gospel of Jesus Christ (see Doctrine and Covenants 65:2; 109:72); however, as we have just seen, this stone will not begin to crush the kingdoms (or governments) of the world until after the council at Adam-ondi-Ahman has commenced.

As mentioned previously, King Nebuchadnezzar's dream of the "great image" has a very similar meaning to the four beasts that were seen in a later vision by Daniel (see Daniel 7:1–7). Most scholars agree that the lion in Daniel's vision represented the Babylonian Empire, the bear represented the Medo-Persian Empire, the leopard represented the Macedo-Grecian Empire, and the fourth beast—which is described as "dreadful and terrible, and strong exceedingly" (Daniel 7:7)—represented not only the Roman Empire but also each of the kingdoms of the world that would be built following the Roman Empire, including those in the latter days.[45] However, unlike King Nebuchadnezzar's dream of the "great image," Daniel's vision of the "four great beasts" includes some additional details regarding their downfall, including some important events surrounding the council at Adam-ondi-Ahman.

In this vision, Daniel saw that in the latter days, a "little horn" (Daniel 7:8) would grow out of the head of this fourth beast. Daniel was told that this "little horn" (Daniel 7:8) represented the prominent leader of a powerful government or kingdom (see Daniel 7:24). Once

---

44. *Journal of Discourses*, 17:313.

45. According to Keil and Delitzsch, "These four kingdoms, according to the interpretation commonly received . . . are the Babylonia, the Medo-Persian, the Macedo-Grecian, and the Roman empires." *Commentary of the Old Testament*, 245, as quoted in Brandt, *The Book of Daniel*, 163. For a more in-depth explanation of why these four beasts should be interpreted in this way, see Brandt, *The Book of Daniel*, 165–81.

given the opportunity, this little horn "made war with the saints, and prevailed against them" (Daniel 7:21).

According to Daniel, this "war with the saints" would only be permitted to occur until the council at Adam-ondi-Ahman, or as Daniel phrased it, "until the Ancient of days came" (Daniel 7:21–22).[46] During this council, Daniel was shown that "judgment was given to the saints of the most High; and the time came that the saints possessed the kingdom" (Daniel 7:22). Also in connection with this council at Adam-ondi-Ahman, Daniel tells us that "the beasts . . . had their dominion taken away" (Daniel 7:12) and their "thrones were cast down" (Daniel 7:9). These events can be likened to the stone cut out of the mountains without hands, which smashed the "great image" shown to King Nebuchadnezzar in his dream (see Daniel 2:44–45).

More of this "little horn" will be discussed hereafter. For now, suffice it to say that these events spoken of by Daniel fall right in line with all that has been discussed in this chapter; namely, that because of this council, Satan's thrones will be cast down, and Christ will be given dominion over His Saints from this time forward.

It is in this way that the council at Adam-ondi-Ahman will, according to Joseph Smith, "prepare [us] for the coming of the Son of Man."[47]

---

46. Joseph Smith defined this phrase, "until the Ancient of days came," as the "council" at Adam-ondi-Ahman (*Teachings of the Prophet Joseph Smith,* 157). He also defined the Ancient of Days as "our Father Adam" (*Teachings of the Prophet Joseph Smith,* 157).

47. *Teachings of the Prophet Joseph Smith,* 157. See also Doctrine and Covenants 116:1.

# 6
# The Redemption of Zion

After the council at Adam-ondi-Ahman has taken place, a few things must still occur before the New Jerusalem can be built. As we shall see, a portion of the Lamanites must first become converted to the gospel of Jesus Christ, for according to the Lord, "the Lamanites shall blossom as the rose" (Doctrine and Covenants 49:24), and it will also be around this time that the Jews will begin to return to Jerusalem.[1]

We are told that after the times of the Gentiles are fulfilled, the Lord will begin to pour out His Spirit upon these two branches of the house of Israel. The prophet Nephi spoke of the conversions that follow:

> And the gospel of Jesus Christ shall be declared among them [the descendants of Lehi]; wherefore, they shall be restored unto the knowledge of their fathers, and also to the knowledge of Jesus Christ, which was had among their fathers. . . .

1. The fulness of the gospel will also be offered to the lost ten tribes after the times of the Gentiles are fulfilled. However, as we shall discuss in chapters 7 and 8, this will not occur at large until after Zion has been built.

> And their scales of darkness shall begin to fall from their eyes; and many generations shall not pass away among them, save they shall be a pure and a delightsome people.
>
> And it shall come to pass that the Jews which are scattered also shall begin to believe in Christ; and they shall begin to gather in upon the face of the land [Jerusalem]; and as many as shall believe in Christ shall also become a delightsome people. (2 Nephi 30:5–7)

## The Jews Return to Jerusalem

According to the prophet Nephi, many of the Jews will be brought to a belief in Jesus Christ before they return to the land of their fathers and inhabit Jerusalem. This is also made clear by the prophet Jacob, who says of the Jews, "When they shall come to the knowledge of their Redeemer, they shall be gathered together again to the lands of their inheritance (2 Nephi 6:11; see also 2 Nephi 25:15-18; Mormon 5:14). This does not necessarily imply that these Jews will fully embrace the Restored Gospel of Jesus Christ at this time—though some may. Rather, as Nephi suggests, many will begin to "believe in Christ," (see 2 Nephi 30:27) which could indicate a broader conversion to Christianity in general during this phase of their conversion.

In any event, after many of these Jews begin to believe in Jesus Christ, many other non-believing Jews will also return to Jerusalem with their brothers. Elder Orson Pratt explained:

> The Jews dispersed among the Gentiles . . . will go to Jerusalem. Some of them will believe in the true Messiah, and thousands of the more righteous, whose fathers did not consent to the shedding of the blood of the Son of God, will receive the Gospel before they gather from among the nations. Many of them, however, will not receive the Gospel, but seeing that others are going to Jerusalem they will go also; and when they get back to Palestine, to the place where their ancient Jerusalem stood, and see a certain portion of the believing Jews endeavoring to fulfill and carry out the prophecies, they also will take hold and assist in the same work. At the same time they will have their synagogues, in which they will preach

against Jesus of Nazareth, "that impostor," as they call him, who was crucified by their fathers.[2]

This will be the scene in Jerusalem until Christ comes. Some of the Jews will have accepted the gospel of Jesus Christ, and some of them, perhaps even the majority, will have not. More about the Jews' conversion will be discussed hereafter.

## A Remnant Converted

The other group that Nephi spoke of who would become converted to the gospel after the times of the Gentiles are fulfilled are the descendants of Lehi (see 2 Nephi 30:5–6).

In the Book of Mormon, the descendants of Lehi are often referred to as the remnant of Jacob (see 1 Nephi 13:34; Alma 46:23; 3 Nephi 20:10–16; 3 Nephi 21:3). This remnant of Jacob, to whom the gospel will be taken at this time, will be the same remnant who previously went among the Gentiles in America "as a young lion among the flocks of sheep" and "treadeth [them] down and teareth [them] in pieces" (3 Nephi 21:12). Although many of them will likely not be converted to the gospel at the time of this conflict, we have reason to believe that this remnant will be a good and honorable people, for we are told that the Lord will have fought this battle for them (see 3 Nephi 20:19).

After this future conflict has passed, but before Zion is built, a portion of this remnant of Jacob must become converted to the gospel of Jesus Christ. Elder Orson Pratt stated, "This people—the Latter-day Saints, before they can ever return to build up the waste places of Zion and receive their inheritances in Jackson County, Missouri, have got to exert themselves to bring the remnants of Joseph to a knowledge of the truth."[3]

The reason why a portion of this remnant must become converted to the gospel before Zion is built is because the Lord made a covenant with the remnant of Jacob that they would be given the privilege and responsibility of building the New Jerusalem along with the Saints. As we know, the Americas were given to the seed of Joseph as an

---

2. *Journal of Discourses*, 18:64–65.

3. *Journal of Discourses*, 17:299.

inheritance (see Genesis 49:22; 1 Nephi 5:14), and the seed of Joseph is largely made up of Church members (Ephraim)[4] and Lamanites (Manasseh) (see Alma 10:3; 1 Nephi 5:14).

Because this remnant makes up a large part of the seed of Joseph to whom the Americas have been given, the Lord has told us that if we Church members are righteous, we can "be numbered among this the remnant of Jacob, unto whom I have given this land for their inheritance; *And they* [righteous Church members] *shall assist my people, the remnant of Jacob* . . . that they may build a city, which shall be called the New Jerusalem" (3 Nephi 21:22–23; emphasis added). Speaking of this scripture, Elder Orson Pratt said:

> Now, a great many, without reading these things, have flattered themselves that we are the ones who are going to do all this work [i.e., building the city Zion]. It is not so; we have got to be helpers, we have got to be those who cooperate with the remnants of Joseph in accomplishing this great work; for the Lord will have respect unto them, because they are of the blood of Israel, and the promises of their fathers extend to them, and they will have the privilege of building that city, according to the pattern that the Lord shall give.[5]

It should be noted that while the remnant of Jacob will play a major role in this latter-day work, the building of Zion will still be done under the direction of our Church leaders. President Joseph Fielding Smith explained, "That the remnants of Joseph, found among the descendants of Lehi, will have part in this great work is certainly consistent, and the great work of this restoration, the building of the temple and the City of Zion, or New Jerusalem, will fall to the lot of the descendants of Joseph, but it is Ephraim who will stand at the head and direct the work."[6]

In this way, with Church members and the remnant of Jacob working together, the New Jerusalem will be built in the Americas.

---

4. *Journal of Discourses*, 10:188; see also George Reynolds, *Are We of Israel?* (Geo. Q. Cannon & Sons Co. Printers, 1883), 36.

5. *Journal of Discourses*, 17:301.

6. Joseph Fielding Smith, *Doctrines of Salvation*, comp. Bruce R. McConkie (Bookcraft, 1954–56), 2:251.

And as we shall see, after Zion has been established, there will be many more Lamanites who will become converted to the gospel and gather to the New Jerusalem with their brethren.

## Return to a Celestial Law

One additional event that must occur before Zion is built is a willingness by the Saints to live the law of consecration. In the words of Hugh Nibley, "The express purpose of the law of consecration is the building up of Zion. . . . We do not wait until Zion is here to observe it; it is rather the means of bringing us nearer to Zion."[7]

President Brigham Young also said, "If the people called Latter-day Saints do not become one in temporal things as they are in spiritual things, they will not redeem and build up the Zion of God upon the earth."[8]

This willingness from the Saints to live the law of consecration will come in part by both the persecution and the destructions that the members of the Lord's Church would have recently endured. The effect of these two events will no doubt strengthen the faith of all surviving Latter-day Saints who endured faithfully, and as a result, many will be eager to live the law of consecration and have all things common among them.

## Led Out of Bondage

It will likely be under these circumstances that the Lord will raise up a righteous leader who will lead the Saints back to Jackson County, Missouri, to redeem Zion. The Lord revealed in the Doctrine and Covenants, "Behold, I say unto you, the redemption of Zion must needs come by power; Therefore, I will raise up unto my people a man, who shall lead them like as Moses led the children of Israel. For ye are the children of Israel . . . and ye must needs be led out of bondage by power, and with a stretched-out arm" (Doctrine and Covenants 103:15–17).

---

7. Hugh Nibley, *Approaching Zion*, ed. Don E. Norton (Deseret Book and FARMS, 1991), 390.

8. *Journal of Discourses*, 13:3.

The bondage referred to here will likely be similar to the persecutions we referenced previously. As discussed in chapter 2, the prophesied persecutions that we will soon face will likely come as a result of us losing our liberties under a United States government violating the Constitution. However, once the times of the Gentiles are fulfilled, a cleansing process will take place in America by way of destructions, and once we reach the council at Adam-ondi-Ahman, "thrones" will be "cast down" (Daniel 7:9), and God will make an "end of all nations" (Doctrine and Covenants 87:6).

No doubt this will also include the United States government, for as Brigham Young stated, "the Government of the United States [will] be shivered to pieces."[9] And yet even after this occurs, we can still expect to be put in some type of bondage prior to the building of Zion. What is this future bondage?

One can naturally conclude that after the governments of Gentile nations are broken to pieces, it will pave the way for Satan to install his one-world government. This one-world government will attempt to put the Saints, and the rest of the world, in bondage. And for a short time at least, it appears that this operation may be successful. "For ye are the children of Israel . . . and ye must needs be led out of bondage by power, and with a stretched-out arm" (Doctrine and Covenants 103:17).

Elder Orson Pratt said of this verse, "This indicates that there may be bondage ahead, and that the Latter-day Saints may see severe times, and that unless we keep the commandments of God, we may be brought into circumstances that will cause our hearts to tremble within us."[10]

What this bondage will look like is largely unknown; however, one possibility comes to us from the vision given to a former Patriarch to the Church, Charles D. Evans, which vision we referenced previously in chapter 4. As the reader may recall, in this vision, Elder Evans was shown a deadly plague that would sweep through the nation, "producing certain death."[11] After being shown this plague, Elder

9. *Journal of Discourses*, 12:119.

10. *Journal of Discourses*, 15:362.

11. *Contributor*, 15:640.

Evans was then shown a foreign power that would attempt to invade America and seize the government. According to his account, "A foreign power had invaded the nation [of the United States] which, from every human indication, it appeared would seize the government and supplant it with monarchy. I stood trembling at the aspect."[12]

It is possible that the foreign invasion that Elder Evans saw will be led by the "little horn" that Daniel saw in his vision (Daniel 7:8), who "made war with the saints, and prevailed against them" for a time (Daniel 7:21). Daniel's record states that this little horn "shall devour the whole earth, and shall tread it down, and break it in pieces" (Daniel 7:23). This certainly qualifies as "bondage" (Doctrine and Covenants 103:17) and also fits the scene described by Elder Evans.

Furthermore, we know from the previous chapter that this "little horn" will wage war with the Saints and will prevail against them "until the Ancient of days came" (Daniel 7:22); therefore, perhaps we can also infer that this "war with the saints" (Daniel 7:8) is one and the same with the foreign invasion described by Elder Evans, and one and the same with the "bondage" reverenced previously by the Lord (see Doctrine and Covenants 103:17).

Perhaps these events were what the Lord was referring to when He said on two separate occasions that Zion would not be redeemed until "after much tribulation" (Doctrine and Covenants 103:12–13; 58:4). Or perhaps these events were what Brigham Young was warning the Saints of when he boldly stated, "If we live, we shall see the nations of the earth arrayed against this people; for that time must come, in fulfillment of prophecy."[13] Or perhaps these events were what President John Taylor was referencing when he said, "I expect one nation after another to rise against us until they will all be broken to pieces . . . and then, if we have not learned it we shall learn that God is our strength, and that in him only can we trust."[14]

According to John Taylor, the nations of the world who rise against us will be "broken to pieces," which is similar to how Elder Evans described the next scene in his vision. After seeing this foreign power

---

12. *Contributor*, 15:640.

13. *Journal of Discourses*, 5:339.

14. *Journal of Discourses*, 9:343.

invade the United States, he said, "I stood trembling at the aspect, when, lo, a power arose in the west . . . [and] to this suddenly rising power every lover of constitutional rights and liberties throughout the nation gave hearty support. The struggle was fiercely contested, but the Stars and Stripes floated in the breeze, and bidding defiance to all opposition, waved proudly over the land."[15]

While we do not know for certain, this scene shown to Elder Evans appears to align closely with both Daniel's vision of the "little horn" in Daniel 7 and the Lord's prophecy that "ye must needs be led out of bondage by power, and with a stretched-out arm" (Doctrine and Covenants 103:17).

## A Man Like Unto Moses

Regardless of how this prophecy plays out, we can rest assured that when the time comes, the Lord will free His people from this bondage by "[raising] up unto my people a man, who shall lead them like as Moses led the children of Israel" (Doctrine and Covenants 103:16).

Who will this man be? Elder Orson Pratt speculated:

> Zion must be led forth out of bondage, as Israel was at the first. In order to do this God has prophesied that he will raise up a man like unto Moses, who shall lead his people therefrom.
>
> Whether that man is now in existence, or whether it is someone yet to be born; or whether it is our present leader who has led us forth into these valleys of the mountains . . . we perhaps may not all know. . . . God is not under the necessity of choosing a young man, he can make a man eighty years of age full of vigor, strength and health, and he may spare our present leader to lead this people on our return to Jackson County. But whether it be he or some other person, God will surely fulfill this promise.
>
> This [revelation] was given before our Prophet Joseph Smith was taken out of our midst. Many of us no doubt thought when that revelation was given that Joseph would be the man. I was in hopes it would be Joseph, for I had no idea that he was going to be slain. . . . But we still were in hopes that he would live and that he

15. *Contributor*, 15:640–41.

> would be the man who, like Moses, would lead this people from bondage. I do not know but he will yet. God's arm is not shortened that he cannot raise him up even from the tomb. We are living in the dispensation of the fullness of times, the dispensation of the resurrection, and there may be some who will wake from their tombs for certain purposes and to bring to pass certain transactions on the earth decreed by the Great Jehovah; and if the Lord sees proper to bring forth that man just before the winding up scene to lead forth the army of Israel, he will do so.[16]

Could Elder Pratt be correct? Would the Lord in fact resurrect the Prophet Joseph Smith to fulfill this purpose? According to Elder Heber C. Kimball, "[Once] the western boundaries of the State of Missouri [are] swept so clean of its inhabitants . . . then the prophet Joseph and others will make their appearance and those who have remained faithful will be selected to return to Jackson County, Missouri, and take part in the upbuilding of that beautiful city, the New Jerusalem."[17]

In addition to this statement made by Elder Kimball, we also have other evidence that suggests that Joseph Smith may indeed be this man raised up "like as Moses," sent to lead the Saints from bondage.

For example, before Zion's Camp was organized, the Lord, in a revelation given to Joseph Smith, gave unto the Church a parable that revealed to them how they were to redeem Zion. In this parable, the Lord said, "And go ye straightway unto the land of my vineyard, and redeem my vineyard; for it is mine; I have bought it with money. Therefore, get ye straightway unto my land; break down the walls of mine enemies; throw down their tower, and scatter their watchmen . . . and possess the land" (Doctrine and Covenants 101:56–58).

In this parable, the Lord appoints "one of his servants" (Doctrine and Covenants 101:55) to organize and lead an army with the purpose of redeeming His vineyard (Zion). Zion's Camp was organized in 1834 with this very intention; however, this camp was abandoned before any of the events in this parable were able to play out. This means that the fulfillment of this parable may yet be future.

---

16. *Journal of Discourses*, 15:362–63.

17. *Deseret News,* May 23, 1931.

The reason why this parable is so insightful is that the Lord later revealed the identity of this servant who is to organize and lead the Saints forth when Zion is redeemed. He said, "Verily, verily I say unto you, that my servant Joseph Smith, Jun., is the man to whom I likened the servant to whom the Lord of the vineyard spake in the parable which I have given unto you" (Doctrine and Covenants 103:21).

It is possible that the servant in this parable, whom the Lord revealed as Joseph Smith, is synonymous with the man who will be raised up "like as Moses" (Doctrine and Covenants 103:16) and that he will assume this same role.[18]

In addition to this parable, Joseph Smith made a statement just before his death that leads us to believe that he would in fact one day fulfill these very prophesies. Addressing the Nauvoo Legion for the last time, he said, "This I will promise to you, that *when I come again to lead you forth*, for I will go to prepare a place for you, so that where I am you shall be with me."[19]

Perhaps this event is what President Brigham Young was referring to when he said, "As quick as Joseph finishes his mission in the spirit world he will be resurrected. . . . When his spirit again quickens his body, he will ascend to heaven, present his resurrected body to the Father and the Son, receive his commission as a resurrected being, and visit his brethren on this earth, as did Jesus after his resurrection."[20]

## The Presence of the Lord

In addition to the man who "shall lead them like . . . Moses" (Doctrine and Covenants 103:16), we are told that there will be many other heavenly beings who will also be with the Saints upon their return to Zion. For example, Joseph Smith spoke of a time in which

---

18. This possibility becomes even more convincing when we consider that the servant in this parable was revealed to be Joseph Smith just five verses after the Lord taught the Saints about the man who would be raised up "like as Moses" (Doctrine and Covenants 103:16, 21).

19. N. B. Lundwall, "Diary of John E. Forsgren" (June 22, 1844), *The Fate of the Prosecutors of the Prophet Joseph Smith* (Bookcraft, 1952), 154.

20. *Journal of Discourses*, 4:285–86. For several other references concerning the resurrection and future mission of the Prophet Joseph Smith, see Richard N. Skousen, *His Return* (Verity Publishing, 2007), 81–96.

he "saw, in a vision, the armies of heaven protecting the Saints in their return to Zion."[21]

In addition to these unseen angels, we are told that the presence of the Lord will also go before the Saints upon their return to Jackson County, Missouri: "And as your fathers were led at the first, even so shall the redemption of Zion be. . . . Mine angels shall go up before you, and also my presence, and in time ye shall possess the goodly land" (Doctrine and Covenants 103:18, 20).

If we are to be "led out of bondage by power" (Doctrine and Covenants 103:17) even "as [our] fathers were led [out of Egypt]" (Doctrine and Covenants 103:19), will we also be guided by a pillar of fire? Elder Orson Pratt concluded that this would indeed be the case. Commenting on the above scriptures, he said:

> We shall go back to Jackson County. Not that all this people will leave these mountains, or all be gathered together in a camp, but when we go back there will be a very large organization consisting of thousands, and tens of thousands, and they will march forward, *the glory of God overshadowing their camp by day in the form of a cloud, and a pillar of flaming fire by night*, the Lord's voice being uttered forth before his army.[22]

## Cities of Zion

As Elder Pratt referenced above, not all the Saints will be selected to build up Jackson County, Missouri. Expounding on this, President Brigham Young asked, "Are we going back to Jackson County? Yes. When? As soon as the way opens up. Are we all going? O no! Of course not. The country is not large enough to hold our present numbers."[23]

What of the rest of the Saints? Where will they settle if not in Jackson County, Missouri? It is likely that many groups of faithful Saints will either be instructed to build up Zion where they are

21. *History of the Church*, 2:381.

22. *Journal of Discourses*, 15:364; emphasis added.

23. *Journal of Discourses*, 18:355. Similarly, President George Q. Cannon said, "We are going back to Jackson county, Missouri. . . . The day will come when Latter–day Saints will be selected—all may not be called at once, but those who are worthy will be called." Conference Report, Apr. 1898, 14.

or be called upon to settle in other surrounding areas outside of Jackson County, Missouri, all according to the inspired direction of our Church leadership. "The New Jerusalem," according to Hyrum Andrus, "was not to be one great city, but a network of small municipalities called *cities of Zion*."[24]

This doctrine was confirmed by the Lord, who said in the Doctrine and Covenants that when the time comes to build up Zion, the Saints are to gather together at the "place appointed" (i.e., Jackson County, Missouri) and that the Saints shall continue to gather there "until the day cometh when there is found no more room for them; and then I have other places which I will appoint unto them" (Doctrine and Covenants 101:20–21).

According to this scripture, when Jackson County, Missouri, is filled to capacity, the Lord will appoint other places for the gathering of His Saints. According to the *History of the Church*, each individual city of Zion would "contain from fifteen to twenty thousand people. . . . [And when a city of Zion] is thus laid off and supplied, lay off another in the same way, and so fill up the world in these last days."[25]

Elder Bruce R. McConkie also alluded to this when he said that "Zion will be built up in many places,"[26] and on a second occasion, he said, "The revealed word relative to the gathering to Independence and its environs will come through the prophet of God on earth. When it does come . . . that call will not be for the saints in general to assemble there. The return to Jackson County will be by delegates, as it were. Those whose services are needed there will assemble as appointed. The rest of Israel will remain in their appointed places."[27]

This phrase "appointed places," suggests that those who are not called upon to settle in Jackson County, Missouri, will be directed to settle in other areas surrounding this center stake of Zion, all according to revelation given to our Church leadership.

---

24. Hyrum L. Andrus, *Doctrines of the Kingdom, Volume III: Foundations of the Millennial Kingdom of Christ* (Deseret Book, 1973), 300; emphasis in original.

25. *History of the Church*, 1:358.

26. Bruce R. McConkie, *The Millennial Messiah* (Deseret Book, 1982), 294.

27. Bruce R. McConkie, *The Millennial Messiah*, 294; emphasis added.

## The Temple at the New Jerusalem

In connection with settling the areas in and around Jackson County, Missouri, the Saints will have quite a bit of work on their hands. The Lord has told us that the Saints "shall return to the lands of their inheritances, and shall build up the waste places of Zion" (Doctrine and Covenants 103:11).

This phrase "waste places" is often used in the scriptures to describe the setting in Zion just before its redemption. Because of the destruction in America that will have occurred just prior to this time, much of the land will have been left desolate and destroyed. It will be necessary, therefore, for the Saints to "build up the waste places of Zion" when they return (Doctrine and Covenants 103:11).

However, while a great deal of work will need to be done by the Saints, it will not be without help from the other side of the veil. According to John Taylor's vision, "It seemed that hosts of angels all helped to get material to . . . build the temple and the city [of Zion]."[28] Perhaps this angelic help is what the prophet Ether was referring to when he prophesied that "the New Jerusalem . . . should come down out of heaven, and the holy sanctuary of the Lord" (Ether 13:3).

This angelic help will allow the Saints to build a large temple directly in the center of Zion at Jackson County, Missouri (see Doctrine and Covenants 84:2–5). Elder Orson Pratt described this temple as follows: "There will be 24 different compartments in the Temple that will be built in Jackson County. The names of these compartments were given to us some 45 or 46 years ago; the names we still have, and when we build these 24 rooms, in a circular form and arched over the center, we shall give the names to all these different compartments just as the Lord specified through Joseph Smith."[29]

Once this New Jerusalem temple has been built, we are told that our Savior Jesus Christ will make an appearance to the Saints who are gathered there and will reign in their midst (see 3 Nephi 21:23–25). We are also told that all the ancient records kept by the Nephites—records that were hid up in the Hill Cumorah long ago—will be transferred

28. "A Vision, Salt Lake City, Night of Dec 16, 1877," in *Wilford Woodruff's Journal*, ed. Scott G. Kenny (Signature Books, 1985), 4:419 (June 15, 1878).

29. *Journal of Discourses*, 24:24.

to this temple. Elder Orson Pratt said, "The grand repository of all the numerous records of the ancient nations of the western continent was located in another department of the hill [Cumorah], and its contents are under the charge of holy angels until the day should come for them to be transferred to the sacred temple of Zion."[30]

In addition to the temple, other buildings will be built in Zion as well. Elder Orson Pratt stated, "Will there be any other buildings excepting those 24 rooms that are all joined together in a circular form and arched over the center—are there any other rooms that will be built—detached from the Temple? Yes. There will be tabernacles, there will be meeting houses for the assembling of the people on the Sabbath day. There will be various places of meeting so that the people may gather together."[31]

Patriarch Charles D. Evans also had much to say about these buildings and about this time period. After seeing the invading foreign power being overcome by the priesthood of God, Elder Evans's vision turned to the building up of Zion:

> The light of the gospel which had but dimly shone because of abomination, now burst forth with a luster that filled the earth. Cities appeared in every direction, one of which, in the center of the continent [the New Jerusalem], was an embodiment of architectural science after the pattern of eternal perfections, whose towers glittered with a radiance emanating from the sparkling of emeralds, rubies, diamonds and other precious stones set in a canopy of gold and so elaborately and skillfully arranged as to shed forth a brilliancy which dazzled and enchanted the eye. . . .
>
> Schools and universities were erected, to which all had access; in the latter Urims were placed, for the study of the past, present and future, and for obtaining a knowledge of the heavenly bodies, and of the constructions of worlds and universes. The inherent properties of matter, its arrangements, laws, [and] mutual relations were revealed and taught and made plain as the primer lesson of a child. The conflicting theories of geologists regarding the formation and age of the earth were settled forever. All learning was based on

30. Orson Pratt, *Millennial Star*, 28:417.

31. *Journal of Discourses*, 24:25.

> eternal certainty. Angels brought forth the treasures of knowledge which had lain hid in the womb of the dumb and distant past.[32]

In connection with this higher form of learning, President Brigham Young stated:

> About the time that the Temples of the Lord will be built and Zion is established—pretty nigh this time, you will see . . . strangers in your midst, walking with you, talking with you: they will enter into your houses and eat and drink with you, go to meeting with you, and begin to open your minds, as the Savior did the two disciples who walked out in the country in days of old. . . .
>
> [They will be] your father and your mother—your ancestors for many generations back—the people that have lived upon the face of the earth. . . . They will expound the Scriptures to you, and open your minds, and teach you of the resurrection of the just and the unjust, of the doctrine of salvation: they will use the keys of the holy Priesthood, and unlock the door of knowledge, to let you look into the palace of truth. You will exclaim, That is all plain: why did I not understand it before? And you will begin to feel your hearts burn within you as they walk and talk with you.[33]

Here, President Young tells us tells us that the faithful Saints in Zion will have "strangers in [our] midst." As we shall see, these "strangers" will likely include both translated and resurrected beings.[34] Elder Heber C. Kimball even gave us the identity of some of these resurrected beings:

> We shall go to Jackson County, Missouri . . . and you will see the day when Presidents Young, Kimball, and Wells, and the Twelve Apostles will be in Jackson County, Missouri, laying out your inheritances. In the flesh? Of course. We should look well without being in the flesh! We shall be there in the flesh, and all our enemies cannot prevent it. Brother Wells, you may write that. You will be there, and Willard will be there, and also Jedediah, and Joseph and Hyrum Smith, and David, and Parley; and the day will be when

32. *Contributor*, 15:641.

33. *Journal of Discourses*, 6:294–95.

34. More of these translated beings will be discussed further in chapter 9.

I will see those men in the general assembly of the Church of the Firstborn.[35]

Here, Elder Kimball speaks of several deceased persons who will be in Jackson County, Missouri, laying out our inheritances "in the flesh," meaning that they will be administering the law of consecration as resurrected beings.

What is remarkable is that section 85 of the Doctrine and Covenants makes a reference to such an event. This sermon begins as follows: "And it shall come to pass that I, the Lord God, will send one mighty and strong, holding the scepter of power in his hand" (Doctrine and Covenants 85:7).

Whom this "one mighty and strong" will be has not yet been revealed to us by the Lord. However, if this "one mighty and strong" is the same individual whom the Lord will "raise up . . . like as Moses" to lead us from bondage (Doctrine and Covenants 103:16), then Joseph Smith would certainly be a leading candidate.

While we are not certain of this person's identity, one thing we do know is that this "one mighty and strong" will be a resurrected being, for according to the Lord, when he comes, he will be "clothed with light for a covering" (Doctrine and Covenants 85:7). We know that this phrase—"clothed with light for a covering"—is describing a resurrected being because as Elder Orson Pratt taught, this "one mighty and strong" was "to be an immortal personage—one that is clothed upon with light."[36]

The Lord revealed that the assignment of this resurrected being would be "to set in order the house of God, and to arrange by lot the inheritances of the saints" (Doctrine and Covenants 85:7), which is another way of saying that this individual would oversee the administering of the law of consecration. No doubt this event is what Elder Heber C. Kimball was referencing when he said that several resurrected beings "will be in Jackson County, Missouri, laying out your inheritances [in the flesh]."[37]

---

35. *Journal of Discourses*, 9:27.

36. *Journal of Discourses*, 21:150.

37. *Journal of Discourses*, 9:27.

## Glory for a Defense

Once Zion's temple has been built, the Lord has told us that "a cloud shall rest upon it, which cloud shall be even the glory of the Lord, which shall fill the house" (Doctrine and Covenants 84:5).

In addition to the temple, this glory will also fall upon the home of every faithful Latter-day Saint. The prophet Isaiah tells us, "And the Lord will create upon every dwelling-place of mount Zion, and upon her assemblies, a cloud and smoke by day and the shining of a flaming fire by night; for upon all the glory of Zion shall be a defence. And there shall be a tabernacle for a shadow in the daytime from the heat, and for a place of refuge, and a covert from storm and from rain" (2 Nephi 14:5–6).

The glory that will be found in Zion will be discussed more hereafter.

## The Righteous Gather to Zion

Once Zion has been built, the righteous from all around the world will gather to it: "And it shall come to pass that the righteous shall be gathered out from among all nations, and shall come to Zion, singing with songs of everlasting joy" (Doctrine and Covenants 45:71).

One of the more miraculous events to occur at this time will be the way in which these righteous individuals will gather to the New Jerusalem. Elder Orson Pratt stated, "Because of your testimony, all the elect of God, of whatever nation, tongue, and people, will be gathered out year after year [to the New Jerusalem]; and by-and-by, the great and last gathering will be done through instrumentality of angels."[38]

Then, referring to a statement made by the Savior in Matthew 24:40–41, Elder Pratt continued: "There will be two, as it were, grinding at a mill; the faithful one will be taken, and the other will be left: there will be two, as it were, sleeping in one bed; one will be picked up by the angels, and the other will be left; and the remnant of the

38. *Journal of Discourses*, 7:187–88.

children of God scattered abroad on all the face of the earth will receive their last gathering by the angels."[39]

As part of this gathering, a second mission to the remnant of Jacob will be launched, this time to that portion of Lehi's descendants who have still not accepted the gospel message. We learn this from the Lord, who, after explaining that the remnant of Jacob will take part in the building of the New Jerusalem, said, "Then . . . this gospel shall be preached among the remnant of this people" (3 Nephi 21:26). Elder Orson Pratt commented on this discourse given by our Savior, saying:

> Do not think that all the [Lamanites] are going to be converted . . . before we can return to Jackson County. Do not think this for a moment, it will only be a remnant; for when we have laid the foundation of that city and have built a portion of it, and have built a Temple therein, there is another work which we have got to do in connection with these remnants of Jacob whom we shall assist in building the city. What is it? We have got to be sent forth as missionaries to all parts of this American continent. Not to the Gentiles, for their times will be fulfilled; but we must go to all those . . . who are scattered through Mexico, and Central and South America, and the object of our going will be to declare the principles of the Gospel unto them, and bring them to a knowledge of the truth. . . .
>
> First, a remnant will be converted; second, Zion will be redeemed, and all among the Gentiles who believe will assist this remnant of Jacob in building the New Jerusalem; third, a vast number of missionaries will be sent throughout the length and breadth of this great continent, to gather all the dispersed of his people in unto the New Jerusalem; fourth, the power of heaven will be made manifest in the midst of this people, and the Lord also will be in their midst . . . and he will instruct and counsel them personally as he did their ancient fathers in the days of their righteousness.[40]

---

39. *Journal of Discourses*, 7:187–88.

40. *Journal of Discourses*, 17:301–2.

## The City of Enoch Returns

At some point after the New Jerusalem has been built,[41] we are told that the city of Enoch will make its return to the earth. The Lord said to Enoch that in the last days, "I shall prepare, an Holy City . . . and it shall be called Zion, a New Jerusalem. . . . *Then shalt thou [Enoch] and all thy city meet them there,* and we will receive them into our bosom, and they shall see us; and we will fall upon their necks, and they shall fall upon our necks, and we will kiss each other" (Moses 7:62–63; emphasis added).

John Taylor said of these verses, "And then when the time comes that these calamities we read of shall overtake the earth, those that are prepared will have the power of translation, as they had in former times, and the city will be translated. And Zion that is on the earth will rise, and the Zion above will descend, as we are told, and we will meet and fall on each other's necks and embrace and kiss each other."[42]

## The Tree of Life

In addition to the return of the city of Enoch, one of the more interesting possibilities to occur in Zion is the return of the tree of life. After the Fall of Adam and Eve, the tree of life was removed from the Garden of Eden and placed "in the midst of the paradise of God" (Revelation 2:7). However, according to Elder Parley P. Pratt, there will come a time when the Lord will "bring again Zion, even Enoch's city," and when this occurs, the Lord will also "bring back the tree of

---

41. The exact timing of the return of the city of Enoch is largely unknown. According to Elder Orson F. Whitney, "When the right time comes, and all things are ready, the pure in heart . . . will go down in the might of the Lord and redeem Zion. . . . Then shall the New Jerusalem be built, and the way prepared for the return of the City of Enoch." Conference Report, Oct. 1919, 74. Thus, the city of Enoch will return sometime after Zion is redeemed, but how long after is still somewhat of a mystery. It is possible that the city of Enoch will not return until the Second Coming, when the righteous are caught up to meet Christ in the clouds of heaven (see Doctrine and Covenants 84:100).

42. *Journal of Discourses*, 21:253; see also *Journal of Discourses*, 25:305.

life which is in the midst of the paradise of God; that you and I may partake of it."[43]

Because the Garden of Eden, and consequently the tree of life, were originally located in Jackson County, Missouri,[44] were the tree of life to be restored back to its original location, it would indeed be planted in Zion, for Jackson County, Missouri, is the revealed site of the New Jerusalem (see Doctrine and Covenants 57:1–3).

---

43. *Millennial Star*, Feb. 1841, 257–58. See also Alma 5:62; Revelation 22:2.

44. President Brigham Young stated, "Joseph the Prophet told me that the garden of Eden was in Jackson [County] Missouri." *Wilford Woodruff's Journal*, 5:15 (Mar. 1847). Furthermore, Elder Heber C. Kimball taught, "The spot chosen for the garden of Eden was Jackson County, in the State of Missouri, where Independence now stands; it was occupied in the morn of creation by Adam and his associates who came with him for the express purpose of peopling this earth" (*Journal of Discourses*, 10:235).

# 7
# The Lost Ten Tribes

As discussed in chapter 3, after the times of the Gentiles are fulfilled, the gospel message will be taken from the Gentiles and offered instead to the literal descendants of the house of Israel. We have already discussed the conversions of two of these groups of people—namely, a portion of the Jews and the remnant of Jacob—but at this point in our story, after Zion has been built, a third branch of the house of Israel will receive the fulness of the gospel and will gather to the New Jerusalem in great numbers. This group is commonly referred to as the lost ten tribes.

In order to fully understand their return, however, it will first be necessary to give a short history of this important group of people.

## History of Israel

This history begins with Abraham, who was chosen by the Lord to be the father of many nations. Through his faithfulness, Abraham was promised that his seed would become the Lord's covenant people. This promise was renewed to his son Isaac and again to Isaac's son Jacob. Jacob (who was later renamed Israel) had twelve sons, the descendants of whom became known as the twelve tribes of Israel.[1]

After the children of Israel were put into bondage in Egypt, and after Moses led them out of bondage, they wandered in the wilderness for forty years until they crossed the Jordan River and settled in Palestine. Soon after, King Saul united Israel as one kingdom. After Saul's reign, David and his son Solomon both reigned as kings over Israel. What happened next is where our story begins.

After the death of Solomon in 922 BC, a controversy over taxes arose (see 1 Kings 12:3–4). This controversy brought on a rebellion in which the northern ten tribes refused to be ruled by Rehoboam, the son of Solomon and the rightful king (see 1 Kings 12:19). In their rebellion, these northern ten tribes separated themselves from the two southern tribes, Judah and (half of) the tribe of Benjamin (see 1 Kings 12:19–21; 1 Kings 11:29–32).[2] From this point forward, Israel was no longer united as one kingdom. Eventually, the Levites left the Northern Kingdom of Israel and traveled south to be part of the Southern Kingdom as well (see 2 Chronicles 29:5–10; see also 2 Chronicles 11:16–17). This left two and a half tribes in the Southern Kingdom and ten and a half tribes in the Northern Kingdom.[3]

After this division, most of the northern ten tribes went apostate. The Lord sent many prophets to get them to repent but to no avail. As a result of their wickedness, in 721 BC the Assyrians, under the reign of Shalmanezer, attacked the northern ten tribes and carried many of them captive back to the land of Assyria.

There, in Assyria, these Israelites remained in bondage for over a hundred years. Under these humbling circumstances, many Israelites

---

1. Because of his faithfulness, Joseph received a double portion of his father's inheritance. Therefore, Joseph's two sons Ephraim and Manasseh each received an equal portion and were numbered among the tribes of Israel, making thirteen tribes total. For all practical purposes, however, they are still referred to as the twelve tribes of Israel.

2. See also Earnest L. Whitehead, *The House of Israel* (Publishers Press, 1972), 52.

3. The thirteen tribes total, with the inclusion of Ephraim and Manasseh, are made up as follows: the Northern Kingdom consisting of the tribes of Ruben, Simeon, Dan, Naphtali, Gad, Asher, Issachar, Zebulon, Ephraim, Manasseh, and half of Benjamin, and the Southern Kingdom consisting of the tribes of Judah, Levi, and the other half of Benjamin.

were likely brought to repentance for their wickedness. In any event, something happened shortly afterward that would allow these Israelites to be freed from bondage and escape into the north.

In 612 BC, the Babylonians attacked and conquered Assyria.[4] With Assyria defeated, the Israelites had a chance to escape.[5] The captive Israelites fled in great numbers from Assyria, journeyed "beyond [the] Euphrates"[6] according to Josephus, then over the Caucasus Mountains, and headed northward.[7] Where were they going? As we shall see, this group was being led by the Lord until they arrived at their final destination.

## SEPARATION FROM THE MAIN BODY

Before they reached their final destination, however, it appears that many Israelites decided to break off from this main group. For whatever reason, several chose to remain behind and settle in whatever lands they happened to be in.[8] As a result, many intermarried with surrounding nations and over time became scattered and lost. The Church's *Old Testament Student Manual* states, "As the ten tribes traveled north, some stopped along the way—many possibly being scattered throughout Europe and Asia."[9]

---

4. Sidney B. Sperry, *The Voice of Israel's Prophets* (Deseret Book, 1953), 353. Specifically, it was Nineveh, the capital city of Assyria, which was captured on this date.

5. Vaughn E. Hansen, *Israel's Lost Ten Tribes: Migrations to Britain and the United States* (Cedar Fort, 2011), 33; W. Cleon Skousen, "The Exciting History of Joseph and Judah," in *Gospel Diamond Dust* (Verify Publishing, 2011), 78; W. Cleon Skousen, *Isaiah Speaks to Modern Times* (Ensign Publishing, 1984), 284.

6. Flavius Josephus, "The Antiquities of the Jews," in *The Complete Works of Josephus*, trans. William Whiston (Thomas Nelson Publishers, 1998), 11:5:2.

7. Skousen, "The Exciting History of Joseph and Judah," 78; Skousen, *Isaiah Speaks to Modern Times*, 284. See also Hansen, *Israel's Lost Ten Tribes*, 33.

8. Hansen, *Israel's Lost Ten Tribes*, 20, 27; W. Cleon Skousen, *The Making of America* (National Center for Constitutional Studies, 1985), 54–55; Skousen, "The Exciting History of Joseph and Judah," 80–84; Hyrum Andrus, Eric Skousen, and W. Cleon Skousen, "The Anglo-Saxon Connection," *Freeman Digest*, Apr. 1984.

9. *Old Testament Student Manual* (2003), 2:115.

Here is what Latter-day Saint scholar George Reynolds said about this group of Israelites:

> Is it altogether improbable that in that long journey . . . from the land of their captivity [Assyria] to the frozen north, some of the backsliding Israel rebelled, turned aside from the main body, forgot their God, by and by mingled with the Gentiles and became the leaven to leaven with the promised seed all the nations of the earth? The account given in the Book of Mormon of a single family of this same house, its waywardness, its stiffneckedness before God, its internal quarrels and family feuds are, we fear, an example on a small scale of what most probably happened in the vast bodies of Israelites who for so many months wended their tedious way northward. Laman and Lemuel had, no doubt, many counterparts in the journeying Ten Tribes.[10]

Hereafter, we will refer to the group of dissenters as those Israelites who were *scattered* throughout the world, and the group who continued their journey north as *the main body.*

## A Rebellious Ephraim

From all that we can gather, it appears that the majority of these scattered Israelites who broke off from the main body were Ephraimites. Reynolds continued: "And who so likely to rebel as stubborn, impetuous, proud and warlike Ephraim? . . . Can it be any wonder then that so much of the blood of Ephraim has been found hidden and unknown in the midst of the nations of northern Europe?"[11]

If Reynolds is correct, it would explain why most of the early missionaries of the Church were sent to European nations in the mid-1800s. It was to seek out those Israelites who had broken off from the main body and intermarried with other nations. Once the descendants of these Israelites joined the Church, many came to America,

---

10. George Reynolds, *Are We of Israel?* (Geo. Q. Cannon & Sons Co. Printers, 1883), 10–11.

11. Reynolds, *Are We of Israel?*, 11. Similarly, Brigham Young said, "The sons of Ephraim are wild and uncultivated, unruly, ungovernable. The spirit in them is turbulent and resolute; they are the Anglo-Saxon race, and they are upon the face of the whole earth. . . . I see a congregation of them before me today." *Journal of Discourses*, 10:188.

received patriarchal blessings, and were told by the Lord that they were from the lineage of Ephraim.[12] This was likely due in part to the many Ephraimites who broke off from the main body of Israelites right around these areas in Europe during their journey to the north country.

President Brigham Young said, "We are now gathering the children of Abraham who have come through the loins of Joseph and his sons, more especially through Ephraim, whose children are mixed among all the nations of the earth. . . . I see a congregation of them before me today."[13]

Why have there not been more Israelites outside of the tribe of Ephraim to join the Church? As we shall see, this is because the main body of Israelites did not settle in these areas. Rather, they continued their northward journey until they reached their final destination.

## Scattered Israel

As it turns out, the scriptures are full of references to each of these two groups. By reviewing these scriptures, we can learn much about each party. While there are many scriptures that refer to scattered Israel, the following scriptures are sufficient to give us an idea of what happened to them.

The prophet Nephi said that "the house of Israel . . . will be scattered upon all the face of the earth, and also among all nations" (1 Nephi 22:3). Moses, when speaking to the tribes of Israel, said, "the Lord shall scatter you among the nations" (Deuteronomy 4:27). In Ezekiel, the Lord said, "[The Israelites] shall know that I am the Lord, when I shall scatter them among the nations, and disperse them in the countries" (Ezekiel 12:15; see also Ezekiel 11:16; Deuteronomy 8:64).

Each of these scriptures state very plainly that many Israelites, at one time or another, would be scattered among all nations.[14] With

12. See, for example, Hansen, *Israel's Lost Ten Tribes*, 94–96.

13. *Journal of Discourses*, 10:188. See also Reynolds, *Are We of Israel?*, 36.

14. In addition to that portion of the ten tribes who were scattered during their journey north, this list likely also refers to Israelites who intermarried with the Assyrians at the time of their captivity, the Lehites and Mulekites who journeyed to the New World, the Jews who were scattered after AD 70, and

this in mind, we shall now examine the scriptures that refer to those Israelites who were not scattered with their brethren but who continued on their journey north.

## The Main Body

We will preface these scriptures with statements from two General Authorities, which will help shed some light on this second group of Israelites. The first statement comes from President Joseph Fielding Smith, who said, "The Ten Tribes were taken by force out of the land the Lord gave them. Many of them mixed with the peoples among whom they were *scattered*. A large portion, however, departed in *one body* into the north and disappeared from the rest of the world."[15]

And Elder James E. Talmage said, "It is plain that, while many of those belonging to the Ten Tribes were diffused among the nations, a sufficient number to justify the retention of the original name were led away as a body."[16]

We make this distinction here because it is important to understand that these two groups will be gathered very differently. The Israelites who were scattered have been, and will continue to be, gathered in through missionary work. The main body of Israelites who continued on their journey north, however, will be gathered much differently, as we shall soon see. As it turns out, the scriptures are very clear in making this distinction.

One such scripture is our tenth article of faith, written by Joseph Smith, which reads, "We believe in the literal gathering of Israel *and* in the restoration of the Ten Tribes" (emphasis added). Here, the Prophet Joseph makes a distinction between the gathering of Israel (through missionary work) and the restoration of the ten tribes (or the eventual return of those who journeyed north).

Similar language was again used by Joseph Smith when he received the keys of the gathering of Israel from Moses in the Kirtland

---

other Israelites who were scattered from time to time, of which we have no knowledge.

15. Joseph Fielding Smith, *The Way to Perfection* (Zion's Publishing Company, 1940), 130; emphasis added.

16. James E. Talmage, *The Articles of Faith* (1968), 340; emphasis added.

Temple. Of this experience, the Prophet said, "Moses appeared before us, and committed unto us the keys of the gathering of Israel from the four parts of the earth, *and* the leading of the ten tribes from the land of the north" (Doctrine and Covenants 110:11; emphasis added).

The *Old Testament Student Manual* gives us more information about this scripture:

> It is apparent from this passage that though the main body of ten of the tribes is lost, there are representatives of all twelve tribes scattered throughout the earth. . . . The scriptures teach that remnants of all the tribes of Israel were scattered among the nations of the earth and in the last days will be gathered out from among these nations and from the four quarters of the earth. The remnant known as the lost ten tribes will return as a body out of the north countries.[17]

Another to comment on this scripture was President John Taylor, who said:

> Moses had held the keys and authority of the gathering of the children of Israel, from the land of Egypt, in a former dispensation, so he was now sent to confer these said keys upon Joseph Smith and Oliver Cowdery. . . . The gathering of Israel from the four quarters of the earth have been committed to Joseph Smith, and he has conferred those keys upon others that the gathering of Israel may be accomplished, *and in due time the same thing will be performed to the tribes in the land of the north.*[18]

Elder Bruce R. McConkie, when speaking of these two scriptures quoted above (Doctrine and Covenants 110:11 and the tenth article of faith), said:

> This inspired language leaves the clear impression that the gathering of Israel is one thing and the restoration of the Ten Tribes is another. Why this distinction? Are not the Ten Tribes a part of Israel? . . .
>
> There is a distinction between Israel as a whole and the Ten Tribes who are the dominant portion of Jacob's seed. All scripture

17. *Old Testament Student Manual,* 2:115.

18. *Journal of Discourses*, 25:180; emphasis added.

> comes by the power of the Holy Ghost and is verily true. When special and unusual language is used, there is a reason. Holy writ is not idle chatter; it is the mind and will of the Lord; it says what he wants said.[19]

Another to comment on the distinction made in these two scriptures was Elder Orson F. Whitney:

> It is maintained by some that the lost tribes of Israel—those carried into captivity about 725 B.C.—are no longer a distinct people; that they exist only in a scattered condition, mixed with the nations among which they were taken by their captors, the conquering Assyrians. If this be true, and those tribes were not intact at the time Joseph and Oliver received the keys of the gathering, why did they make so pointed a reference to "the leading of the ten tribes from the land of the north?" This, too, after a general allusion to "the gathering of Israel from the four parts of the earth." What need to particularize as to the Ten Tribes, if they were no longer a distinct people? And why do our Articles of Faith give those tribes a special mention?[20]

The prophet Jeremiah was another to distinguish between these two groups of people. He said that in the last days, people would say, "The Lord liveth, that brought up the children of Israel from the land of the north [i.e., the main body], *and* from all the lands whither he had driven them [i.e., scattered Israel]" (Jeremiah 16:15; emphasis added). On another occasion, Jeremiah also said that the Lord will "bring them [the main body of Israelites] from the north country *and* gather them [i.e., scattered Israel] from the coasts of the earth" (Jeremiah 31:8; emphasis added).

The prophet Ether was yet another to teach of this distinction. He said that the gathering of Israel will consist of those "who were scattered and gathered in from the four quarters of the earth [i.e., scattered Israel], *and* from the north countries [i.e., the main body]" (Ether 13:11; emphasis added).

Isaiah was also careful to distinguish between scattered Israelites and the main body of the ten tribes. Notice the words he uses to

---

19. Bruce R. McConkie, *The Millennial Messiah* (Deseret Book, 1982), 319.

20. Orson F. Whitney, *Saturday Night Thoughts* (Deseret Book, 1921), 174.

describe them: "[The Lord] shall set up an ensign for the nations, and shall assemble the *outcasts* of Israel, *and* gather together the *dispersed* of Judah from the four corners of the earth" (Isaiah 11:12; emphasis added).

Elder Parley P. Pratt, when commenting on this passage in Isaiah, said, "Here you behold an ensign to be reared for the nations; not only for the dispersed of Judah, but the outcast of Israel. The Jews are called *dispersed*, because they are scattered among the nations; but the ten tribes are called *outcasts*, because they are cast out from the knowledge of the nations into a land by themselves."[21]

As one Latter-day Saint scholar said about this verse in Isaiah, "Notice that the Ten Tribes are described as '*outcasts*,' whereas the Jews are described as '*dispersed*' among the nations. . . . This would indicate that wherever the Ten Tribes are located, they are intact as a people and not 'dispersed' to the four corners of the earth as are the Jews."[22]

President Joseph Fielding Smith also explained, "The 10 tribes were led off captive and later went into the north, and where they are no man knows; but among the children of Israel many were scattered among the nations."[23]

From this information, we can conclude that the gathering of Israel will involve not one but two groups of people: the gathering of scattered Israel from the four quarters of the earth *and* the restoration of the ten tribes (the main body) from the north country.[24]

---

21. Parley P. Pratt, *Voice of Warning* (H. S. Eldridge, 1871), 22. President Joseph Fielding Smith said of this book, "I advise you to get a copy of Parley Pratt's *Voice of Warning*. It was published first in the year 1837 and received the endorsement of the Prophet Joseph Smith and was published in several editions during the lifetime of the Prophet. . . . This work should be read by all members of the Church and all good men everywhere. It was approved by the Prophet Joseph Smith." Joseph Fielding Smith, *The Signs of the Times* (Deseret Book, 1952), 159, 237.
22. Skousen, *Isaiah Speaks to Modern Times*, 249–50.
23. Joseph Fielding Smith, *Doctrines of Salvation*, comp. Bruce R. McConkie (Bookcraft, 1954–56), 3:165.
24. 1 Nephi 22:3–4 states that the "more part" of the Israelites were scattered, which means the rest of the Israelites were not scattered but were actually "separated" as it states in 3 Nephi 15:20.

With this distinction in mind, we now turn to the story of the main body to find out what happened to them during their journey north.

## The Second Book of Esdras

While there is no scriptural record of this event, there is one apocryphal source that gives us a little glimpse of what may have occurred to this group along their journey.[25] It comes from 2 Esdras, and it reads as follows:

> The ten tribes, which were carried away prisoners out of their own land . . . took this counsel among themselves, that they would leave the multitude of the heathen [Assyria], and go forth into a further country, where never mankind dwelt, That they might there keep their statutes, which they never kept in their own land. And they entered into Euphrates by the narrow places of the river. For the most High then shewed signs for them, and held still the flood, till they were passed over. For through that country there was a great way to go, namely, of a year and a half: and the same region is called Arsareth. Then dwelt they there until the latter time.[26]

While this short passage is all we have on Israel's departure from Assyria, it is helpful because it reveals some important things. First, it tells us that by the time they left Assyria, this group had repented of their apostate ways. It states that these Israelites desired to escape so they could "keep their statutes, which they never kept in their own land." Of this, Elder Orson Pratt wrote, "They must have repented of

25. Referring to the Apocrypha, Hugh Nibley asked, "What are the Apocrypha? They are a large body of writings, Jewish and Christian, existing alongside the Bible, each of which has at some time or other been accepted as true revealed scriptures by some Christian or Jewish group. Where do they come from? The actual manuscripts are as old as our Bible manuscripts and are sometimes written by the same hands, but their contents betray widely scattered sources, some of which are orthodox and some of which are not. Then why bother about them? Because writers of the Bible respect them and sometimes quote them, thus including excerpts of the Apocrypha in our Bible, while the fathers of the church in the first three centuries accept many of them as genuine and quote them as scripture." Hugh Nibley, *Since Cumorah*, ed. John W. Welch (Deseret Book and FARMS, 1988), 29.

26. *Apocrypha*, 2 Esdras 13:40–46.

their sins or God would not have miraculously divided the river for them to pass over."[27]

Second, it tells us that because they had repented, the Lord was guiding and preparing the way for them to reach their final destination. It states that "the most High . . . shewed signs for them, and held still the flood, till they were passed over."[28] The Lord, in the Book of Mormon, confirmed that the Father was leading this group of people when He said, "Concerning the other tribes of the house of Israel, *whom the Father hath led away* out of the land" (3 Nephi 15:15).

We should also mention that in addition to being led by the Father, these ten tribes also had inspired prophets guiding them during this journey. Of this, Elder Bruce R. McConkie said, "The Lost Tribes are not lost unto the Lord. In their northward journeyings they were led by prophets and inspired leaders. They had their Moses and their Lehi, were guided by the spirit of revelation, kept the law of Moses, and carried with them the statutes and judgments which the Lord had given them in ages past."[29]

Or, as Reynolds put it, "[The ten tribes] were doubtless guided by inspired leaders, who, by Urim and Thummim, or through dreams and visions, pointed out the paths ahead. Perhaps, as in the days of the deliverance from Egypt, a pillar of cloud by day and of fire by night guided their footsteps."[30]

Third, this passage from 2 Esdras tells us that they journeyed "a year and a half" before reaching their final destination in the "region . . . called Arsareth" (wherever that may be).

Fourth, it tells us that the land where the ten tribes arrived was completely isolated from any civilization. It was a "country where never mankind dwelt." This is important because it lets us know that this particular group of Israelites did not intermarry with other nations. This would allow them to remain separate until their return to Zion in the latter days.

---

27. *Millennial Star*, Mar. 30, 1867, 200.

28. Speaking of the Euphrates River.

29. Bruce R. McConkie, *Mormon Doctrine*, 2nd ed. (Bookcraft, 1966), 457.

30. Reynolds, *Are We of Israel?*, 30.

## The Ten Tribes' Journey to the Arctic Ocean

Where exactly is this "country where never mankind dwelt"? As we follow their trail, we speculate that they traveled north until they reached the Arctic Ocean. Elder Orson Pratt concluded that at this time, the Israelites "evidently had a highway made for them in the midst of the Arctic Ocean," which would have allowed them to cross.[31] Or, as Reynolds stated, "They did cross [the Arctic Ocean], but how, we know not—perhaps on the ice of winter, perhaps the Lord threw up a highway or divided the waters as he did aforetime, that they passed through dry shod."[32]

If the Israelites did make it this far, where did they go from here? While we do not know for certain, enough has been revealed about this group of people to fill in some of the details.

The first thing we know is that this group was still in a single body over 600 years after they arrived at the Arctic Ocean.[33] We know this because after Christ's Resurrection, He appeared to the Nephites in the Americas and told them that He soon would personally visit the ten tribes: "I go unto the Father, and also to show myself unto the lost tribes of Israel, for they are not lost unto the Father, for he knoweth whither he hath taken them" (3 Nephi 17:4).

And on another occasion, the Lord said of these lost tribes:

> And verily, verily, I say unto you that I have other sheep, which are not of this land, neither of the land of Jerusalem, neither in any parts of that land round about whither I have been to minister.
>
> For they of whom I speak are they who have not as yet heard my voice; neither have I at any time manifested myself unto them.
>
> *But I have received a commandment of the Father that I shall go unto them, and that they shall hear my voice,* and shall be numbered among my sheep, that there may be one fold and one shepherd;

---

31. *Millennial Star*, 29:200–201.

32. Reynolds, *Are We of Israel?*, 32.

33. According to 2 Esdras, their journey to the north took a year and a half. If they left Assyria in 612 BC, they would have arrived in the north about 611–610 BC. Jesus's Resurrection occurred around AD 32–33, making it over 640 years later.

> therefore I go to show myself unto them. (3 Nephi 16:1–3; emphasis added)

From these passages of scripture, Elder Bruce R. McConkie concluded, "[The ten tribes] were still a distinct people many hundreds of years [after their departure from Assyria], for the resurrected Lord visited and ministered among them following his ministry on this continent among the Nephites."[34]

President Joseph Fielding Smith agreed: "These lost tribes were in a body somewhere when the Savior visited the Nephites on this continent. We believe he went to them and established his Church among them with an organization similar to that given to the Nephites."[35]

It should also be noted that this visit from the Savior to the ten tribes was recorded by them and will one day be available to us. This was made clear by the Lord, who said, "I shall also speak unto the other tribes of the house of Israel, which I have led away, and they shall write. . . . And the Nephites and the Jews shall have the words of the lost tribes of Israel; and the lost tribes of Israel shall have the words of the Nephites and the Jews" (2 Nephi 29:12–13).

Elder Orson Pratt concluded from this scripture that "the ten tribes in the north country will have a record as well as the Jews, a Bible of their own, if you please."[36] Speaking of this scriptural record, Elder McConkie wrote, "Obviously [Christ] taught them in the same way and gave them the same truths which he gave his followers in Jerusalem and on the American continent; and obviously they recorded his teachings, thus creating volumes of scripture comparable to the Bible and Book of Mormon."[37]

Daniel H. Ludlow, when commenting on these scriptural records, said:

> The Lord promises that in the mouths of three great scriptural witnesses the divinity of Christ would be established. It is of interest to note that evidently the resurrected Jesus Christ appeared to all

---

34. Bruce R. McConkie, *Mormon Doctrine*, 457.
35. Joseph Fielding Smith, *The Way to Perfection*, 131.
36. *Journal of Discourses*, 19:172.
37. Bruce R. McConkie, *Mormon Doctrine*, 457.

> of the peoples who were to write these great scriptural witnesses. He appeared as a resurrected being to the Jews, from whom we get the Bible; he appeared as a resurrected being to the Nephites, from whom we get the Book of Mormon; and he promises here that he is going to appear as a resurrected being to the lost tribes of Israel, from whom shall come the third great scriptural witness.[38]

Elder James E. Talmage added:

> The prophecy stands that the tribes shall be brought forth from their hiding place . . . [and their] scriptures shall become one with the scriptures of the Jews, the Holy Bible, and with the scriptures of the Nephites, the Book of Mormon, and with the scriptures of the Latter-day Saints as embodied in the volumes of modern revelation.[39]

According to Doctrine and Covenants 133:30, when the ten tribes return, they will bring their "rich treasures" with them. Many have interpreted these rich treasures as the scriptural record that these Israelites have kept. For example, Wilford Woodruff tells us that "their records, and their choice treasures they will bring with them to Zion."[40] Furthermore, in April 1845, the Council of the Twelve made a proclamation to the world, which stated that "the ten tribes of Israel should also be revealed in the north country, together with their oracles and records."[41]

It is exciting to think that more scripture will someday be given to us, scripture which will have more words of Christ and no doubt will also give an account of what really happened to the ten tribes during and after their departure from Assyria. Until then, however, we will have to be content with what the Lord has given us on the subject and do the best we can to piece the rest together.

---

38. Daniel H. Ludlow, *A Companion to Your Study of the Book of Mormon* (Deseret Book, 1978), 271.

39. Conference Report, Apr. 1916, 130.

40. *Journal of Discourses*, 21:301.

41. Issued Apr. 6, 1845, in New York City.

## Still in a Group Today

The next thing we know about this group of people is that they are still in a group today. President Joseph Fielding Smith said:

> The Ten Tribes were taken by force out of the land the Lord gave them. Many of them mixed with the peoples among whom they were *scattered*. A large portion, however, departed in *one body* into the North and disappeared from the rest of the world. Where they went and where they are we do not know. That they [the main body] *are intact we must believe*, else how shall the scripture be fulfilled? There are too many prophecies concerning them and their return in a body for us to ignore the fact.[42]

Elder James E. Talmage also stated, "It is plain that, while many of those belonging to the Ten Tribes were *diffused* among the nations, a sufficient number to justify the retention of the original name were led away as a *body* and *are now in existence* in some place where the Lord has hidden them."[43]

President Joseph Fielding Smith also wrote, "All I know about [the present location of the ten tribes] is what the Lord has revealed, and He declares that they will come from the North. He has also made it very clear and definite that these lost people are separate and apart from the scattered Israelites now being gathered out."[44]

Elder Orson Pratt, when speaking of the missionary efforts to the house of Israel, said that the elders in this dispensation would have to search out the Israelites who are "scattered among [the] nations" and then went on to say that "there are some from the ten tribes among [the scattered nations]; but the body of the ten tribes are in the north country."[45]

## John the Revelator

The next thing we know is that John the Revelator has been, and is now, among this group of Israelites who journeyed north. His mission

42. Joseph Fielding Smith, *The Way to Perfection*, 130; emphasis added.

43. Talmage, *Articles of Faith*, 340; emphasis added.

44. Smith, *Signs of the Times*, 186.

45. *Journal of Discourses*, 7:187.

is to prepare these tribes for their long-awaited return. According to the *History of the Church*, "The Spirit of the Lord fell upon Joseph [Smith] in an unusual manner, and he prophesied that John the Revelator was then among the Ten Tribes of Israel who had been led away by Shalmaneser, king of Assyria, to prepare them for their return from their long dispersion, to again possess the land of their fathers."[46]

Daniel Allen testified, "I heard Joseph the prophet say that he had seen John the Revelator and had a long conversation with him, who told him that he John was their leader, Prophet, Priest and King, and said that he was preparing that people [the ten tribes] to return and further said there is a mighty host of us."[47]

In addition to John the Revelator, these Israelites will also have other prophets among them. Elder Orson Pratt said, "Do not think that we are the only people who will have Prophets. God is determined to raise up Prophets among that people. . . . John the Revelator will be there, teaching, instructing and preparing them."[48]

Elder Melvin J. Ballard also testified of this, saying, "My witness and testimony is that . . . even now their prophets prophesy of their deliverance and are preparing that people."[49]

From President Spencer W. Kimball, we learn that the ten tribes "will return with their prophets, and their sacred records will be a third witness for Christ."[50] Elder Orson Pratt even said that there is also a quorum of Twelve Apostles "that were called among the ten tribes of Israel in the north country."[51] President Joseph Fielding Smith agreed:

> When the Savior taught the Nephites, he informed them that he had "other sheep" which were not of the Nephites, neither of the

---

46. *History of the Church*, 1:176. See also Revelation 10:9–10; Doctrine and Covenants 77:14; 133:26.

47. *Minutes of the School of the Prophets*, 157 (Aug. 17, 1872). More of this "mighty host" will be discussed later.

48. *Journal of Discourses*, 18:25.

49. Conference Report, Oct. 1920, 82.

50. Conference Report, Oct. 1959, 61. For more information about prophets among the ten tribes, see *Journal of Discourses*, 2:200–201; 4:231.

51. *Journal of Discourses*, 17:187.

> land of Jerusalem, and these also were to hear his voice and be ministered to by him. It is reasonable for us to conclude that among these others, who were hidden from the rest of the world, he likewise chose disciples—perhaps twelve—to perform like functions and minister unto their people with the same fulness of divine authority.[52]
>
> They had their prophets and kept a record. . . . The time has not yet arrived for the writings of the Lost Tribes to be made known, but this must shortly come to pass.[53]

It is important to remember that these ten tribes are not only currently in one body, but as we shall see in the next chapter, they will also return in one body as well.

52. Joseph Fielding Smith, *Doctrines of Salvation,* 3:159.

53. Joseph Fielding Smith, *The Way to Perfection,* 131–33.

# 8

# The Return of the Lost Ten Tribes

As we have just seen, there is some evidence to suggest that after the ten tribes escaped from Assyria, they journeyed north until they reached (and crossed) the Arctic Ocean. If true, then it was at this time that one of the greatest mysteries of all time occurred: They completely vanished from the knowledge of humankind. Where they went and where they are now, we are not quite certain. What we do know, however, is that these same lost ten tribes will make their return to Zion after the New Jerusalem has been established in Jackson County, Missouri (see Doctrine and Covenants 133:32). Elder Orson Pratt made this clear when he said that "the ten tribes will come from the north; but after Zion is built in Jackson County, and after the Temple is built."[1]

Note that when we speak of the return of the lost ten tribes, we are not referring to the group of Israelites who were scattered throughout the world. Scattered Israel will be gathered through missionary work. Rather, the return of the lost ten tribes will consist of those Israelites

1. *Journal of Discourses*, 18:68. See also *Journal of Discourses*, 18:23–25.

who journeyed north until they reached their final destination. They arrived in the north as a group, and they will return to Zion as a group.[2]

When these Israelites do make their return, it will be spoken of as one of the greatest miracles of all time. The prophet Jeremiah prophesied, "The days come, saith the Lord, that it shall no more be said, The Lord liveth, that brought up the children of Israel out of the land of Egypt; But, The Lord liveth, that brought up the children of Israel from the land of the north" (Jeremiah 16:14–15).

In other words, the events surrounding the return of the lost ten tribes will be even more impressive than the events that surrounded the Exodus of the children of Israel from Egypt! This prophecy is truly remarkable when we consider all the miracles, from the ten plagues to the parting of the Red Sea, which "brought up the children of Israel out of the land of Egypt" (Jeremiah 16:14). As one Latter-day Saint scholar said about this scripture in Jeremiah:

> Every year the Jews celebrate Passover, remembering the exodus (on the first day of Passover) and the parting of the Red Sea to pass over to freedom (on the last day of Passover). What would it take to get them to cease referring to those events and replace them with another? . . . Would it not take an even more miraculous event to eclipse the great miracles of Moses?[3]

With this Jeremiah passage in mind, it is natural to wonder what might happen upon the ten tribes' return. While we do not have all the details, the Lord has given us some of this information. Section 133 of the Doctrine and Covenants reads as follows:

> And they who are in the north countries [i.e., the main body of the lost ten tribes] shall come in remembrance before the Lord; and their prophets shall hear [the Lord's] voice, and shall no longer stay themselves; and they shall smite the rocks, and the ice shall flow down at their presence.
>
> And an highway shall be cast up in the midst of the great deep.

---

2. See chapter 7.

3. John Pratt, "A Volcanic Highway for the Lost Tribes?," *Meridian Magazine,* Sept. 15, 2005, http://www.johnpratt.com/items/docs/lds/meridian/2005/highway.html.

> Their enemies shall become a prey unto them,
>
> And in the barren deserts there shall come forth pools of living water; and the parched ground shall no longer be a thirsty land.
>
> And they shall bring forth their rich treasures unto the children of Ephraim, my servants.
>
> And the boundaries of the everlasting hills shall tremble at their presence.
>
> And there shall they fall down and be crowned with glory, even in Zion, by the hands of the servants of the Lord, even the children of Ephraim.
>
> And they shall be filled with songs of everlasting joy.
>
> Behold, this is the blessing of the everlasting God upon the tribes of Israel, and the richer blessing upon the head of Ephraim and his fellows. (Doctrine and Covenants 133:26–34)

While these scriptures are rather brief, they do teach us some very important things regarding the return of the lost ten tribes.

First, they teach us that this return will consist of those Israelites in the "north countries" (verse 26). In other words, they are speaking of the main body and not of Israelites who were scattered throughout the world.

Second, they teach us that the ten tribes will have prophets among them when they return. The scripture says, "their prophets shall hear [the Lord's] voice" (verse 26).

Third, we learn that upon their return there will be great changes in nature: "rocks" will be smitten, "ice" will melt, and a "highway" will be cast up that will run through the ocean, or "the great deep" (verses 26–27). Furthermore, "barren deserts" will produce "pools of living water" (verse 29), and a great earthquake will cause the "everlasting hills [to] tremble" (verse 31). Here is how Elder Orson Pratt described these events:

> To show that they come with power, they come on a highway cast up for them; the ice feels the power of God and flows down, making room for them; and the barren deserts of the north . . . will yield forth pools of living water to quench their thirst. As they come to sing in the height of Zion, the everlasting hills, this great Rocky Mountain range, extending from the arctic regions south to the central portions of America, will tremble beneath the power of

> God at the approach of that people. . . . But where have this great company been, where has this mighty host come from? They have come from their hiding place in the north country; they have been led thence by the Prophets of the Most High God, the Lord going before their camp, talking with them out of the cloud, as he talked in ancient days with the camp of Israel.[4]

Fourth, we learn from these verses that any enemies who might oppose these Israelites along their way to Zion will "become a prey unto them" (verse 28), which tells us that they will return with power.

Fifth, we learn that these returning tribes will bring their "rich treasures" with them (verse 30). These rich treasures, as discussed previously, have been interpreted by many General Authorities to be the records that these Israelites kept throughout their journey.[5] We learn here that these records will be brought "unto the children of Ephraim" (verse 30), or the members of the Church in Zion.

Sixth, we learn that these returning tribes will come to Zion to be "crowned with glory . . . by the hands of the servants of the Lord, even the children of Ephraim" (verse 32). As we shall soon see, being crowned with glory has reference to receiving all the saving ordinances of the temple.

These verses in Doctrine and Covenants 133 are extremely helpful in understanding the return of the lost ten tribes and will be referred to often throughout the remainder of this chapter.

## A Great Host

The next thing we need to determine is just how large this group will be. In other words, how many Israelites will return? While the exact number is unknown, it has been revealed that we can expect a massive group of people.

This fact is made clear by the prophet Isaiah, who said that when the ten tribes return, they will outnumber the members of the Church. The prophet stated, "More are the children of the desolate than the children of the married wife, saith the Lord" (Isaiah 54:1).

---

4. *Journal of Discourses*, 18:24.

5. See for example, *Journal of Discourses*, 21:301.

Here is what one Latter-day Saint commentator said about this verse: "The 'children of the desolate' represent the large number of people from the [lost ten] tribes of Israel who will gather to Zion following the building of the New Jerusalem. There will be many more of them than the remnant who will already have gathered and built the New Jerusalem, or those whom Isaiah calls the 'children of the married wife.'"[6]

Furthermore, a second Latter-day Saint commentator also wrote:

> The Ten Tribes will suddenly appear to inhabit the desolate cities of America. All these will add millions to the membership of the Church. Because the Ten Tribes have been lost from the knowledge of both Jews and Christians for around 2,500 years, it has been assumed that they are like an abandoned wife which has remained "desolate" and without children. However, Isaiah said that when the Ten Tribes put in their appearance in the latter days, the members of the Church (the married wife) will look upon these multitudes and say, "More are the children of the desolate [ten tribes] than the children of the married wife."[7]

If there will indeed be more returning Israelites than members of the Church at this time, then we can safely conclude that there will be millions of returning Israelites. To illustrate how this could be possible, if we consider that this group of Israelites who arrived in the north has had over 2,500 years to multiply, then we may begin to get an idea of just how large this group could be when they return.

Here is what Latter-day Saint scholar Rodney Turner said about the number of Israelites taken captive to Assyria: "The annals of Sargon II state that 27,290 Israelites were taken captive. However, this figure is probably limited to these more prominent citizens taken

---

6. Monte S. Nyman, *Great Art the Words of Isaiah* (Horizon Publishers, 1980–2002), 211. Nyman continues, "The symbolic marriage of Christ to Israel is here represented, with the members of the Church being considered the children of that covenant relationship."

7. W. Cleon Skousen, *Isaiah Speaks to Modern Times* (Ensign Publishing, 1984), 668–69.

in the fall of Samaria; the actual number exiled to Assyria through the years was undoubtedly much larger."[8]

Latter-day Saint scholar Earnest Whitehead even went as far as estimating the number of Israelites who fled Assyria to be as large as "a hundred thousand people."[9] While these numbers do not represent the number of people who arrived in the north, it does give us an idea of how many Israelites may have had a chance to escape Assyrian bondage and flee north. Even if relatively few made it to their final destination, it still could have been a very large group if they did in fact begin their journey with as many as 100,000 people. If this group has had over 2,500 years to multiply, then the returning Israelites could be very large indeed.

With this information, it is easy to see why the prophet Jeremiah spoke of their return with such amazement. Such a large number of returning Israelites will naturally require a very large amount of land to settle on once they arrive in Zion. We are told that because of the destruction that will have occurred in America just prior to this time, much of its desolate land will be given to these returning Israelites. Joseph Smith prophesied:

> I am prepared to say by the authority of Jesus Christ, that not many years shall pass away before the United States shall present such a scene of bloodshed as has not a parallel in the history of our nation; pestilence, hail, famine, and earthquake will sweep the wicked of this generation from off the face of the land, *to open and prepare the way for the return of the lost tribes of Israel from the north country.*[10]

As it turns out, the land that will have been left desolate may reach much farther than just the United States. In fact, it may extend to much of North and South America. Joseph Smith taught that while the center stake of Zion will be located in Jackson County, Missouri

---

8. Rodney Turner, *The Footstool of God* (Grandin Book Company, 1983), 147. It is important to note that the Bible records this number as much larger. See Clay McConkie, *The Ten Lost Tribes: A People of Destiny* (Springville: Bonneville Books 2002), 37.

9. Earnest L. Whitehead, *The House of Israel* (Publishers Press, 1972), 88.

10. *Teachings of the Prophet Joseph Smith*, sel. Joseph Fielding Smith (1976), 17; emphasis added.

(see Doctrine and Covenants 57:1–5), the boundaries of Zion will eventually extend to all of North and South America. He said, "There has been great discussion in relation to Zion—where it is . . . but I will make a proclamation that will cover a broader ground. The whole of America is Zion itself from north to south."[11] And on a second occasion, he said, "The redemption of Zion is the redemption of all N[orth] & S[outh] America."[12]

If the boundaries of Zion extend to all of North and South America, then it is very possible that this prophesied destruction may extend into parts of each of these two lands prior to Zion being built. Once desolate, portions of these lands would be available for the ten tribes to settle on. Upon their return, we are told that these Israelites will proceed to "build up the waste places of Zion" (Doctrine and Covenants 101:18).

The prophet Isaiah often spoke of these events. All throughout his record, Isaiah gives us many details regarding this stage of their return. He begins by telling us that when the ten tribes return, the Lord will instruct the Saints living in Zion to "enlarge the place of thy tent, and . . . stretch forth the curtains of thine habitations" (Isaiah 54:2). In other words, the Saints will be instructed to find more room for the returning Israelites! In the next verse, we find out why. Isaiah says that this will be done so that the returning ten tribes may "inherit the [land of the] Gentiles, and make the desolate cities to be inhabited" (Isaiah 54:3).

What is remarkable about this event is that even after all the destruction that will have occurred in these lands, Isaiah tells us that these returning Israelites will still have a hard time finding enough room to settle. He said that "the land of thy destruction, shall even now be too narrow by reason of the [new] inhabitants" (Isaiah 49:19). Isaiah then tells us that when this occurs, the ten tribes will say to the Saints in Zion that "the place is too strait [i.e., crowded] for me: give place to me that I may dwell" (Isaiah 49:20).

---

11. *Teachings of Joseph Smith*, 362. See also Articles of Faith 1:10; Andrew F. Ehat and Lyndon W. Cook, *The Words of Joseph Smith* (Bookcraft, 1980), 363.

12. Ehat and Cook, *Words of Joseph Smith,* 415. Brigham Young also taught this principle. He said that "North and South America are Zion" (*Journal of Discourses*, 11:324).

Isaiah then tells us what the reaction of the Saints will be when this occurs: "Lift up thine eyes round about, and behold: all these gather themselves together, and come to thee. . . . Then shalt thou say in thine heart, Who hath begotten me these, seeing I have lost my children, and am desolate, a captive, and removing to and fro? and who hath brought up these? Behold, I was left alone; these, where had they been?" (Isaiah 49:18, 21).

These remarkable verses give us an idea of just how many Israelites could be returning at this time. They also give us some indication of just how much strength these new Israelites will add to the Church in Zion.

## The Current Location of the Lost Ten Tribes

Knowing what we now know about their history and return, it is natural to wonder what happened to this group of Israelites once they crossed the Arctic Ocean. Where did they go? And where are they today?

While these answers are unknown to everyone except the Lord, it has not stopped us from speculating. After all, who doesn't love a good conspiracy theory? With that said, here are the most common theories as to the current whereabouts of the lost ten tribes.

## Polar Regions

In the earlier days of the Church, many Latter-day Saint scholars took the position that once the ten tribes crossed the Arctic Ocean, they settled in the polar regions of the north, in or around the Arctic Circle. One such scholar was George Reynolds, who said, "The Ten Tribes [are] hidden by Divine Providence in the far off frozen regions of the north, and environed by a belt of snow and ice so impenetrable that no man in modern days has reached them."[13]

13. George Reynolds, *Are We of Israel?* (Geo. Q. Cannon & Sons Co. Printers, 1883), 10.

Another to take this view was Elder W. W. Phelps, who said, "There may be a continent at the north pole, of more than 1300 square miles, containing thousands of millions of Israelites."[14]

Elder Orson Pratt was another to discuss this possibility. He said:

> The Lord God . . . [will bring] them forth from those dreary, desolate, cold arctic regions. . . .
>
> I do know, from that which is reported by those who have tried to find a passage to the pole, that there is a warmer country off there. . . . There is a tract of country around the pole, some seven or eight hundred miles in diameter, that no man among the nations that we are acquainted with, has ever explored. But how much of that land may be fit for habitation I am not prepared to say, for I do not know. I know it would be a very easy matter for the Lord God, by the aid of great mountain ranges encircling them around about, to produce a band of ice which would prevent other nations and people very easily reaching them.[15]

During this time in Church history, this theory was very popular, but it did not last long. There was at the time much unexplored land in the north, but as time went by, and as more and more explorations took place, there quickly seemed to be less and less land where the ten tribes could be living. Turner wrote, "This was generally accepted in the 19th century when the polar regions were largely unexplored, but in the main it has not been publicly advocated by Church authorities for well over half a century."[16]

Here is another explanation for why this polar region theory may have lost some of its steam: "In 1875 . . . there were still many unexplored areas in the north countries. As time went on, Robert Peary's expedition claimed victory over the North pole in 1909. The accuracy and coverage of our maps improved, and there appeared to be fewer and fewer places where the northern tribes could be residing.

---

14. Letter of W. W. Phelps to Oliver Cowdery, *Messenger and Advocate* 2, no. 1 (Oct. 1835): 94.
15. *Journal of Discourses*, 18:23–26.
16. Rodney Turner, *This Eternal Earth* (Granite Publishing, 2000), 205.

As that happened, some LDS writers shifted to a more figurative interpretation."[17]

## Scattered Remnants Only: A Figurative Interpretation

This figurative interpretation reasons that if the ten tribes are not currently in the north, then they must have all been scattered at one time or another.

Those who advance this theory also take the stance that the ten tribes are not in a group today, and therefore their return to Zion, as described in the book of Isaiah and Doctrine and Covenants 133, must be referring to scattered Israel. However, because these particular passages seem to be describing a group of Israelites who return all at once—and since the house of Israel has, in these last days, been gathered one by one through missionary work—those who advance this theory have assumed that these passages must be interpreted figuratively rather than literally.

One General Authority to take this stance was Elder B. H. Roberts. When commenting on section 133 of the Doctrine and Covenants, he said, "We of course must be prepared to take into account the figurative language they speak. It is possible that if we fail to do this, we shall misapprehend, in part, some material fact of their message. Especially should one be on his guard in such highly picturesque matters as the return of the lost tribes from their long dispersion—from the lands of the north."[18]

Another General Authority to take this stance was Elder Bruce R. McConkie, who said:

> There is something mysterious and fascinating about believing the Ten Tribes are behind an iceberg somewhere in the land of the north. . . . A common cliché asserts: "If we knew where the Lost Tribes were, they would not be lost." True it is that they are lost from the knowledge of the world; they are not seen and recognized as the

---

17. Pratt, "A Volcanic Highway." Pratt continued, "The idea of multitudes of people existing at some unknown location on the earth is now so remote that scientists would allow virtually zero chance of that happening."

18. B. H. Roberts, *Defense of the Faith and the Saints* (Deseret News, 1907), 2:481.

> kingdom they once were; but in general terms, their whereabouts is known. They are scattered in all the nations of the earth, primarily in the nations north of the lands of their first inheritance.[19]
>
> The Ten Tribes . . . will be gathered one by one as their hearts are touched by the Spirit of Christ.[20]

To explain section 133 of the Doctrine and Covenants, Elder McConkie suggests that the highway to be cast up in the great deep is merely symbolic of the straight and narrow path,[21] that the scriptures they bring with them will be none other than our current standard works,[22] and so forth.[23]

This figurative interpretation would seem to be the stance you would have to take if you believed that the ten tribes were all scattered throughout the world at one time or another. However, those of us who believe that there was indeed a group of Israelites who remained together in one body after they arrived in the north prefer a different theory. This theory is that the ten tribes are not on this earth but were taken, much like Enoch's city, to another sphere after they crossed the Arctic Ocean.

## Another Sphere

If the Lord did indeed remove the ten tribes from the earth, it certainly would not have been the first time that He performed such an act. Earlier, the Lord did this with Enoch's city (see Moses 7:69) and again with Melchizedek's city of Salem (see Joseph Smith Translation, Genesis 14:32–34 [in the Bible appendix]). It is also possible that the

---

19. Bruce R. McConkie, *A New Witness of the Articles of Faith* (Deseret Book, 1985), 520.
20. Bruce R. McConkie, *A New Witness for the Articles of Faith*, 542.
21. Bruce R. McConkie, *The Millennial Messiah* (Deseret Book, 1982), 327.
22. Bruce R. McConkie, *The Millennial Messiah*, 217.
23. For those who are interested in reading the remainder of Elder McConkie's figurative interpretation of Doctrine and Covenants 133, see *Millennial Messiah,* 216–17, 319–28. For more information regarding this figurative interpretation, see Donald W. Parry and Jay A. Parry, *Understanding the Signs of the Times* (Deseret Book, 1999), 104–106.

Lord may have done this at other times as well.[24] In each of these cases, the Lord took an entire civilization, with their land, and relocated them to another part of our galaxy. The Lord is said to be the same yesterday today and forever, and if He has done this in the past, He certainly could have repeated this process again for the lost ten tribes. After all, what better way of keeping the ten tribes hidden than by removing them from the earth?

Something else worth mentioning is that if these ten tribes were indeed taken from this earth, John the Revelator would still be able to minister unto them because John is a translated being, and as Joseph Smith said about translated beings, "Their place of habitation is that of the terrestrial order, and a place prepared for such characters [the Lord] held in reserve to be ministering angels unto many planets."[25] This would allow John to minister unto the lost ten tribes, even if they are not currently on this earth.

As it turns out, we have evidence that indicates that many of the early Church leaders taught these very ideas. President Brigham Young, for example, was asked in 1859 if the explorations that were being made in northern Canada would result in the discovery and return of the lost ten tribes. He replied, "The nations will have nothing to do with the preparing of the way for their return. But when the time has come for their return, the Lord will do the work. They are on a portion of earth separated from this globe in the north which cannot be seen from this earth."[26]

In addition, Wilford Woodruff told of a conversation he had with President Brigham Young. He recorded in his journal, "President Young said he heard Joseph Smith say that the Ten Tribes of Israel were on a Portion of Land separated from this Earth."[27] He also noted,

---

24. Parley Pratt spoke of the "fragments, which have been broken off from the earth from time to time, in the mighty convulsions of nature. Some in the days of Enoch, some perhaps in the days of Peleg, some with the ten tribes, and some at the crucifixion of the Messiah" (*Millennial Star*, Feb. 1841, 257).

25. *Teachings of the Prophet Joseph Smith*, 170.

26. *Wilford Woodruff's Journal*, ed. Scott G. Kenny (Signature Books, 1985), 6:363 (Sept. 8, 1867).

27. *Wilford Woodruff's Journal*, 6:363 (Sept. 8, 1867).

"A portion of the North Country containing the ten tribes may be separated from the Earth."[28]

Again, we find recorded in the biography of Wilford Woodruff, "The leaders on their return from Provo made a visit to Logan. Here, President Young is quoted as saying that the ten tribes of Israel are on a portion of the earth—a portion separated from the main land."[29]

Eliza R. Snow, plural wife of the Prophet Joseph Smith, recorded in poetry:

> And when the Lord saw fit to hide
> The "ten lost tribes" away,
> Thou, earth, wast sever'd to provide
> The orb on which they stay.[30]

When curious where Eliza Snow got the idea for the lyrics to this hymn, one person asked her, "Eliza, where did you get your ideas about the ten lost tribes being taken away as you explain it in your wonderful hymn?" She answered, "Why my husband [the Prophet Joseph] told me about it."[31]

Elder Orson Pratt also wrote:

> The Prophet Joseph once in my hearing advanced his opinion that the Ten Tribes were separated from the Earth; or a portion of the Earth was by a miracle broken off, and that the Ten Tribes were taken away with it, and that in the latter days it would be restored to the Earth or be let down in the Polar regions. Whether the Prophet founded his opinion upon revelation or whether it was a matter of mere speculation with him, I am not able to say.[32]

---

28. *Wilford Woodruff Journal*, 6:368 (Sept. 25, 1859).

29. Matthias F. Cowley, *Wilford Woodruff: History of His Life and Labors* (Bookcraft, 1964), 448.

30. Eliza R. Snow, "An Address to Earth," *Sacred Hymns and Spiritual Songs of the Church of Jesus Christ of Latter-Day Saints* (Deseret News, 1891), 322. See also Eliza R. Snow, *Millennial Star* 13:272 (Sept. 1852).

31. Robert W. Smith, *The Last Days*, 6th ed., comp. Robert W. and Elisabeth A. Smith (Pyramid Press, 1943), 217.

32. Orson Pratt, *Letter Box of Orson Pratt,* Church Historian's Office, Letter to John C. Hall, Dec. 13, 1875, as quoted in R. Clayton Brough, *The Lost Tribes* (Horizon Publishers, 1979), 50.

If the lost ten tribes were indeed taken with a piece of this earth and relocated somewhere in our galaxy, how then would they then return in the latter days? As it turns out, this question may be answered by the description of their return, as recorded in section 133 of the Doctrine and Covenants. If we examine this section with this new information, we find the following.

We first read that "they who are in the north countries shall come in remembrance before the Lord" (Doctrine and Covenants 133:26). If the ten tribes returned from another sphere or planet, they would logically return to the same place from whence they disappeared, which would be somewhere in the north, near the Arctic Ocean. From here, these Israelites in the "north countries" would begin their journey toward Zion.

As we continue in section 133 of the Doctrine and Covenants, we learn that "their prophets shall hear [the Lord's] voice, and shall no longer stay themselves; and they shall smite the rocks" (verse 26). As discussed in chapter 7, these Israelites will have prophets among them. Here, we learn that these prophets, as they lead their people to Zion from the north countries, will no longer "stay themselves" (verse 26). In other words, they will no longer be kept hidden from the knowledge of the world but will be revealed. Furthermore, if a portion of earth was taken when the ten tribes were relocated, then it would naturally be restored again to its original location when the ten tribes return. If this were to occur, and a portion of earth came in contact with our planet, it would truly "smite the rocks" (verse 26).

To illustrate, while referring to Revelation 6:13, Elder Parley P. Pratt was asked the question "How can the stars fall from heaven to earth, when they (as far as we know) are much larger than the earth?" This was his answer:

> The stars which will fall to earth, are fragments which have been broken off from the earth from time to time, in the mighty convulsions of nature. Some in the days of Enoch, some perhaps in the days of Peleg, some with the ten tribes, and some at the crucifixion of the Messiah. These all must be restored again at the "times of restitution of all things." This will restore the ten tribes of Israel; and also bring again Zion, even Enoch's city. It will bring back the tree of life which is in the midst of the paradise of God; that you and

> I may partake of it. (See Rev. 2:7). When these fragments . . . are brought back and joined to this earth, it will cause a convulsion of nature . . . mountains will flow down, the valleys rise, the sea retire to its own place, the islands and continents will be removed, and earth be rolled together as a scroll. The earth will be many times larger than it is now.[33]

Once the land mass containing the lost ten tribes is restored to its mother earth, the heat of this meteor, as it comes in contact with the frozen regions of the Arctic, will cause mountains of ice to melt and "flow down at their presence" (Doctrine and Covenants 133:26).

As we continue in Doctrine and Covenants 133, we learn that "an highway shall be cast up in the midst of the great deep" (verse 27). Once this land is restored unto its original location in the north, the returning Israelites will still have to pass through the Arctic Ocean in order to get to Zion. In order for this to occur, the Lord tells us He will produce a miracle similar to the ancient miracle of parting of the Red Sea. We are told that a "highway" will be cast up "in the midst of the great deep" (verse 27), allowing the Israelites to cross. As Elder Orson Pratt explained, "The Israel of the latter day has got to cross the sea dry shod, just as ancient Israel did."[34] This seems to agree with the account in 2 Esdras, which states that the ten tribes will remain hidden until "the latter time; and now when they shall begin to [return], the Highest shall stay the springs of the stream again, that they may go through."[35]

Section 133 continues: "And they shall bring forth their rich treasures unto the children of Ephraim" (verse 30). As discussed previously, these rich treasures will undoubtedly include the scriptural record that these Israelites kept when the resurrected Lord ministered unto them.[36]

Section 133 continues: "And there shall they fall down and be crowned with glory, even in Zion, by the hands of the servants of the Lord, even the children of Ephraim" (verse 32). The children of

33. *Millennial Star*, Feb. 1841, 257–58.

34. *Journal of Discourses*, 18:23.

35. *Apocrypha*, 2 Esdras 13:46–47.

36. See, for example, *Journal of Discourses*, 21:301.

Ephraim are the members of the Church who will already be in Zion at this time. Elder Orson Pratt therefore asked:

> Now what does this mean? A people that have had such mighty power, a people before whose camp the Lord of hosts has been seen, and his glory by day and by night; a people before whom the mountains and the hills tremble and flee; shall a people of that description fall down and be crowned by another people? Who are this other people, that is, these highly favored children of Ephraim? What particular blessing has the Lord for Ephraim? He holds the birthright. "Ephraim is my first-born," saith the Lord in the 31st chapter of Jeremiah. The first-born in the great latter-day work, holding the keys of blessing for all the twelve tribes of Israel. . . . God did not take away the birth-right of Reuben, the first-born of Israel, and transfer it to the heads of the sons of Joseph for a purpose that was of no particular account; but he transferred the birth-right from Reuben to Joseph that they might hold it as the first-born among all the tribes of Israel, to bless them in the latter days.[37]

In other words, the birthright of Ephraim is to crown the ten tribes with glory once they make their way to Zion (see Doctrine and Covenants 133:32). But what exactly does it mean to be crowned with glory? As it turns out, being "crowned with glory" (Doctrine and Covenants 133:32) is synonymous with receiving the fulness of the priesthood, or having your calling and election made sure. The Lord made this clear when He said that the righteous will "possess eternal life, *and be crowned with celestial glory*" (Doctrine and Covenants 101:65; emphasis added).

Thus, once Zion is built, the children of Ephraim (worthy members of the Church) will administer this highest of temple ordinances to the returning lost ten tribes and thereby crown them with glory. Elder Orson Pratt explained, "Do not think that we are the only people who will have Prophets. God is determined to raise up Prophets among that people [the ten tribes], *but he will not bestow upon them all the fulness of the blessings of the Priesthood. The fulness will be reserved to be given to them after they come to Zion.* But Prophets will be

---

37. *Journal of Discourses*, 18:24–25.

among them while in the north, and a *portion* of the Priesthood will be there."[38]

This important doctrine will be important to remember as our story progresses.

Section 133 continues: "Behold, this is the blessing of the everlasting God upon the [ten] tribes of Israel, and the richer blessing upon the head of Ephraim and his fellows" (verse 34).

This scripture tells us that while the ten tribes will be blessed by receiving the fulness of the priesthood, there will be an even richer blessing upon "Ephraim and his fellows" for their part in administrating these temple ordinances to their brethren. If the majority of Church members are from the tribe of Ephraim, who then are Ephraim's fellows?

Ephraim's "fellows" will be the members of the Church who belong to the house of Israel but who are descendants of tribes other than Ephraim. This group will include any Israelites who helped build Zion prior to the return of the lost ten tribes and who were told in their patriarchal blessing that they were from the tribes of Reuben, Simeon, Levi, Judah, Dan, Naphtali, Gad, Asher, Issachar, Zebulun, Benjamin, or Manasseh. They will be individuals who were gathered to the Church through missionary work and should not be confused with the main body of the returning lost ten tribes. These individuals have been designated Ephraim's "fellows" because they will assist the Ephraimites in crowning the returning ten tribes with celestial glory through the ordinances of the temple once the ten tribes make their return from the north.

## Benjamin Brown's Account

The following excerpt, from Robert W. Smith's book entitled *The Last Days*, is a transcript of an interview with Homer Brown, a former Patriarch to the Church. During this interview, Brother Brown tells of a conversation between his grandfather, Benjamin Brown, and the Prophet Joseph Smith:

---

38. *Journal of Discourses*, 18:25; emphasis added.

One evening in Nauvoo, just after dark, somebody rapped at the door very vigorously. Grandfather said he was reading the Doctrine and Covenants. He rose hurriedly and answered the summons at the door, where he met the Prophet Joseph Smith.

He said, "Brother Brown, can you keep me over night, the mobs are after me?" Grandfather answered, "Yes, sir. It will not be the first time, come in." . . .

Afterward they were in conversation relative to the principles of the Gospel. During the conversation the ten lost tribes were mentioned. Grandfather said, "Joseph, where are the ten tribes?" He said, "Come to the door and I will show you, come on Sister Brown, I want you both to see."

It being a starlight night the Prophet said: "Brother Brown, can you show me the Polar Star?" "Yes, sir," he said, pointing to the North Star. "There it is." . . .

The Prophet answered: "You are correct. Now," he said, pointing toward the star, "do you discern a little twinkler to the right and below the Polar Star, which we would judge to be about the distance of 20 feet from here?"

Grandfather answered, "Yes, sir."

The Prophet said: "Sister Brown, do you see that star also?"

Her answer was, "Yes, sir."

"Very well then," he said, "Let's go in." After re-entering the house, the Prophet said: "Brother Brown, I noticed when I came in that you were reading the Doctrine and Covenants. Will you kindly get it."

He did so. The Prophet turned to Section 133 and read, commencing at the 26th verse and throughout to the 34th verse. He said, after reading the 31st verse, "Now let me ask you what would cause the everlasting hills to tremble with more violence than the coming together of two planets. And the place whereon they reside will return to this Earth. Now," he said, "Scientists will tell you that it is not scientific: that two planets coming together would be disastrous to both; but, when two planets or other objects are traveling in the same direction and one of them with a little greater velocity than the other, it would not be disastrous, because one traveling faster would overtake the other. Now, what would cause the mountains of ice to melt quicker than the heat caused by the friction of the two planets coming together?" And then he asked the question,

> "Did you ever see a meteor falling that was not red hot? So that would cause the mountains of ice to melt.
>
> "And relative to the Great Highway, which should be cast up when that planet returns to its place in the great Northern Waters, it will form a highway and waters will recede and roll back." He continued, "Now as to their coming back from the Northern Waters; they will return from the north because their planet will return to the place from whence it was taken.
>
> "Relative to the waters rolling back to the north. If you take a vessel of water and swing it rapidly around your head you won't spill any, but if you stop the motion gradually, it will begin to pour out. Now, Brother Brown, at the present time this earth is rotating very rapidly. When this planet returns it will make the earth that much heavier, and it will then revolve slower, and that will account for the waters receding from the earth for a great while, but it has now turned and is proceeding rapidly eastward." . . .
>
> The Prophet added . . . "When [Enoch's city] comes back, that and the planet on which the lost tribes are, the earth will receive its equilibrium, and will revolve as it naturally was."[39]

One witness of this statement was Israel Call, who, after hearing the above statement, said, "My father, Anson Call, was a particular friend of the Prophet Joseph. I heard him say on a number of occasions that the Prophet told him in company with others that the ten tribes were on a portion of this earth, that had been taken away."[40]

While this account is not a firsthand experience, it does seem to fall right in line with many of the things we have discussed above.

## Other Accounts

In addition to Benjamin Brown's account, there have also been many others who have testified that the Prophet Joseph taught them

39. Smith, *The Last Days*, 217–21. We should point out that according to Latter-day Saint author R. Clayton Brough, Benjamin Brown's view "is not acceptable to modern science because it defies some of the basic laws or theories of physics and astronomy" (Brough, *The Lost Tribes*, 49).

40. Smith, *The Last Days*, 221.

very similar things.[41] For example, Bathsheba W. Smith reported the following: "Joseph taught that . . . the ten tribes were not on this globe, but a portion of this earth cleaved off with them, went flying into space, and when the Earth reels to and fro like a drunken man, and the stars from heaven fall, it would join on again."[42]

Furthermore, here are some excerpts from Charles L. Walker's journal:

> Br. Everett said that he heard Joseph say that the earth had been divided and parts taken away, but the time would come when all would be restored.[43]

> [Jacob Gates] said he heard Joseph Smith say . . . concerning the ten Lost Tribes, They are hid from us by land and air. . . . Yes, said Joseph, by land and air; they are hid from us in such a manner and at such an angle that the Astronomers cannot get their telescopes to bear of them from this Earth.[44]

> Sister Green, stat[ed] that she heard Eliza Snow speak of the nine and one-half lost tribes being on an orb and would eventually come back to their former place.[45]

> At night paid Sister Eliza R. Snow a Short Visit and had some conversation with her on the Dividing of the Earth. She told me that she heard the Prophet Joseph say that when the 10 tribes were taken away the Lord cut the Earth in two, Joseph striking his left hand in the center with the edge of his right to illustrate the idea, and that they (the 10 tribes) were on an orb or planet by themselves, and when they returned with the portion of this Earth that was taken away with them, the coming together of these 2 bodies or

---

41. The following accounts are taken from Turner, *This Eternal Earth*, 210–16, 257.

42. *Juvenile Instructor*, 27:344.

43. *Journal of Charles L. Walker* (1862), 2:505, digitized by Utah State University's Merrill-Cazier Library.

44. *Journal of Charles L. Walker*, 2:539.

45. *Journal of Charles L. Walker*, 2:532.

> orbs would cause a shock and make the "Earth reel to and fro like a drunken Man."[46]

Daniel Allen testified, "I heard Joseph the Prophet say . . . [the Ten Tribes] were upon a portion of this planet that had been broken off and which was taken away and the sea rushed in between Europe and America, and that when that piece returns there would be a great shake; the sea would then move to the north where it belonged in the morning of creation."[47]

Wandle Mace, an associate of Joseph Smith, was once troubled with this question: If the ten tribes were indeed together in a large group, where on earth could there possibly be enough room to hide them? He asked himself, "Where is there habitable earth for this vast amount of people who are hidden from the rest of mankind?" After hearing the Prophet speak on the subject, his autobiography records:

> In the course of his remarks he spoke of the earth being divided at various times. He said, "When Enoch and his city was taken away, a portion of earth was taken and would again be restored. Also in the days of Peleg, the earth was divided . . . " He then referred to the 'Ten Tribes,' saying, "You know a long time ago in the days of Shalmanezer King of Assyria when the Ten Tribes was taken away, and never been heard of since." He said, "The earth will be restored as at the beginning, and the last taken away will be the first to return, for the last shall be first, and the first shall be last in all things" . . . These remarks satisfied me, it was no longer necessary to hunt the place on this earth where the Ten Tribes were so long hidden, for the earth was divided and taken away, and will be the first to return, as it was the last taken away.[48]

Once again, Wandle Mace quoted Joseph Smith as saying, "Some of you brethren have been coming up the river, on a Steamboat, and while seated at the table, the Steamboat runs against a snag upsetting the table and scattering the dishes. So it will be when these portions

---

46. *Journal of Charles L. Walker*, 2:540.

47. *Minutes of the School of the Prophets*, 156–57 (Aug. 17, 1872).

48. *Autobiography of Wandle Mace*, Church History Library, 35.

of earth return. It will make the Earth reel to and fro like a drunken man."[49]

In his journal, Samuel H. Rogers recorded that the Prophet Joseph taught the following:

> We also read in the Scriptures that the earth shall reel to and fro like a drunken man. What shall cause this earth to reel to and fro like a drunken man? We read that the stars shall fall to the earth like a fig falling from a fig tree. When these stars return to the place where they were taken from, it will cause the earth to reel to and fro. Not that the planets will come squarely against each other, in such case both planets would be broken to pieces. But in their rolling motion they will come together where they were taken from which will cause the earth to reel to and fro.[50]

Of these testimonials, Latter-day Saint scholar Rodney Turner stated:

> We might dismiss one or two such statements as being mere second and third had hearsay, but what are we to do with a pattern of them from prominent, responsible individuals who were closely associated with the Prophet for a number of years? . . . The combined testimonies of such close associates of the Prophet as Brigham Young, Wilford Woodruff, Parley P. Pratt, Eliza R. Snow, Bathsheba W. Smith, and Wandle Mace should not be lightly dismissed. . . . These witnesses are united in testifying that Joseph Smith consistently and repeatedly located the Lost Tribes beyond the Earth.[51]

Regardless of which theory regarding the lost ten tribes turns out to be true, it is clear that when they make their return, it will be spoken of as one of the greatest events to transpire in these latter days (see Jeremiah 16:14–15).

---

49. *Autobiography of Wandle Mace*, 35.

50. *Journal of Samuel Holister Rogers*, Church History Library, 17.

51. Turner, *This Eternal Earth*, 215–16.

# 9
# The Sealing of the 144,000

In the early chapters of this book, we discussed the vision of the last days that was given to the prophet Nephi. Near the end of this recorded vision, right after Nephi saw the building up of Zion,[1] his record states:

> And the angel said unto me: Behold one of the twelve apostles of the Lamb.
>
> Behold, he shall see and write the remainder of these things. . . .
>
> And I, Nephi, heard and bear record, that the name of the apostle of the Lamb was John, according to the word of the angel.

---

1. After Nephi sees our Church firmly established throughout the world (see 1 Nephi 14:12), and after he sees the persecution that the Saints will have to endure (see 1 Nephi 14:13), Nephi then sees the "wrath of God" being poured out upon the wicked (1 Nephi 14:17), which is likely the destruction that will occur in the Americas just prior to the redemption of Zion. Nephi then said, "Then, at that day, the work of the Father shall commence, in preparing the way for the fulfilling of his covenants, which he hath made to his people who are of the house of Israel" (1 Nephi 14:17). This covenant includes the gathering of the house of Israel to the lands of their inheritances (see 3 Nephi 20:29; 1 Nephi 19:15–16) and the building up of Zion (see 3 Nephi 20:21–22).

> And behold, I, Nephi, am forbidden that I should write the remainder of the things which I saw and heard. (1 Nephi 14:20–21, 27–28)

Because Nephi was here forbidden to tell us about the events that are to take place after Zion is built, we must turn to the Apostle John's record in the book of Revelation to learn of these things. Before we examine John's record, however, a brief overview of its contents may be helpful, as it has often been the cause of some confusion among its readers.

## The Book of Revelation

The book of Revelation, written by the Apostle John, contains a vision that he received while he was banished to the Isle of Patmos. In this vision, John saw the entire 7,000-year period of the earth's existence, from the Fall of Adam to the end of the Millennium.

As mentioned in chapter 1, the Lord showed John this vision by unsealing a scroll that was sealed with seven seals. The scroll represented the earth, and each seal represented one thousand years of the earth's existence (see Doctrine and Covenants 77:6–7). When the first seal was opened, John saw the first thousand years of the earth's history; when the second seal was opened, John saw the second thousand years; and so on until all seven seals had been opened and shown to John.

We are currently living in the sixth seal, which simply means that we are nearing the end of the earth's sixth thousand-year period of history.

It is also important to understand that not only are we currently living in the sixth seal, but every event we have discussed up to this point, including the building of Zion and the return of the lost ten tribes, will also occur in the sixth seal. Therefore, when the sixth seal was opened and shown to John, he no doubt saw each of these events in great detail.

However, while John may have *seen* each of these events, there was only one event in the sixth seal that John chose to write about. His record states, "And I beheld when [the angel] had opened the sixth seal, and, lo, there was a great earthquake. . . . And the stars of heaven fell unto the earth, even as a fig tree casteth her untimely figs, when she is shaken of a mighty wind" (Revelation 6:12–13).

We have reason to believe that the earthquake that John is referring to here is the shaking of the earth that will occur when the lost ten tribes make their return from the north, or, as it is written in the Doctrine and Covenants, when "the boundaries of the everlasting hills shall tremble at their presence" (Doctrine and Covenants 133:31). The reason for this assumption comes from a statement made by Elder Parley P. Pratt, who was asked about these verses in Revelation: "How can the stars fall from heaven to the earth when they (as far as we know) are much larger than the earth?"[2] This was Elder Pratt's answer:

> We are not here given to understand that all the stars will fall, or even many of them: but only as a fig tree casteth her untimely figs when she is shaken by the wind. The stars which will fall to the earth are fragments which have been broken off from the earth from time to time in the mighty convulsions of nature . . . *some with the [departure of the lost] ten tribes. . . . When these fragments . . . are brought back and joined to this earth, it will cause a convulsion of nature. . . .* These all must be restored again at the "times of restitution of all things." *This will restore the ten tribes of Israel.*[3]

In other words, the earthquake and falling stars that were seen by John at the end of the sixth seal (see Revelation 6:12–13) were, according to Elder Pratt, the return of the lost ten tribes. Because the return of the lost ten tribes was the last event to be discussed in this work, it will be here, at this point in John's record, where we begin our commentary on the book of Revelation.

## The Four Angels

After John saw the return of the lost ten tribes, he writes, "And after these things I saw four angels standing on the four corners of the earth" (Revelation 7:1).

These four angels will be sent to earth shortly after the ten tribes return. But for what purpose? According to John, these angels will have the power "to hurt the earth and the sea" (Revelation 7:2), meaning

2. *Millennial Star,* Feb. 1841, 257–58.

3. *Millennial Star,* Feb. 1841, 257–58; emphasis added.

that they will be authorized to pour out destructions of all kinds upon the entire earth. However, before these four angels are given permission to unleash these destructions, John tells us, "And I saw another angel ascending from the east . . . and he cried with a loud voice to the four angels, to whom it was given to hurt the earth and the sea, Saying, Hurt not the earth, neither the sea, nor the trees, till we have sealed the servants of our God in their foreheads" (Revelation 7:2–3).

This angel "from the east" here persuades these other four angels to postpone the destruction that they were about to pour out upon the earth. But this destruction is not to be postponed for long—only until the servants of God have been "sealed . . . in their foreheads" (Revelation 7:3).

To be sealed in your forehead simply means that you are sealed up unto eternal life. It is the equivalent of receiving the fulness of the priesthood, or having your calling and election made sure. Joseph Smith said, "Four destroying angels holding power over the four quarters of the earth until the servants of God are sealed in their foreheads, which signifies sealing the blessing upon their heads, meaning the everlasting covenant, thereby making their calling and election sure."[4]

John then tells us how many servants are to be sealed in their foreheads at this time: "And I heard the number of them which were sealed [in their foreheads]: and there were sealed an hundred and forty and four thousand of all the tribes of the children of Israel" (Revelation 7:4).[5]

John then proceeds to tell us that these 144,000 will be made up of 12,000 from each of the twelve tribes of Israel (see Revelation 7:5–8),[6] which is also helpful in clarifying that at this point in John's

4. *Teachings of the Prophet Joseph Smith*, sel. Joseph Fielding Smith (1976), 321. See also *Teachings of the Prophet Joseph Smith*, 366; *Journal of Discourses*, 14:242–43.

5. According to Joseph Smith, "If the first Seventy are all employed, and there is a call for more laborers, it will be the duty of the seven presidents of the first Seventy to call and ordain other Seventy and send them forth to labor in the vineyard, until, if needs be, they set apart seven times seventy, and even until there are one hundred and forty–four thousand thus set apart for the ministry" (*Teachings of the Prophet Joseph Smith*, 75).

6. Note that in these passages, the tribe of Dan is omitted and is replaced by Joseph's double portion of Ephraim and Manasseh.

revelation, the ten tribes have indeed made their return, for that is the most plausible way that 12,000 from each tribe could be called and set apart.

It should be noted that we are unsure whether this figure of 144,000 will be literal or symbolic. For example, in ancient Israel, the number twelve represented the priesthood and priesthood power,[7] and according to Latter-day Saint scholar Alonzo L. Gaskill, "Because the number twelve symbolizes priesthood, multiples of twelve are traditionally understood to be a symbol for the fulness of the priesthood, or making one's calling and election sure."[8]

Since 144,000 is a multiple of twelve (12 x 12,000 = 144,000), and since the number 144,000 represents the fulness of the priesthood, it may very well end up being the case that the number of individuals who make up this group will far exceed 144,000 when all is said and done. In fact, Joseph Smith alluded to this when he said, "There will be 144,000 saviors on Mount Zion, *and with them an innumerable host* that no man can number."[9]

## The Mission of the 144,000

What will the mission of this 144,000 be? In section 77 of the Doctrine and Covenants, Joseph Smith asked, "What are we to understand by sealing the one hundred and forty-four thousand, out of all the tribes of Israel—twelve thousand out of every tribe?" (Doctrine and Covenants 77:11).

This was the revealed answer as he heard it: "We are to understand that those who are sealed are high priests, ordained unto the holy order of God, to administer the everlasting gospel . . . to bring as many as will come to the church of the Firstborn" (Doctrine and Covenants 77:11).

---

7. See Mick Smith, *The Book of Revelation: Plain, Pure, and Simple* (Bookcraft, 1998), 288–89; Alonzo L. Gaskill, *The Lost Language of Symbolism: An Essential Guide for Recognizing and Interpreting Symbols of the Gospel* (Deseret Book, 2003), 134.

8. Gaskill, *The Lost Language of Symbolism*, 135.

9. *Teachings of the Prophet Smith*, 366; emphasis added.

Here Joseph Smith learns that these 144,000 are "to bring as many as will come to the church of the Firstborn" (Doctrine and Covenants 77:11).

We should here point out that the Church of the Firstborn is not equivalent with The Church of Jesus Christ of Latter-day Saints. Rather, members of the Church of the Firstborn are those who will inherit the highest degree of the celestial kingdom. In section 88 of the Doctrine and Covenants, the Lord said, "I give unto you . . . eternal life, even the glory of the celestial kingdom; Which glory is that of the church of the Firstborn" (Doctrine and Covenants 88:4–5; see also Doctrine and Covenants 76:50, 55–58, 71, 92–95; 93:21–22; 107:18–19; 78:21).

It is therefore possible to belong to The Church of Jesus Christ of Latter-day Saints and not belong to this Church of the Firstborn. Not until Latter-day Saints receive their calling and elections and are thereby sealed up unto eternal life will they become members of the Church of the Firstborn.

The mission of the 144,000, therefore, is to first receive this seal themselves at the hand of Ephraim (see Doctrine and Covenants 133:32),[10] and second, to get others to receive this seal as well (see Doctrine and Covenants 77:11). In other words, their mission is to seek out and invite all who are worthy to become members of the Church of the Firstborn by receiving their calling and elections.

The 144,000 will be sent out as missionaries to all the world, inviting all who have a desire to join the Saints in Zion become members of Christ's true Church and eventually receive this ordinance as well. They will be instrumental in the final last gathering spoken of in section 45 of the Doctrine and Covenants: "And it shall come to pass that the righteous shall be gathered out from among all nations, and shall come to Zion, singing with songs of everlasting joy" (Doctrine and Covenants 45:71).

10. Since Doctrine and Covenants 133:32 has reference to the returning ten tribes being "crowned with glory" (or receiving one's calling and election made sure), it is therefore very likely that this phrase is also referring to the sealing of the 144,000 because this group is made up of 12,000 from each tribe (see Revelation 7:5–8).

Much of this gathering will no doubt be the direct result of the ministry of these 144,000, who are to be sealed in their foreheads before the four waiting angels pour out destruction upon the earth.

As we discuss this future destruction, it must be remembered that this destruction is different from the destruction that will have occurred in the Americas after the times of the Gentiles are fulfilled. After the destruction in the Americas, Zion will be built, the ten tribes will return, and the 144,000 will be called and sealed. The 144,000 will then "bring as many as will come to the church of the Firstborn" (Doctrine and Covenants 77:11) so that they may receive this seal as well. Once this has occurred, a second period of destruction, as prophesied in the book of Revelation, will begin.

## The Day of Power

In order to understand why the four angels in the book of Revelation are told to postpone pouring out destruction until these 144,000 Israelites have been called and sealed in their foreheads, we need to understand that this sealing will actually provide a literal physical protection from these future destructions, not only for the 144,000 but for all the Saints who receive it. In section 84 of the Doctrine and Covenants, we read:

> And the sons of Moses and of Aaron [i.e., worthy holders of the Melchizedek and Aaronic Priesthoods] shall be filled with the glory of the Lord, upon Mount Zion in the Lord's house [i.e., in the temple in the New Jerusalem]. . . .
>
> For whoso is faithful unto the obtaining these two priesthoods of which I have spoken, and the magnifying their calling, are sanctified by the Spirit *unto the renewing of their bodies.*
>
> They become . . . the elect of God.
>
> And also all they who receive this priesthood . . . receiveth my Father's kingdom; therefore all that my Father hath shall be given unto him. (Doctrine and Covenants 84:32–35, 38; emphasis added)

In other words, all who are faithful and found worthy of their respective priesthoods at the time the temple at the New Jerusalem is built will enter into that temple and receive the fulness of the priesthood—which, as discussed in chapter 5, is an ordinance performed in the temple that seals the recipient up to eternal life. It is the equivalent of having your calling and election made sure. It is also the equivalent of being sealed in your forehead. Thus, according to section 84, those who receive the fulness of the priesthood at the temple in Zion will become the "elect of God," which means they will receive their calling and election and as a result will be given "all that [the] Father hath" (Doctrine and Covenants 84:38). Once this occurs, section 84 tells us that these individuals will be "sanctified by the Spirit unto the renewing of their bodies" (Doctrine and Covenants 84:33).

This phrase—"sanctified by the Spirit unto the renewing of their bodies"—has reference to a literal physical protection, as mentioned previously, that will come to all those who received this seal placed upon them at this time. Elder Orson Pratt explained:

> When the Temple [in New Jerusalem] is built the sons of the two Priesthoods, that is, those who are ordained to the Priesthood of Melchizedek . . . and those who have been ordained to the Priesthood of Aaron . . . will enter into that Temple . . . and all of them who are pure in heart will behold the face of the Lord and that too before he comes in his glory in the clouds of heaven, for he will suddenly come to his Temple, and he will purify the sons of Moses and of Aaron. . . . In doing this, he will purify not only the minds of the Priesthood in that Temple, *but he will purify their bodies until they shall be quickened, renewed and strengthened*, and they will be partially changed, not to immortality, but changed in part that they can be filled with the power of God, and they can stand in the presence of Jesus, and behold his face in the midst of that Temple.
>
> This will prepare them for further ministrations among the nations of the earth, it will prepare them to go forth in the days of tribulation and vengeance upon the nations of the wicked, when God will smite them with pestilence, plague and earthquake, such as former generations never knew. Then the servants of God will need to be armed with the power of God, they will need to have that sealing blessing pronounced upon their foreheads *that they can stand forth in the midst of these desolations and plagues and not be overcome by them*. When John the Revelator describes this scene he says he saw four angels sent forth, ready to hold the four

> winds that should blow from the four quarters of heaven. Another angel ascended from the east and cried to the four angels, and said, "Smite not the earth now, but wait a little while." "How long?" "Until the servants of our God are sealed in their foreheads." What for? *To prepare them to stand forth in the midst of these desolations and plagues, and not be overcome.* When they are prepared, when they have received a renewal of their bodies in the Lord's Temple, and have been filled with the Holy Ghost and purified as gold and silver in a furnace of fire, then they will be prepared to stand before the nations of the earth and preach glad tidings of salvation in the midst of judgments that are to come like a whirlwind upon the wicked.[11]

According to Elder Pratt, those who have received this seal "can stand forth in the midst of these desolations and plagues and not be overcome,"[12] and this because their bodies will be "quickened, renewed and strengthened, and . . . partially changed"[13] so that they are "filled with the power of God."[14] It is very likely that those who receive this seal will be translated, much like the Three Nephites of old (see 3 Nephi 28:4–23), for according to President John Taylor, those in Zion "will have the power of translation."[15]

In fact, President Taylor even went as far as saying that eventually, the entire "city [of Zion] will be translated."[16] Having this "power of translation,"[17] or receiving this protective seal, will be the only way to guarantee survival from the destruction that these four angels will unleash upon the world.

---

11. *Journal of Discourses*, 15:365–66; emphasis added.

12. *Journal of Discourses*, 15:366.

13. *Journal of Discourses*, 15:365.

14. *Journal of Discourses*, 15:365–66.

15. *Journal of Discourses*, 21:253. See also Bruce R. McConkie, *The Millennial Messiah* (Deseret Book, 1982), 119.

16. *Journal of Discourses*, 21:253. For a discussion on the translation of Zion's citizens before the Second Coming, see John M. Pontius, *The Triumph of Zion* (Cedar Fort, 2010), chapter 3.

17. *Journal of Discourses*, 21:253.

## History Repeats Itself

As it turns out, this will certainly not be the first time God will have protected only those who have received His seal or mark. During the first Passover, God instructed all the children of Israel to kill a "lamb . . . without blemish," and spread its blood "on the two side posts and on the upper door post of the houses" (Exodus 12:5–7). The Lord then said, "For I will pass through the land of Egypt this night, and will smite all the firstborn in the land of Egypt. . . . And the blood shall be to you for a token upon the houses where ye are: and when I see the blood, I will pass over you, and *the plague shall not be upon you to destroy you*, when I smite the land of Egypt" (Exodus 12:12–13; emphasis added).

Here, the Lord preserved all who had received God's mark or token upon their houses and destroyed the rest.[18]

A second example is found in a vision that Ezekiel received just prior to the destruction of Jerusalem by the Babylonians in 587 BC. In this vision, Ezekiel saw the Lord instructing one of His angels to pass through the city of Jerusalem and set a spiritual mark on the foreheads of all those who had sorrow in their hearts for the abominations being done in the city. Those who received this spiritual mark were saved from the destruction while the rest were slain (see Ezekiel 9:1–7).

## The Mark of the Beast

During this time period, God will not be the only one who will be sealing the children of men in their foreheads, for as John the Revelator tells us, "And he [one of Satan's followers] causeth all, both small and great, rich and poor, free and bond, to receive a mark in their right hand, or in their foreheads: And that no man might buy or sell, save he that had the mark, or the name of the beast, or the number of his name" (Revelation 13:16–17).

According to Latter-day Saint scholar G. Erik Brandt:

> These marks carry both spiritual and physical significance. Spiritually, the mark of the beast serves as a contrast to God's seal.

18. A second example is found in Ezekiel 9:4–6.

> It is a counter mark representing opposition to those who are sealed in their foreheads. . . .
>
> Marking one's right hand and forehead means that one's deeds and thoughts are devoted to a cause, in this case the cause of the beast. Those who outwardly immerse themselves in the worship of the beast receive this mark, as a natural consequence of their works and thoughts.[19]

And just as those who receive God's seal are sealed up unto eternal life, so also will those who receive this mark of the beast be sealed up unto eternal damnation. An angel revealed to John:

> If any man worship the beast and his image, and receive his mark in his forehead, or in his hand,
>
> The same shall drink of the wine of the wrath of God, which is poured out without mixture into the cup of his indignation; and he shall be tormented with fire and brimstone in the presence of the holy angels, and in the presence of the Lamb:
>
> And the smoke of their torment ascendeth up for ever and ever: and they have no rest day nor night, who worship the beast and his image, and whosoever receiveth the mark of his name. (Revelation 14:9–11)

## Protective Seal

By contrast, those who receive God's seal will be protected from God's wrath. In fact, when John learned of the four angels who would pour out destructions upon the earth, he wrote, "And it was commanded them that they should not hurt the grass of the earth, neither any green thing, neither any tree; *but only those men which have not the seal of God in their foreheads*" (Revelation 9:4; emphasis added).

Another to speak of this sealing protection was Wilford Woodruff. In 1894, President Woodruff spoke of a vision that he received concerning this time period:

> Can you tell me where the people are who will be shielded and protected from these great calamities and judgments which are even

19. G. Eric Brandt, *The Book of Revelation: Things Which Must Shortly Come to Pass* (Granite Publishing, 2009), 298.

now at our doors? I'll tell you. The priesthood of God who honor their priesthood, and who are worthy of their blessings are the only ones who shall have this safety and protection. They are the only mortal beings. No other people have a right to be shielded from these judgments. They are at our very doors; not even this people will escape them entirely. They will come down like the judgments of Sodom and Gomorrah. And none but the priesthood will be safe from their fury.

> God has held the angels of destruction for many years, lest they should reap down the wheat with the tares. But I want to tell you now, that those angels have left the portals of heaven, and they stand over this people and this nation now, and are hovering over the earth waiting to pour out the judgments. . . . If you do your duty, and I do my duty, we'll have protection, and shall pass through the afflictions in peace and in safety. Read the scriptures and the revelations. They will tell you about all these things. . . . It's by the power of the Gospel that we shall escape.[20]

Elder Orson Pratt said that "we could not, with our narrow comprehensions of mind, perceive the power that will then follow," adding that "in the day of his power, you [missionaries] . . . will be armed with that glory, power, and majesty, and clothed upon from on high to that degree that no power on earth can stay you."[21] In addition, the prophet Nephi said:

> For the time soon cometh that the fulness of the wrath of God shall be poured out upon all the children of men; for he will not suffer that the wicked shall destroy the righteous.
>
> Wherefore, *he will preserve the righteous by his power*, even if it so be that the fulness of his wrath must come, and the righteous be preserved, even unto the destruction of their enemies by fire. Wherefore, the righteous need not fear; for thus saith the prophet, they shall be saved, even if it so be as by fire. . . .
>
> For behold, *the righteous shall not perish; for the time surely must come that all they who fight against Zion shall be cut off.* (1 Nephi 22:16–17, 19; emphasis added)

---

20. *Young Woman's Journal*, Aug. 1894, 11:512–13.

21. *Journal of Discourses*, 7:187.

The Savior, when giving a discourse on the last days, warned, "Watch ye therefore, and pray always, and keep my commandments, *that ye may be counted worthy to escape all these things which shall come to pass*, and to stand before the Son of Man when he shall come clothed in the glory of his Father" (Joseph Smith Translation, Luke 21:36 [in Luke 21:36, footnote *d*]; emphasis added).

Those who are "counted worthy to escape" will be those with the seal of the living God placed upon their foreheads. Latter-day Saint scholars Donald and Jay Parry wrote, "God figuratively marks and seals the righteous with his seal, making them his and placing them under his protection."[22]

Similarly, Elder Bruce R. McConkie, when speaking of these future destructions that the angels in the book of Revelation will unleash, said, "Only those in Zion who are sealed up unto eternal life have power to withstand the onslaught."[23]

Joseph Smith also taught this principle:

> Without Zion, and a place of deliverance, we must fall; because the time is near when the sun will be darkened, and the moon turn to blood, and the stars fall from the heaven, and the earth reel to and fro. Then, if this is the case, and if we are not sanctified and gathered to the places God has appointed . . . we must fall; we cannot stand; we cannot be saved; for God will gather out his Saints from the Gentiles, and then comes desolation and destruction, and *none can escape except the pure in heart who are gathered.*[24]

Similarly, as the Lord said unto Enoch, "As I live, even so will I come in the last days . . . but before that day . . . great tribulations shall be among the children of men, but *my people will I preserve*" (Moses 7:60–61; emphasis added).

## The Glory in Zion

The prophet Isaiah was another to teach us that those in Zion will be protected during this time period: "And the Lord will create upon

22. Donald W. Parry and Jay A. Parry, *Understanding the Signs of the Times* (Deseret Book, 1999), 90.

23. Bruce R. McConkie, *The Millennial Messiah*, 385.

24. *Teachings of the Prophet Joseph Smith*, 71; emphasis added.

every dwelling place of mount Zion, and upon her assemblies, a cloud and smoke by day, and the shining of a flaming fire by night: for upon all the glory shall be a defence. And there shall be a tabernacle for a shadow in the daytime from the heat, and for a place of refuge, and for a covert from storm and from rain" (Isaiah 4:5–6).

Similarly, in section 115 of the Doctrine and Covenants, we read, "Arise and shine forth . . . that the gathering together upon the land of Zion, and upon her stakes, may be for a defense, and for a refuge from the storm, and from wrath when it shall be poured out without mixture upon the whole earth" (Doctrine and Covenants 115:5–6).

For this reason, section 45 of the Doctrine and Covenants states:

> And it shall be called the New Jerusalem, a land of peace, a city of refuge, a place of safety for the saints of the Most High God;
>
> And the glory of the Lord shall be there, and the terror of the Lord also shall be there, insomuch that the wicked will not come unto it, and it shall be called Zion. . . .
>
> And it shall come to pass among the wicked: Let us not go up to battle against Zion, for the inhabitants of Zion are terrible; wherefore we cannot stand. . . .
>
> And it shall come to pass that the righteous shall be gathered out from among all nations, and shall come to Zion, singing with songs of everlasting joy. (Doctrine and Covenants 45:66–67, 70–71)

Elder Orson Pratt said of this verse:

> There must be something wonderful, indeed, to attract the attention of all nations; unless there is to be a very great power manifested, it would not attract the attention of the people afar off. . . . No wonder that the nations afar off flow to Zion. Did you ever hear tell of a whole city lighted up in that manner? . . . not on one house alone, but upon every dwelling place, "a cloud and smoke by day, and the shining of a flaming fire by night." The nations will be struck with wonder, and will say, "If that people have such great power, let us leave our own lands and countries; for it must be that those people are the people of God, for their houses are enveloped

> in a flame of fire every night, because of His glory: let us go up there, and know what His will is concerning us."[25]

Elder Pratt also stated:

> The Lord God has decreed that Zion shall become a strong nation, that the armies of Israel shall become very great, and not only very great, but they will be sanctified before him, and there will be such a power made manifest in their midst, that their banners will be terrible to all the nations of the earth. They will not be terrible because we outnumber the nations, but this terror of Zion which will be among the nations, will be because of the power of the great Jehovah that will be manifested in their midst. . . . Fear will seize upon the nations of the earth, and the banners of Zion will be terrible.[26]

This glory of Zion will be a direct result of its citizens receiving the seal of the living God in their foreheads. We are told that as a result of their righteousness, they will be "sanctified by the Spirit unto the renewing of their bodies" (Doctrine and Covenants 84:33), meaning that their bodies will be "quickened" and "filled with the power of God."[27] This will cause many in Zion to "have the power of translation,"[28] which will result in the entire city of Zion being filled with God's glory and will thus be protected from the terrible series of destructions that are about to be poured out upon the earth.

---

25. *Journal of Discourses*, 2:298.

26. *Journal of Discourses*, 17:306.

27. *Journal of Discourses*, 15:365–66.

28. *Journal of Discourses*, 21:253.

# 10
# The Seven Trumpets

Once the 144,000 have been sealed in their foreheads and have brought "as many as will come to the church of the Firstborn" (Doctrine and Covenants 77:11), destructions of all kinds will begin to be poured out upon the earth. And, as discussed in the previous chapter, in the midst of these destructions, only those who have received the seal of the living God will have the promise of protection.

## A Great Sign in Heaven

Just prior to these destructions, however, we are told that a great sign shall appear in the heavens.[1] We read in the Doctrine and Covenants, "And immediately there shall appear a great sign in heaven, and all people shall see it together" (Doctrine and Covenants 88:93).

---

1. This sign in heaven is placed at this point in our study because once the 144,000 have been sealed, the book of Revelation tells us that there will follow a "silence in heaven about the space of half an hour" (see Revelation 8:1). The Lord, in Doctrine and Covenants 88, also speaks of a "silence in heaven for the space of half an hour" (verse 95). If this silence here spoken of is the same silence mentioned in the book of Revelation (as we may suppose), then we learn from section 88 that immediately preceding this half hour of silence, a great sign shall appear in the heavens (see Doctrine and Covenants 88:97).

Of this sign, Joseph Smith said:

> There will be wars and rumors of wars, signs in the heavens above and on the earth beneath, the sun turned into darkness and the moon to blood, earthquakes in divers places, the seas heaving beyond their bounds; then will appear one grand sign of the Son of Man in heaven. But what will the world do? They will say it is a planet, a comet, etc. But the Son of Man will come as the sign of the coming of the Son of Man, which will be as the light of the morning cometh out of the east.[2]
>
> It will be small at its first appearance and gradually becomes larger until every eye shall see it. Shall the Saints understand it? Oh yes. Paul says so. Shall the wicked understand? Oh no, they attribute it to a natural cause. They will probably suppose it is two great comets coming in contact with each other. It will be small at first and will grow larger and larger until it will be all in a blaze so that every eye shall see it.[3]

Another to comment on this sign was Elder Orson Pratt:

> There will be a great sign in the heavens. It is not to be limited so that some few only of the human family can see it; but it is said, "All people shall see it together!" At least, it is to be like our sun seen over one entire side of the globe, and then passing immediately round to the other, or else it will encircle the whole earth at the same time. But the bridegroom does not come then. These are only the preceding events to let the Latter-day Saints and the pure in heart know that these are the times that they may trim up their lamps and prepare for the triumphant appearing of their Lord.[4]

We learn from President Wilford Woodruff that this "great sign in heaven" (Doctrine and Covenants 88:93) will be one of many signs to appear in the heavens in the last days. In 1889, he told of a vision he received: "I saw a great many signs that were presented before me, by

---

2. *Teachings of the Prophet Joseph Smith*, sel. Joseph Fielding Smith (1976), 286–87.

3. Andrew F. Ehat and Lyndon W. Cook, *The Words of Joseph Smith* (Bookcraft, 1980), 181 (spelling and grammar corrected). See also *History of the Church*, 5:290–91.

4. *Journal of Discourses*, 8:51.

[a heavenly messenger]; and among the rest, there were seven lions, as of burning brass, set in the heavens. [The messenger] says, 'That is one of the signs that will appear in the heavens before the coming of the Son of Man. It is a sign of the various dispensations.'"[5]

## The Seventh Seal Is Opened

It is important to understand that the sign in the heavens, along with the sealing of the 144,000, are among the last events to occur in the sixth seal.[6] Once these events have passed, the seventh seal will be opened. Once the seventh seal is opened, we are told there will be a half hour of silence. John records:, "And when [the angel] had opened the seventh seal, there was silence in heaven about the space of half an hour" (Revelation 8:1).

## The Half Hour of Silence

This half hour of silence marks the opening of the seventh seal. Of this silence, Elder Orson Pratt stated, "During the period of silence all things are perfectly still; no angels flying during that half hour; no trumpets sounding; no noise in the heavens above."[7]

Note that this silence is to be observed in heaven during this half hour period, as opposed to on the earth. The earth during this time will no doubt be very active as wickedness and corruption will be prevalent throughout. Comparatively, we can assume that the Saints in Zion will also be active in building up the kingdom of God on earth during this time.

Elder Orson Pratt also said of this half hour, "Whether the half hour here spoken of is according to our reckoning—thirty minutes, or whether it be according to the reckoning of the Lord we do not

---

5. Wilford Woodruff, "Administration of Angels," Mar. 3, 1889, in *Collected Discourses Delivered by President Wilford Woodruff, His Two Counselors, the Twelve Apostles, and Others*, ed. Brian H. Stuy (BHS Publishing, 1987–1992), 1:217.

6. According to Revelation 8:1, a half hour of silence marks the beginning of the seventh seal. Both the sign in heaven and the sealing of the 144,000 immediately precede this event (see Doctrine and Covenants 88:93–95; Revelation 6:12; 7:8).

7. *Journal of Discourses*, 16:328.

know . . . for aught we know the half hour during which silence is to prevail in heaven may be quite an extensive period of time."[8]

If this silence is to be found in heaven, then it would seem likely that this half hour would indeed be "according to the reckoning of the Lord," as Elder Pratt has suggested. Furthermore, Elder Bruce R. McConkie reasoned, "If the time here mentioned is 'the Lord's time' in which one day is a thousand years, the half hour would be some twenty-one of our years (Abr. 3:4; 2 Pet. 3:8)."[9]

If this half hour does in fact last "some twenty-one of our years," as Elder McConkie has suggested, then perhaps this will be the time period that the 144,000 will be sent forth as missionaries "to bring as many as will come to the church of the Firstborn" (Doctrine and Covenants 77:11). In other words, perhaps this half hour will be the Lord's way of giving the inhabitants of the earth one last chance to repent and join His Saints in Zion so that all who will may receive His seal and be protected.

Whether or not this is the purpose and duration of the half hour of silence still remains to be seen, as its meaning has yet to be revealed by the Lord.[10]

## The Seven Angels

After this half hour of silence has passed, John records, "And I saw the seven angels which stood before God; and to them were given seven trumpets" (Revelation 8:2).

Whether or not these seven angels include the four angels that were mentioned in the previous chapter is unknown; however, the mission of these seven angels will be the same as the former. They are sent to pour out destructions upon the earth. John revealed, "And the seven angels which had the seven trumpets prepared themselves to sound" (Revelation 8:6).

And thus the tribulation begins. We read further, "The first angel sounded, and there followed hail and fire mingled with blood, and

---

8. *Journal of Discourses*, 16:328.

9. Bruce R. McConkie, *The Millennial Messiah* (Deseret Book, 1982), 382.

10. Bruce R. McConkie, *The Millennial Messiah*, 635.

they were cast upon the earth: and the third part of trees was burnt up, and all green grass was burnt up" (Revelation 8:7).

The Lord begins by sending hail fire to the earth—not upon people directly but upon the "trees" and "green grass" that are upon the earth. In fact, the majority of these seven angels do not pour out their destructions with the intent to destroy people. Rather, they are meant to humble humankind and encourage repentance.

The Lord did something similar in Egypt at the time of Moses. Of the ten plagues, only one was intended to kill the Egyptians. The other nine were meant to alter Egypt's surroundings in an effort to soften Pharaoh's heart. The Nile was turned to blood (see Exodus 7:19). Frogs, lice, flies, locusts, and boils were all sent, not to kill but to be a pestilence unto Egypt (see Exodus 8:1–32). Egypt's cattle were destroyed by both a grievous hailstorm (see Exodus 9:19) and deadly plagues (see Exodus 9:3). And finally, thick darkness covered the land for three days (see Exodus 10:22). It was only after the Lord gave Pharaoh and the rest of Egypt ample opportunity to repent and let the Israelites go that He sent His destroying angel.

So too will it be with these destructions poured out by the seven angels. The majority do not destroy people but rather people's surroundings in an attempt to encourage repentance. Furthermore, just as the Israelites of old were protected from the majority the ten plagues (see Exodus 8:22; 9:4–6; 9:25–26; 10:22–23; 12:12–13), so too will the modern-day Israelites who have been sealed in their foreheads be protected from these latter-day plagues.

John continues: "And the second angel sounded, and as it were a great mountain burning with fire was cast into the sea: and the third part of the sea became blood; And the third part of the creatures which were in the sea, and had life, died; and the third part of the ships were destroyed" (Revelation 8:8–9).

"John," according to Brandt, "does not say exactly what the calamity of this trumpet is, but volcanoes are certainly the leading candidates. Thousands can be found circling the Pacific Ocean, known as the 'rim of fire;' and many others dot the globe from Africa, to the Atlantic Ocean, to the Mediterranean and beyond. The trumpet calls forth fire which is thrown, without regard, into the seas, causing death to the sea life, turning the waters as blood."[11] Thankfully, those who have been sealed in their foreheads will be unaffected by this plague.

John continues: "And the third angel sounded, and there fell a great star from heaven, burning as it were a lamp, and it fell upon the third part of the rivers, and upon the fountains of waters; And the name of the star is called Wormwood: and the third part of the waters became wormwood; and many men died of the waters, because they were made bitter" (Revelation 8:10–11).

Wormwood was a bitter herb that contaminated clean drinking water in the ancient world (see Jeremiah 9:15; 23:15). Here, John tells us that God will send this Wormwood to a third part of the earth's natural fountains, making their waters unfit to drink. Again, those who have been sealed in their foreheads will be unaffected by this plague.

John continues: "And the fourth angel sounded, and the third part of the sun was smitten, and the third part of the moon, and the third part of the stars; so as the third part of them was darkened, and the day shone not for a third part of it, and the night likewise" (Revelation 8:12).

This fourth plague will affect not only the earth but the heavens also, as the lights of the sky darken. Again, those who have been sealed in their foreheads will be unaffected by this darkness, for Isaiah tells us that "upon every dwelling place" in Zion, there will be found "a cloud and smoke by day, and the shining of a flaming fire by night" (Isaiah 4:5).

## The Three Remaining Angels

As severe as these first four plagues seem to be, they are nothing compared to the three which are to follow. John records: "And I beheld, and heard an angel flying through the midst of heaven, saying with a loud voice, Woe, woe, woe, to the inhabiters of the earth by reason of the other voices of the trumpet of the three angels, which are yet to sound!" (Revelation 8:13).

---

11. G. Eric Brandt, *The Book of Revelation: Things Which Must Shortly Come to Pass* (Granite Publishing, 2009), 183.

The next plague to be poured out upon the earth will have a devastating effect on the inhabitants of the earth: "And the fifth angel sounded, and I saw a star fall from heaven unto the earth: and to him was given the key of the bottomless pit" (Revelation 9:1).

Stars are often used throughout the scriptures to represent the spirit children of our Heavenly Father (see Job 38:7; Revelation 12:4). According to Brandt, "The fallen star spoken of by John is a clear reference to Lucifer, the 'son of the morning,' who once sat in authority in the premortal existence."[12] When this fifth angel sounds his trump, Lucifer will be given the key to the "bottomless pit." Brandt continues: "Scripturally, the term pit is used synonymously with hell, . . . the symbolic holding of the devil and his hosts."[13]

As Elder Bruce R. McConkie stated, "The bottomless pit is the depths of hell."[14] In other words, it is where Satan and all his followers, the one-third who were cast out during the War in Heaven, currently reside. "During the previous six thousand years," writes Latter-day Saint scholar Mick Smith, "the Lord had power over the key and controlled, so to speak, the powers of the adversary, but now [when the fifth angel sounds his trump] it is in possession of the Destroyer and he will do all he can to afflict and torment man."[15]

How will this occur? John tells us in the next verses, "And [Satan] opened the bottomless pit; and there arose a smoke out of the pit, as the smoke of a great furnace; and the sun and the air were darkened by reason of the smoke of the pit. And there came out of the smoke locusts upon the earth: and unto them was given power, as the scorpions of the earth have power" (Revelation 9:2–3).

These "locusts" that John refers to are undoubtedly none other than those who currently reside in the bottomless pit. They are the "third part of the hosts of heaven" (Doctrine and Covenants 29:36) who followed Satan in the premortal life. Once cast to the earth,

---

12. Brandt, *The Book of Revelation*, 194. See also Doctrine and Covenants 76:25–27; Isaiah 14:12–17; Luke 10:18.

13. Brandt, *The Book of Revelation*, 194.

14. Bruce R. McConkie, *Doctrinal New Testament Commentary* (Bookcraft, 1973), 3:570.

15. Mick Smith, *The Book of Revelation: Plain, Pure, and Simple* (Bookcraft, 1998), 90.

they were allowed to tempt and try man, although their power has always been limited by God.[16] However, when the fifth angel sounds his trump and Satan is authorized to open this bottomless pit, these satanic angels will be loosed, and God will temporarily give them a longer leash.

When this occurs, John tells us that they will be "given power, as the scorpions of the earth have power" (Revelation 9:3). He also tells us that this power will be used to torment man. He records: "And to them it was given that they should not kill [man], but that they should be tormented five months: and their torment was as the torment of a scorpion, when he striketh a man. And in those days shall men seek death, and shall not find it; and shall desire to die, and death shall flee from them" (Revelation 9:5–6).

While these satanic spirits will, at this time, be allowed more power, John here tells us that this power will still in fact be limited by God. They are not to kill man, only torment them for a time. Furthermore, John tells us, "And it was commanded them that they should not hurt the grass of the earth, neither any green thing, neither any tree; *but only those men which have not the seal of God in their foreheads*" (Revelation 9:4; emphasis added).

Here again we find further evidence that those who have been sealed in their foreheads are to be protected from these terrible plagues. Latter-day Saint scholars Donald and Jay Parry write, "[Just as] locusts ravage green plants and trees, [Satan's] armies will scourge the men and women of the earth, save those who are citizens of Zion and who possess the seal of the living God on their foreheads. . . . These events are designed to encourage people to repent of their sins and to acknowledge God as their Lord and King."[17]

---

16. See, for example, Mark 5:1–16; Mark 1:34; Job 2:6; *Teachings of the Prophet Joseph Smith*, 181. Hugh Nibley stated, "God does not fight Satan: a word from him and Satan is silenced and banished. There is no contest there; in fact we are expressly told that all the power which Satan enjoys here on earth is granted to him by God. 'We will allow Satan, our common enemy, to try man and to tempt him.'" Hugh Nibley, *Nibley on the Timely and Timeless* (Bookcraft, 1978), 288.

17. Donald W. Parry and Jay A. Parry, *Understanding the Signs of the Times* (Deseret Book, 1999), 253.

John continues, "And the sixth angel sounded, and I heard a voice from . . . the golden altar which is before God, Saying to the sixth angel which had the trumpet, Loose the four angels which are bound in the bottomless pit. And the four angels were loosed" (Joseph Smith Translation, Revelation 9:13–15 [in Revelation 9:14, footnote *a*]).

Here again we find four more demonic spirits, spirits who likely hold a position of authority in this spirit prison, released from the bottomless pit. The mission of these four satanic angels is simple: gather the children of the earth together for war. We read that after no time, these demonic spirits will have influenced 200 million people into taking up arms: "And the number of the army of the horsemen were two hundred thousand thousand [i.e., 200 million]" (Revelation 9:16).

It should be noted that this army of 200 million will be made up of mortals as opposed to demonic spirits (contrast, for example, the locusts mentioned in Revelation 9:3, who are made up of demonic spirits only). We learn from John that this army of 200 million will eventually kill one-third of the earth's entire population "by the fire, and by the smoke, and by the brimstone, which issued out of their mouths" (Revelation 9:18).

What will happen to the remaining two-thirds of the earth's population? "And the rest of the men which were not killed by these plagues yet repented not of the works of their hands" (Revelation 9:20).

During this time period, fewer and fewer will be able to remain neutral in this war between good and evil, for as the Lord said in the Doctrine and Covenants, "The day speedily cometh; the hour is not yet, but is nigh at hand, when peace shall be taken from the earth, and the devil shall have power over his own dominion. And also the Lord shall have power over his saints, and shall reign in their midst, and shall come down in judgment upon . . . the world" (Doctrine and Covenants 1:35–36).[18]

It is important to understand that those in Zion will not be compelled to join this army, for the Lord in the Doctrine and Covenants has said:

---

18. See also *Journal of Discourses*, 7:189; 2 Nephi 30:10.

> And it shall come to pass among the wicked, that every man that will not take his sword against his neighbor must needs flee unto Zion for safety.
>
> And there shall be gathered unto it out of every nation under heaven; and it shall be the only people that shall not be at war one with another.
>
> And it shall be said among the wicked: Let us not go up to battle against Zion, for the inhabitants of Zion are terrible; wherefore we cannot stand. (Doctrine and Covenants 45:68–70)

Outside of Zion, however, no such promise is given, as we are told that millions upon millions will be joining this satanic army.

John even tells us how the devil will have assembled such a massive army in such a short period of time. He said that during this time, there will be "spirits of devils, working miracles, which go forth unto the kings of the earth and of the whole world, to gather them to the battle. . . . And he [the devil] gathered them together into a place called in the Hebrew tongue Armageddon" (Revelation 16:14, 16).

And thus the battle of Armageddon begins as this massive army, after destroying everyone in their path, set its sights on Jerusalem. Elder Orson Pratt said:

> [Satan] will gather up millions upon millions of people into the valleys around about Jerusalem in order to destroy the Jews after they have gathered. How will the Devil do this? He will perform miracles to do it. The Bible says the kings of the earth and the great ones will be deceived by these false miracles. It says there shall be three unclean spirits that shall go forth working miracles, and they are spirits of devils. Where do they go? To the kings of the earth; and what will they do? Gather them up to battle unto the great day of God Almighty. Where? Into the valley of Armageddon.[19]

As we shall see in the next chapter, this battle of Armageddon will play an important role in the winding-up scenes before the Savior makes His return to the earth.

---

19. *Journal of Discourses*, 7:189.

# 11
# Armageddon

To recap, after the fifth angel sounds his trump, Satan and all his hosts of evil spirits will be loosed from the bottomless pit. When this occurs, they will be allowed to use more of their power and influence to tempt and afflict humankind. Currently, God has set limits on what Satan and his one-third are able to do; however, at this point in our story, God will have sufficiently warned the wicked inhabitants of the earth by way of the first four angels, and those who have still chosen not to repent by this time will be delivered into Satan's power (see Doctrine and Covenants 1:35).[1]

We are told that once the sixth angel sounds his trump, Satan and his hosts will use this added power to assemble together a "mighty army" (Ezekiel 38:15), which, according to John the Revelator, will consist of 200 million soldiers (see Revelation 9:16; Revelation 16:14–16). The prophet Zechariah even tells us that this army will be made up of all nations of the earth (see Zechariah 14:2), which seems to suggest a one-world government and which also helps explain its large numbers. In fact, only those living in Zion will be out of its reach (see Doctrine and Covenants 45:66–70).

1. See also *Journal of Discourses*, 7:189.

## Gog and Magog

The prophet Ezekiel tells us that this army will be led by a man whom he calls "Gog" (Ezekiel 38:2). According to Ezekiel, this "Gog" will come from "the land of Magog" (Ezekiel 38:2), which is located somewhere in or around modern-day Russia.[2]

Because Gog is said to be from the land of Magog, his army has often been referred to as Magog as well.[3] Therefore, the common phrase "Gog and Magog" simply refers to a military leader (Gog) and his army (Magog).

Gog is referred to by other titles in the scriptures as well, including the "little horn" (Daniel 7:8), the "antichrist" (1 John 2:18), "the beast" (Revelation 13:2), and "that man of sin" (2 Thessalonians 2:3). We were introduced to this individual in chapter 5 where we learned of a "little horn," as seen by Daniel (Daniel 7:8), who "made war with the saints" prior to the council at Adam-ondi-Ahman (Daniel 7:21). After the Saints have been "led out of bondage by power" (Doctrine and Covenants 103:17), Daniel tells us that Gog will eventually turn his attention to the Jews at Jerusalem (see Daniel 7:23–25).

We learn from the prophet Joel that the army assembled by Gog will be the strongest army that the world has ever seen up to this point in time: "A great people and a strong; there hath not been ever the like, neither shall be any more after it" (Joel 2:2).[4]

While Gog will be unsuccessful at conquering Zion, Joel tells us that Gog's army will go forth conquering every other nation in their path: "A fire devoureth before them; and behind them a flame burneth: the land is as the garden of Eden before them, and behind them a desolate wilderness; yea, and nothing shall escape them" (Joel 2:3).

In the midst of this rampage, we are told by the prophet Zechariah that Gog and Magog will attempt to come up "against Jerusalem to battle" (Zechariah 14:2; see also Joel 3:1; Zechariah 12:1–2).

---

2. Grant R. Jeffery, *Armageddon: Appointment With Destiny* (WaterBrook Press, 1997), 103–108. See also G. Eric Brandt, *The Book of Revelation: Things Which Must Shortly Come to Pass* (Granite Publishing, 2009), 205; *Old Testament Student Manual* (2003), 2:292.

3. *Old Testament Student Manual*, 2:284.

4. See also *Old Testament Student Manual*, 2:293.

## The Setting at Jerusalem

By this time, the Jews who were previously scattered throughout the world will have gathered together at Jerusalem. We are told that some of these Jews will have been converted to Christianity by this time (see 2 Nephi 30:7; see also 2 Nephi 6:11; 25:15–18; 30:5–7; Mormon 5:14). However, the majority of the Jews will not have. Elder Orson Pratt explained:

> The Jews dispersed among the Gentiles . . . will go to Jerusalem. Some of them will believe in the true Messiah, and thousands of the more righteous, whose fathers did not consent to the shedding of the blood of the Son of God, will receive the Gospel before they gather from among the nations. Many of them, however, will not receive the Gospel, but seeing that others are going to Jerusalem they will go also; and when they get back to Palestine, to the place where their ancient Jerusalem stood, and see a certain portion of the believing Jews endeavoring to fulfill and carry out the prophecies, they also will take hold and assist in the same work. At the same time they will have their synagogues, in which they will preach against Jesus of Nazareth, "that impostor," as they call him, who was crucified by their fathers.[5]

Once the Jews have gathered at Jerusalem, the Lord will raise up a righteous leader among them whom the scriptures call "David" (Jeremiah 30:9; Ezekiel 34:23–24)[6] or "The Branch" (Zechariah 6:12). Whether this David will be converted to the restored gospel of Jesus Christ we do not know. However, we do know that he will be a very righteous man and that he will come from Jewish descent, being a literal descendant of King David (see Jeremiah 23:5–6).[7]

---

5. *Journal of Discourses*, 18: 64–65.

6. See also *History of the Church*, 6:253.

7. It should be noted that there are two schools of thought regarding the identity of this latter-day David. The first is the interpretation presented above; the second is that this David is none other than Christ Himself (see, for example, Bruce R. McConkie, *The Promised Messiah*, 192–95). However, because the Jewish Temple will be rebuilt under David's direction (see Zechariah 6:12), and because this temple will be built before Christ appears to the Jews at Jerusalem during the battle of Armageddon (*Teachings of the Prophet Joseph Smith*, 286),

Under the direction of this great Jewish leader, we are told that the third Jewish temple will be rebuilt. Zechariah prophesied, "Behold the man whose name is The BRANCH . . . and he shall build the temple of the Lord" (Zechariah 6:12).

Of this temple, Joseph Smith said, "Judah must return, Jerusalem must be rebuilt, and the temple . . . and all this must be done before the Son of Man will make His appearance."[8]

As Joseph Smith here indicates, the Jewish temple is to be rebuilt at Jerusalem *before* Christ makes his appearance. This will be important to remember as our story progresses.

We are told that once rebuilt, this third Jewish temple will be similar in size and shape to first and second Jewish temples,[9] and it will likely be built in the same place where the two previous Jewish temples once stood. Elder Orson Pratt said that "Jerusalem shall be redeemed *and a temple established upon its former foundation* in the holy land."[10]

It is important to point out that this temple cannot be rebuilt at the present time. As a result of the Arab–Israeli war of 1967, the Jews gained control of Jerusalem and, subsequently, the mount where the original temple of Solomon once stood. This means that the Jews could technically begin construction on this temple any time they desire. However, the Jews have made it very clear that they will not begin construction at any time in the immediate future. Why not? Because currently, this Temple Mount is being occupied by a beautiful Muslim shrine known as the Dome of the Rock.

## The Dome of the Rock

The Dome of the Rock, built by the Muslims in the seventh century AD, was constructed over a sacred limestone rock, which, according to the Islamic religion, was the same rock from which their

---

this author has chosen to treat David as a separate person from Christ in this work.

8. *Teachings of the Prophet Joseph Smith*, 286.

9. A model of the third temple has already been made by the Jews and is available at https://thirdtemple.org/en/architecture/.

10. *Journal of Discourses*, 20:148; emphasis added.

prophet Muhammad ascended into heaven during a night vision.[11] Furthermore, this rock is also the traditional spot where Abraham, the great ancestor of both Arabs and Jews, offered up his son Isaac as a sacrifice.[12]

There is also a Jewish tradition, however, that states that beneath the Dome of the Rock "lies the white outcropping of rock which is supposed to have been the spot occupied by the Holy of Holies belonging to Solomon's temple."[13]

If this tradition proves to be accurate, then before the third Jewish temple could be rebuilt in its original location, the Dome of the Rock must first, somehow, be demolished. This is what Elder Charles W. Penrose predicted would occur: "The work is moving on for the gathering of the Jews to their own land that they may build it up as it was in former times; that the temple may be rebuilt and the mosque of the Moslem which now stands in its place may be moved out of the way; that Jerusalem may be rebuilt upon its original site."[14]

What makes this complicated, however, is the fact that Islamic leaders have made it clear that if the Jews were to remove this sacred shrine, "there would be Jehad—Holy War!"[15] Therefore, out of respect for the Islamic religion, and to avoid a conflict, the Jews have stated that they would not tear down the Dome of the Rock in order to rebuild their temple.[16]

But what is more, even if the Dome of the Rock were to collapse or be damaged in any way, either by natural disasters or by other means

---

11. W. Cleon Skousen, *Fantastic Victory: Israel's Rendezvous with Destiny* (Bookcraft, 1967), 160.
12. Skousen, *Fantastic Victory*, 160.
13. Skousen, *Fantastic Victory*, 160.
14. *Journal of Discourses*, 24:215.
15. Skousen, *Fantastic Victory*, 15; see also page 268.
16. According to Grant R. Jeffery, "Since the Six–Day War in 1967, Israel has controlled the entire city of Jerusalem, including the Temple Mount. However, Israel allows the Supreme Muslim Religious Council (the Waqf) to control religious activities and to police (without firearms) all activities on the Temple Mount. This area is the location of the Dome of the Rock and the Al-Aqsa Mosque." Grant R. Jeffery, *The New Temple and the Second Coming* (WaterBrook Press, 2007), 4.

outside of Jewish control, "Israeli law would demand that it be rebuilt as it was originally constructed."[17] Thus, the possibility of rebuilding the Jewish temple in place of the Dome of the Rock, at least at the present time, appears to be impossible barring a miracle from God.

Of course, there is also the possibility that the original temple of Solomon was not built where the Dome of the Rock now stands but on the ground next to it. Back in 2005, "the Sanhedrin considered the three logical possibilities for the historical location of the First and Second [Jewish] Temples. The first possibility: Solomon's temple was centered with its Holy of Holies on the rock that today sits within the thirteen-hundred-year-old Dome of the Rock. The second possibility: Solomon's temple was located to the north of the Dome of the Rock on an east–west line directly opposite the eastern gate. The third possibility: the temple was built to the south of the Dome of the Rock near the location of the Al-Aqsa Mosque, close to the southern wall of the Temple Mount."[18]

This means that as of today, the jury is still out as to where exactly the temple of Solomon was located. However, if the Sanhedrin are able to one day determine, either through archaeology or some other means, that Solomon's temple occupied the space next to the Dome of the Rock, then the Jewish temple and the Dome of the Rock could potentially, one day, coexist together on the same Temple Mount. In fact, this may be what John the Revelator was describing when, during his vision of the battle of Armageddon, an angel told him to "rise, and measure the temple of God, and the altar, and them that worship therein. *But the court which is without the temple leave out, and measure it not; for it is given unto the Gentiles*" (Revelation 11:1–2).

In analyzing this verse, we must ask ourselves why it was that an angel told John that the courtyard of the newly rebuilt third Jewish temple would belong to the Gentiles during the battle of Armageddon. Was it because the third temple will be rebuilt *next* to the Dome of the Rock on the Temple Mount? If this proves to be true, then the future courtyard of this third Jewish temple—coincidently called "the court of the Gentiles" (Bible Dictionary, "Temple of Herod")—could

17. Jeffery, *The New Temple and the Second Coming*, 21–22.

18. Jeffery, *The New Temple and the Second Coming*, 108.

potentially overlap with, and therefore occupy the same space as, the Dome of the Rock.

While this scenario seems more likely than the first, we must still consider that as of right now, constructing a Jewish temple next to Dome of the Rock on the Temple Mount would also require a miracle. According to a 2009 article published in *The Jerusalem Post*, the founder of the Islamic Movement in Israel, Sheikh Abdulla Nimar Darwish, warned against any attempt to rebuild the temple next to the Dome of the Rock, stating, "As long as there is a Muslim alive, no Jewish Temple will be built on [the Temple Mount]. The status quo must be maintained, otherwise there will be bloodshed."[19]

Nevertheless, we are told that eventually, somehow, the Jews will rebuild their temple, and it will most likely be erected where the original temple of Solomon once stood.

Naturally, once this temple has been rebuilt, the Jews will once again have a place for performing the animal sacrifices that were originally required under the law of Moses. As we shall see, this is exactly what the Jews will proceed to do once this temple is rebuilt.

## The Ark of the Covenant

One of the more interesting possibilities that may occur in connection with the rebuilding of the Jerusalem temple is the return of the ark of the covenant.

The ark of the covenant was originally built during the first year of Israel's wandering in the wilderness, when the Lord instructed Moses to "make an ark of [acacia] wood. . . . And thou shalt overlay it with pure gold" (Exodus 25:10–11).

The ark was also covered by a "mercy seat of pure gold" (Exodus 25:17), which included two winged cherubs that faced each other (see Exodus 25:18–20). Inside the ark, there were, among other sacred

---

19. Matthew Wagner, "Can Third Temple Be Built Without Destroying Dome of the Rock?," *The Jerusalem Post*, June 21, 2009, https://www.jpost.com/jewish-world/jewish-features/can-third-temple-be-built-without-destroying-dome-of-the-rock.

objects, the Ten Commandments that were written on tables of stone by the hand of God.[20]

With a few exceptions, the ark rested in the innermost sanctuary of the tabernacle—the Holy of Holies—from the time of Moses until the temple of Solomon was built at Jerusalem. Once the temple of Solomon was built, "the priests brought in the ark of the covenant . . . into the oracle of the [temple], to the most holy place" (1 Kings 8:6).

The last time the ark of the covenant was mentioned in the Bible was during the reign of King Josiah (see 2 Chronicles 35:3), who lived at Jerusalem several hundred years after the ark was first placed inside Solomon's temple. Not long after King Josiah's reign, the Babylonians, in 586 BC, attacked Jerusalem, destroyed the temple, and carried off many objects that were located in the temple (see 2 Kings 24:13; 25:13–18; 2 Chronicles 36:18–19; Jeremiah 52:17–23). Strangely enough, however, of all the items that the Bible lists as being removed from Solomon's temple during this conquest, the most sacred and valuable of all Israelite objects—the ark of the covenant—is not among them.

This has led many scholars to believe that the ark was removed from Solomon's temple and hidden somewhere prior to this Babylonian conquest. Where the ark was taken exactly has been somewhat of a mystery, and the theories are many. Some believe that the prophet Jeremiah hid the ark, possibly in a cave at Mount Nebo prior to the Babylonian siege of Jerusalem.[21] Others believe from Ethiopian official historical records and other sources that the ark of the covenant, along with the tables of stone that were placed in it, were secretly taken to Ethiopia by one of Solomon's descendants, where it has been closely guarded for nearly 3,000 years beneath the Church of Zion of Mary, and where it still remains even today.[22] Others yet believe that the ark

---

20. See Exodus 25:2; Joseph Smith Translation, Deuteronomy 10:1–5. See also Edward J. Brandt, "What Was the Ark of the Covenant, and Does It Exist in Any Form Today?," *New Era*, May 1973.

21. This theory originates from the apocryphal record of 2 Maccabees 2.

22. Jeffery, *Armageddon*, 140–47. According to a 1935 article in the Jewish magazine *B'nai B'rith Messenger*, "The Tablets of the Law received by Moses on Mount Sinai and the Ark of the Covenant [are] both said to have been brought to Ethiopia from Jerusalem by Menelik, the son of King Solomon and

was hidden by priests prior to the Babylonian siege in one of the many underground catacombs located below the Jerusalem Temple Mount. For example, the Temple Institute, which is the organization currently overseeing the rebuilding of this third Jewish temple, is on record as saying:

> Solomon . . . oversaw the construction of a vast system of labyrinths, mazes, chambers and corridors underneath the Temple Mount complex. He commanded that a special place be built in the bowels of the earth, where the sacred vessels of the Temple could be hidden in case of approaching danger. Midrashic tradition teaches that King Josiah of Israel, who lived about forty years before the destruction of the First Temple, commanded the Levites to hide the Ark, together with the original menorah and several other items, in this secret hiding place which Solomon had prepared.
>
> This location is recorded in our sources, and today, there are those who know exactly where this chamber is. *And we know that the ark is still there, undisturbed, and waiting for the day when it will be revealed.*[23]

While we are unsure of the present location of the ark, there is an exciting possibility that the ark may one day be brought forth in connection with the rebuilding of the Jerusalem temple. According to Jeremiah, "In [the last] days, saith the Lord, they shall say no more, The ark of the covenant of the Lord: neither shall it come to mind: neither shall they remember it; neither shall they visit it; neither

---

the Queen of Sheba." Martha Neumark, "Lights of New York" *B'nai B'rith Messenger*, Aug. 9, 1935.

23. Temple Institute, "Where is the Ark of the Covenant Located?," accessed Feb. 14, 2025, https://templeinstitute.org/frequently-asked-questions/; emphasis added. Once some of these underground tunnels and catacombs were discovered by Israeli archaeologists following the 1967 Arab–Israeli war, "Muslim authorities," according to Jeffery, "furiously demanded that this newly discovered [underground tunnel area] be immediately sealed, and the Israeli government agreed to limit the archaeological digging for the moment. Several of the individuals who entered this tunnel, including Rabbi Getz, the rabbi of the Western Wall, declared later that they had seen, at a distance, some of the golden Temple objects. However, they were not able to closely examine these objects" (Jeffery, *Armageddon*, 131).

shall that be done any more. At that time they shall call Jerusalem the throne of the Lord" (Jeremiah 3:16–17).

Biblical scholar Grant R. Jeffery said of these verses:

> In other words, Jeremiah prophesied that once the Battle of Armageddon is over and the millennial kingdom has commenced, Israel will stop talking about the Ark, they will stop thinking about the Ark, and they will stop visiting the Ark. The reason the Ark of the Covenant will no longer be important to Israel is that Jesus Christ will be present to be worshipped directly as their Messiah-King.
>
> However, consider the fact that the Jews have not publicly talked about, thought about, or visited the Ark of the Covenant for almost three thousand years since it disappeared. . . . This prophecy of Jeremiah 3:16–17 does not make sense unless the lost Ark of the Covenant will be rediscovered and unless, in the years leading up to Israel's final great crisis, the Ark will play a pivotal role in the spiritual life of the nation. . . .
>
> The return of the Ark of the Covenant to the Holy of Holies of a rebuilt Temple would signal for Israel the final ushering in of the long-awaited messianic era.[24]

While we are unable to say for certain that the ark of the covenant will be brought forth at some future point in time, one thing we do know is that the Jewish temple will be rebuilt, likely in its original location, and as this occurs, Jerusalem will begin to prosper.

## Gog Sets His Sights on Jerusalem

As Jerusalem begins to prosper, its wealth and beauty will attract the attention of Gog and his army. Ezekiel prophesied, "Thus saith the Lord God . . . thou [Gog] shalt think an evil thought; And thou shalt say, I will go up to the land of unwalled villages [of Jerusalem]; I will go to them that are at rest, that dwell safely . . . To take a spoil, and to take a prey . . . to carry away silver and gold, to take away cattle and goods, to take a great spoil" (Ezekiel 38:10–13).

Referring to this scripture, Elder Charles W. Penrose said, "The bankrupt nations, envying the wealth of the sons of Judah, will seek a

---

24. Jeffery, *Armageddon*, 153.

pretext to make war upon them, and will invade the holy land to take a prey and a spoil."[25]

Wilford Woodruff stated that "fleeing Jews [will] take back their gold and silver to Jerusalem and rebuild their city and temple, and they will do this as the Lord lives. Then the Gentiles will say, 'Come let us go up to Jerusalem; let us go up and spoil her. The Jews have taken our gold and silver from the nations of the earth—come let us go up and fight against Jerusalem.'"[26]

With that, Gog and his army Magog will prepare to go "against Jerusalem to battle" (Zechariah 14:2; see also Joel 3:1; Zechariah 12:1–2). Ezekiel describes the scene that follows: "Thou [Gog] shalt ascend and come like a storm, thou shalt be like a cloud to cover the land, thou, and all thy bands, and many people with thee. . . . And thou shalt come up against my people of Israel, as a cloud to cover the land; it shall be in the latter days, and I will bring thee against my land . . . O Gog" (Ezekiel 38:9, 16).

On their way to Jerusalem, we are told that Gog and his army will assemble in the valley of Megiddo,[27] a valley located north of Jerusalem. This valley of Megiddo is the valley from which the term *Armageddon* derives its name.[28] According to Brandt, "Historically, Megiddo represented the key fortification that any invader must capture and hold, if they wished to make their way south to lay siege to or capture Jerusalem and the surrounding area."[29]

And thus the famous battle of Armageddon begins as Gog and Magog make their way to Jerusalem to attack the city.

## Peace Treaty with Israel Violated

It should be noted that the prophet Daniel prophesied that some three and a half years before this attack, Gog will have entered into a

---

25. "The Second Advent," *Millennial Star*, Sept. 10, 1859, 21:582–83, as quoted in *Old Testament Student Manual*, 2:295.

26. *Journal of Discourses*, 22:173.

27. *Journal of Discourses*, 7:189.

28. *Old Testament Student Manual*, 2:291.

29. G. Eric Brandt, *The Book of Revelation: Things Which Must Shortly Come to Pass* (Granite Publishing, 2009), 203.

"covenant" or peace treaty with the Jews at Jerusalem (Daniel 9:27). This peace treaty was originally supposed to have lasted for seven years (see Daniel 9:27)[30]; however, Daniel says that "in the midst" of this peace treaty—or three and a half years into it—Gog will change his mind, break his oath, and command his army to attack Jerusalem (see Daniel 9:27).

When this occurs, Zechariah tells us that Gog and his army will invade and take half of Jerusalem. We read, "The city shall be taken, and the houses rifled, and the women ravished; and half of the city shall go forth into captivity" (Zechariah 14:2).

We also learn from Zechariah that two-thirds of the Jews living in Jerusalem at this time will be slain. He said that "in all the land, saith the Lord, two parts therein shall be cut off and die; but the third shall be left therein" (Zechariah 13:8).

As Gog and his army make their way through the city, they will be determined to take possession of the Jewish temple. According to Smith, "The battle will progressively move towards Jerusalem and the 'mountain of the Lord's house,' or in other words . . . to the temple of the Lord. . . . The battle must come to the house of the Lord, for if [Satan and his followers] are to have dominion over the earth, they must destroy the seat, or resting place, of their foe, the Lord."[31]

Once they reach the temple, we are told that either Gog, or someone from his army, will set up an idol in the holy place of the newly rebuilt Jewish temple. The scriptures call this event "the abomination of desolation" (Mark 13:14) or "the abomination that maketh desolate" (Daniel 12:11).[32]

---

30. The time period in which Daniel here refers (one week) should be interpreted as seven years, not seven days. The Hebrew word for *weeks* (*sheva*) should be interpreted as "seven." Thus, in this context, the *week* that Daniel refers to has reference to a seven-year period, not a seven-day period.

31. Mick Smith, *The Book of Revelation: Plain, Pure, and Simple* (Bookcraft, 1998), 182

32. It should be noted that in addition to this interpretation, the Bible Dictionary states, "In a general sense, abomination of desolation also describes the latter-day judgments to be poured out upon the wicked wherever they may be" (Bible Dictionary, "Abomination of Desolation").

To understand this "abomination of desolation," we need to understand that an event very similar to this has already occurred once at the temple at Jerusalem. In 167 BC, the Greek king Antiochus IV Epiphanes invaded Jerusalem, captured the city, and placed a statue of Zeus in the Jewish temple.[33] Daniel, who lived several hundred years before this event took place, saw this event in vision and described it as follows: "And they [the Greeks under Antiochus IV Epiphanes] shall pollute the sanctuary of strength . . . and they shall place [in the temple] the abomination that maketh desolate" (Daniel 11:31).

Although the Jews, led by Judas Maccabaeus in 164 BC, were eventually able to defeat Antiochus IV Epiphanes and cleanse the sanctuary, Jesus tells us that the future Jewish temple also will be desecrated in a similar manner: "And *again* shall the abomination of desolation, spoken of by Daniel the prophet, be fulfilled" (Joseph Smith—Matthew 1:32; emphasis added).

In other words, the first abomination of desolation in 167 BC was but a type and shadow of the second. Daniel was shown that in the latter days, "the abomination that maketh desolate" will again be "set up" in the sanctuary (Daniel 12:11; see also Daniel 9:27). Latter-day Saint scholar Stephen E. Robinson wrote, "In Daniel, the abomination of desolation is that thing so hateful to God that its presence in the temple causes the divine presence to depart, leaving the sanctuary desolate."[34]

The Apostle Paul also penned something in one of his epistles that has led many scholars to believe that the idol which will be placed in the Holy Place of the Jewish temple during this struggle will be an idol made in the image of Gog. Paul stated that just prior to Christ's coming, a "man of sin" (2 Thessalonians 2:3) would "[exalt] himself above all that is called God, or that is worshipped; *so that he as God sitteth*

33. Randall Price, *Rose Guide to the Temple* (Rose Publishing, 2012), 63.

34. Stephen E. Robinson, "Nephi's 'Great and Abominable Church,'" *Journal of Book of Mormon Studies* 7, no. 1 (1998): 32. Robinson continued, "In the Old Testament, the terms translated into English as abominable or abomination are usually associated with idolatrous worship or gross sexual immortality."

*in the temple of God, shewing himself that he is God*" (2 Thessalonians 2:4).[35]

Whether or not this idol will be in the image of Gog or not remains to be seen; however, one thing we do know is that once Gog has desecrated the Jewish temple with idolatry, his next item of business will be to put an end to all animal sacrifices that were previously restored at the temple by the Levite priests. Daniel stated that Gog "shall cause the sacrifice and the oblation to cease" (Daniel 9:27), and "the daily sacrifice shall be taken away" (Daniel 12:11).

These two important events, the idol set up in the holy place and Gog putting an end to animal sacrifice, mark the beginning of a very critical three-and-a-half-year time period for the Jews. Daniel stated that "from the time that the daily sacrifice shall be taken away, and the abomination that maketh desolate set up, there shall be a thousand two hundred and ninety days [or three and a half years]" of tribulation (Daniel 12:11). During this time period, Daniel tells us that Gog, or the "little horn" (Daniel 7:8), "shall wear out the saints [in Jerusalem] . . . and they shall be given into his hand until a time and times and the dividing of time [or three and a half years]" (Daniel 7:25).[36] John the Revelator echoed this timeline as well, stating that "the holy city shall they [the Gentiles] tread under foot forty and two months [or three and a half years]" (Revelation 11:2).

As terrible as this may seem for the Jews, the Lord revealed to the prophet Zechariah that this tragedy will "refine them as silver" (Zechariah 13:9). The Lord said that as a result, the Jews "shall call on my name, and I will hear them" (Zechariah 13:9).

## The Lord Defends Israel

With Gog in command of such a powerful army, one might ask why he was only able to take "half of the city" (Zechariah 14:2) during this three-and-a-half-year period as opposed to capturing the

---

35. For more information regarding the desecration of this Jewish temple, see Donald W. Parry and Jay A. Parry, *Understanding the Signs of the Times* (Deseret Book, 1999), 268; Bruce R. McConkie, *The Millennial Messiah* (Deseret Book, 1982), 474; Richard N. Skousen, *His Return* (Verity Publishing, 2007), 225.

36. From a Biblical standpoint, "time" refers to one year, "times" refers to two years, and "the dividing of time" refers to half of one year.

entire city of Jerusalem. The answer comes to us from the prophet Zechariah, who said, "In that day shall the Lord defend the inhabitants of Jerusalem" (Zechariah 12:8).[37]

For the next three and a half years, we are told that the Lord will protect His people by sending them "two prophets [who] are to be raised up to the Jewish nation in the last days" (Doctrine and Covenants 77:15). Isaiah tells us that these two prophets will be "full of the fury of the Lord" (Isaiah 51:20; see also Ezekiel 38:18). They will singlehandedly, for the next three and a half years, prevent Gog and Magog from taking the entire city of Jerusalem, and we are told that they will do so by the power of God. The Lord said to the Apostle John:

> And I will give power unto my two witnesses, and they shall prophesy a thousand two hundred and threescore days [or three and a half years]. . . .
>
> And if any man will hurt them, fire proceedeth out of their mouth, and devoureth their enemies: and if any man will hurt them, he must in this manner be killed.
>
> These have power to shut heaven, that it rain not in the days of their prophecy: and have power over waters to turn them to blood, and to smite the earth with all plagues, as often as they will. (Revelation 11:3, 4–6)

Apocrypha scholar Jonah R. Barnes noted of these verses, "Clever readers will recognize this as a parallel account. . . . John appear[s] to be reading from something like the apocryphal *Apocalypse of Elijah*. John and Elijah are both addressing the same cataclysms of the Last Days. [Either] John thought the *Apocalypse of Elijah* was kosher or an angel revealed the same things to John as he had to Elijah."[38]

The *Apocalypse of Elijah*, referenced by Barnes, identifies these two prophets as being the translated beings Elijah and Enoch. It states that "when Elijah and Enoch hear that the shameless one [Gog] has

37. Ezekiel also prophesied that the Jews at Jerusalem "shall dwell safely all of them" (Ezekiel 38:8; see also Ezekiel 38:14).

38. Jonah R. Barnes, *The Key to the Keystone: How Apocryphal Texts Unlock the Book of Mormon's Brass Plates* (Plain and Precious Publishing, 2024), 183.

revealed himself in the holy place, they will come down and fight with him."[39]

Whether or not these two prophets will be Elijah and Enoch remains to be seen. However, one thing that we do know is that these two witnesses will be given the same powers that Elijah and Enoch were once endowed with. Elder Bruce R. McConkie taught, "They shall have power like Elijah who called down fire from heaven to consume his enemies, and who sealed the heavens that it rained not in all Israel for the space of three and a half years, and like Moses by whose word blood and plagues lay heavily upon the Egyptians."[40]

Furthermore, Elder McConkie also gave us an alternative theory for the identity of these two prophets. He said, "And these two shall be followers of that humble man Joseph Smith, through whom the Lord of Heaven restored the fulness of his everlasting gospel in this final dispensation of grace. No doubt they will be members of the Council of the Twelve or of the First Presidency of the Church."[41]

If true, this statement would help to explain why these two prophets will have such power, for if these two prophets are indeed members of The Church of Jesus Christ of Latter-day Saints, then we can safely assume that they will have also been sealed in their foreheads prior to this time. As a result of this seal, these two prophets will have the same protection from God that many of the Saints living in Zion will have. As discussed in chapter 9, this sealing protection is how the righteous are protected from the seven plagues poured out by the seven angels and the very reason why Zion will be so terrible for her enemies to fight against.

At the end of this three-and-a-half-year period, however, the Lord will allow these two prophets to be killed. John the Revelator said, "And when they shall have finished their testimony, the beast that ascendeth out of the bottomless pit shall make war against them, and shall overcome them, and kill them. And their dead bodies shall lie

---

39. Albert Pietersma, Susan Turner Comstock, and Harold A. Attridge, *The Apocalypse of Elijah* (Society of Biblical Literature, 1981), 49.

40. Bruce R. McConkie, *Doctrinal New Testament Commentary* (Bookcraft, 1973), 3:510.

41. Bruce R. McConkie, *Doctrinal New Testament Commentary*, 3:509.

in the street of the great city . . . where also our Lord was crucified" (Revelation 11:7–8; see also Isaiah 51:19–20).

When this occurs, Gog and his army will celebrate their hard-fought victory. John describes their reaction to the death of these two prophets as follows: "And they that dwell upon the earth shall rejoice over them, and make merry, and shall send gifts one to another; because these two prophets tormented them that dwelt on the earth" (Revelation 11:10).

After these two prophets have been killed, Gog and his army will prevent anyone from giving them a proper burial. Instead, they will allow their dead bodies lie in the streets for three and a half days. John records, "And they of the people and kindreds and tongues and nations shall see their dead bodies three days and an half, and shall not suffer their dead bodies to be put in graves" (Revelation 11:9).

Just as soon as Gog and Magog proceed to take the remainder of the city, we are told that these two prophets will be resurrected and will ascend into heaven. John describes this event as follows: "And after three days and an half the Spirit of life from God entered into them, and they stood upon their feet; and great fear fell upon them which saw them. And they heard a great voice from heaven saying unto them, Come up hither. And they ascended up to heaven in a cloud; and their enemies beheld them" (Revelation 11:11–12).

Elder Parley P. Pratt summarized these events as follows:

> After the city and temple are rebuilt by the Jews, the Gentiles will tread it under foot forty and two months [or three and a half years], during which time there will be two prophets continually prophesying and working mighty miracles. And it seems that the Gentile army shall be hindered from utterly destroying and overthrowing the city, while these two prophets continue.
>
> But, after a struggle of three years and a half, they will at length succeed in destroying these two prophets and then overrunning much of the city; they will send gifts to each other because of the death of the two prophets, and in the meantime will not allow their dead bodies to be put in graves, but suffer them to lie in the streets of Jerusalem three days and a half, during which time the armies of the Gentiles, consisting of many kindreds, tongues and nations,

> passing through the city, plundering the Jews, will see their dead bodies lying in the street.
>
> But after three days and a half, on a sudden, the spirit of life from God will enter them; they will arise and stand upon their feet, and great fear will fall upon them that see them. And then they shall hear a voice from heaven saying, "Come up hither," and they will ascend up to heaven in a cloud, with enemies beholding them . . . then comes the shaking spoken of by Ezekiel, and the rending of the Mount of Olives spoken of by Zechariah.[42]

As Elder Pratt here references, once the two prophets have been raised up and have ascended into heaven, Christ will descend and set His foot upon the Mount of Olives. Zechariah prophesied, "Then shall the Lord go forth, and fight against those nations, as when he fought in the day of battle. And his feet shall stand in that day upon the mount of Olives, which is before Jerusalem on the east" (Zechariah 14:3–4; see also Doctrine and Covenants 45:48).

We are told that this event will cause a great earthquake, which will cause the Mount of Olives to split in two. Zechariah prophesied that "the mount of Olives shall cleave in the midst thereof toward the east and toward the west, and there shall be a very great valley; and half of the mountain shall remove toward the north, and half of it toward the south" (Zechariah 14:4; see also Doctrine and Covenants 45:48; Ezekiel 38:19).

When this occurs, Zechariah informs us that the Jews will "flee" from the army of Gog "to the valley of the mountains" (Zechariah 14:5). As the Jews flee to safety around this Messiah who has come to save them, the Lord says:

> And then shall the Jews look upon me and say: What are these wounds in thine hands and in thy feet?
>
> Then shall they know that I am the Lord; for I will say unto them: These wounds are the wounds with which I was wounded in the house of my friends. I am he who was lifted up. I am Jesus that was crucified. I am the Son of God.

42. Parley P. Pratt, *Voice of Warning* (H. S. Eldridge, 1871), 33.

> And then shall they weep because of their iniquities; then shall they lament because they persecuted their king. (Doctrine and Covenants 45:51–53; see also Zechariah 12:10–11; 13:6)

This sacred event will convert the entire Jewish nation to the gospel of Jesus Christ: "So the house of Israel shall know that I am the Lord their God from that day and forward" (Ezekiel 39:22).

## Magog Destroyed by Fire

Meanwhile, once the Jews have gathered around the Savior in safety, the Lord says, "And I will send a fire on Magog" (Ezekiel 39:6). On a second occasion, the Lord said, "I will rain upon [Gog], and upon his bands, and upon the many people that are with him, an overflowing rain, and great hailstones, fire, and brimstone" (Ezekiel 38:22).

Ezekiel tells us that this fire and brimstone will destroy five-sixths of Gog's entire army (see Ezekiel 39:2). And as for Gog, the Lord says, "I will give unto Gog a place there of [in the] graves in Israel" (Ezekiel 39:11).

The prophet Zechariah also spoke of the fate of those who will have fought against Jerusalem. He said, "And this shall be the plague wherewith the Lord will smite all the people that have fought against Jerusalem; Their flesh shall consume away while they stand upon their feet, and their eyes shall consume away in their holes, and their tongue shall consume away in their mouth" (Zechariah 14:12).

Furthermore, the Lord said in Ezekiel, "I will give thee [Gog and Magog] unto the ravenous birds of every sort, and to the beasts of the field to be devoured. Thou shalt fall upon the open field: for I have spoken it, saith the Lord God" (Ezekiel 39:4–5; see also Joel 2:20).

The Lord has said that this destruction will be so great that it will take Israel seven months just to bury Gog and his army of fallen soldiers. We read in Ezekiel, "And it shall come to pass in that day, that I will give unto Gog a place there of graves in Israel . . . and there shall they bury Gog and all his multitude . . . And seven months shall the house of Israel be burying of them, that they may cleanse the land" (Ezekiel 39:11–12).

## A Triumphal Entry

After the army of Gog has been destroyed, the Jews will then lead Jesus back to the Jerusalem temple to honor Him as their Savior (see Ezekiel 44:1–2), at which time "then shall the sanctuary be cleansed" by the Lord (Daniel 8:14).[43] As a result of this cleansing, Ezekiel saw that "the glory of the Lord filled the house of the Lord" (Ezekiel 44:4).

In connection with this cleansing process, and perhaps as a result of the earthquake mentioned previously, we are told that a river of water shall also proceed forth from underneath the temple (see Ezekiel 47:1–2; see also Zechariah 13:1; Joel 3:18), which is another sign that this temple has been accepted by the Lord once more.[44]

Once the temple has been cleansed, and once the Jews have been purified and are converted to the gospel of Jesus Christ, the Doctrine and Covenants tells us that the "sons of Levi" will "offer again an offering unto the Lord in righteousness" (Doctrine and Covenants 13:1). Of this offering, the Prophet Joseph Smith said:

> It is generally supposed that [animal] sacrifice was entirely done away when . . . the Lord Jesus was offered up, and that there will be no necessity for the ordinance of sacrifice in the future; but those who assert this are certainly not acquainted with the duties, privileges and authority of the Priesthood, or with the Prophets. . . .
>
> These [animal] sacrifices, as well as every ordinance belonging to the Priesthood, will, when the Temple of the Lord shall be built [in Jerusalem], and the sons of Levi be purified, be fully restored . . . else how can the restitution of all things spoken of by the Holy Prophets be brought to pass?[45]

---

43. Technically, Daniel 8:14 is in reference to the second Jewish temple, which was desecrated by Antiochus IV Epiphanies in 167 BC and subsequently cleansed by the Jews during the Maccabean Revolt in 164 BC. However, as mentioned previously, these historical events serve as a type and shadow of the events that will unfold in the latter days.

44. *Teachings of the Prophet Joseph Smith*, 286.

45. *History of the Church*, 211–12. President Joseph Fielding Smith added, "The law of sacrifice will have to be restored. . . . It will be necessary, therefore, for the sons of Levi, who offered the blood sacrifices anciently in Israel, to offer such a sacrifice again to round out and complete this ordinance in this dispensation. Sacrifice by the shedding of blood was instituted in the days

Thus, after the Lord has purified the sons of Levi, He will instruct them to again offer animal sacrifices upon the altar of the temple, and they will do so "in righteousness" (Doctrine and Covenants 13:1). This means that they will do so worthily and, according to the Prophet Joseph Smith, under direction of the priesthood.[46]

Soon after the Levites have offered up their sacrifices "unto the Lord in righteousness" (Doctrine and Covenants 13:1), we are told that the Lord will no longer require blood sacrifices from their hands. President Joseph Fielding Smith explained that the "sacrifice of animals will be done to complete the restoration when the temple spoken of is built" but then added that "blood sacrifices will be performed [only] long enough to complete the fulness of the restoration in this dispensation. Afterwards sacrifice will be of some other character."[47]

## After Armageddon

At some point after these events have transpired, a new temple, as seen by the prophet Ezekiel (see Ezekiel 40–43), will be built somewhere in Jerusalem. It should be mentioned that the temple that Ezekiel saw in vision will be a different structure from the third Jewish temple that we have been discussing. We know this because the temple that Ezekiel described is much too large to fit on the Temple Mount, which means it will need to be built elsewhere. What is more, Ezekiel's temple will not be used for animal sacrifices under the law of Moses but will instead be used for the higher ordinances of the priesthood. President Joseph Fielding Smith explained, "Ezekiel predicted the building of a temple in Jerusalem *which will be used for ordinance work* after the gathering of Israel from their long dispersion and when they are cleansed from their transgressions."[48]

Once Jerusalem has been converted, word will spread to the surrounding nations that the Lord again dwells with his people. As a result, we are told that many nations surrounding Jerusalem will also

of Adam and of necessity will have to be restored." Joseph Fielding Smith, *Doctrines of Salvation*, comp. Bruce R. McConkie (Bookcraft, 1954–56), 3:94.

46. *Teachings of the Prophet Joseph Smith*, 172.

47. Joseph Fielding Smith, *Doctrines of Salvation*, 3:94.

48. Joseph Fielding Smith, *Doctrines of Salvation*, 2:244; emphasis added.

become converted to the gospel of Jesus Christ. Zechariah prophesied, "Yea, many people and strong nations shall come to seek the Lord of hosts in Jerusalem, and to pray before the Lord. Thus saith the Lord of hosts; In those days it shall come to pass, that ten men . . . shall take hold of the skirt of him that is a Jew, saying, We will go with you: for we have heard that God is with you" (Zechariah 8:22–23; see also Doctrine and Covenants 45:54; Zechariah 14:16; Ezekiel 38:23; 39:7, 21; Isaiah 19:20–23).

## The Seventh Angel

As we thus approach the Second Coming, the seventh and final angel will sound his trump. John records, "And the seventh angel sounded; and there were great voices in heaven, saying, The kingdoms of this world are become the kingdoms of our Lord, and of his Christ; and he shall reign for ever and ever" (Revelation 11:15).

Sometime after this seventh angel has sounded his trump, the Lord will make His final appearance in the clouds of heaven.

# 12
# Red in His Apparel

Shortly after His Resurrection, the Savior ministered for forty days to several of his disciples who were at Jerusalem (see Acts 1:3). When the forty days were ended, the New Testament states, "[Jesus] was taken up; and a cloud received him out of their sight. And while they looked steadfastly toward heaven as he went up, behold, two [angels] stood by them in white apparel; Which also said, Ye men of Galilee, why stand ye gazing up into heaven? this same Jesus, which is taken up from you into heaven, shall so come in like manner as ye have seen him go into heaven" (Acts 1:9–11).

Of this scripture, Elder Orson Pratt said, "That is, [Jesus] was received into a cloud, taken up in a cloud, and when he comes the second time he will come in a cloud."[1]

## The Clouds of Heaven

Sometime after the battle of Armageddon has ended, the Lord will make His final appearance to the world prior to ushering in the

1. *Journal of Discourses*, 18:170.

Millennium.[2] As part of this appearance, the Lord will appear in the clouds of heaven and be seen by all. The Savior said, "I will come; and they shall see me in the clouds of heaven, clothed with power and great glory; with all the holy angels" (Doctrine and Covenants 45:44).

John the Revelator added, "Behold, he cometh with clouds; and every eye shall see him" (Revelation 1:7).

To understand how it would be possible for every eye to behold the Lord at this moment, we need to understand that there is currently a veil covering our earth that separates us from the presence of God. However, when Christ makes this final appearance in the clouds, this veil will be removed and the entire world will suddenly come into the presence of the Lord. The Lord said in the Doctrine and Covenants, "The veil . . . which hideth the earth, shall be taken off, and all flesh shall see me together" (Doctrine and Covenants 101:23).

It is interesting to note that the removal of this veil applies not only to us mortals on earth but also to those living in the spirit world. Elder Orson Pratt taught, "[The Second Coming] will be an event that will be seen by all—all flesh shall see the glory of the Lord; when he reveals himself the second time, every eye, not only those living at that time in the flesh, in mortality on the earth, but also the very dead themselves."[3]

This veil is more than just a symbolic divider between us and God. Rather, our earth is actually covered by a very literal, physical veil. As we shall see, this veil was created and placed over our earth by the Lord to shield our earth from beholding too much light coming from the outside universe. However, to more fully understand this veil and what happens when it is removed, we must first understand more about this outside light, including where it originates from and what it actually is.

---

2. Scripturally speaking, the Millennium will actually begin much earlier—specifically once the seventh seal is opened (see Doctrine and Covenants 77:12). However, the thousand years of peace associated with the Millennium will not begin until after this final appearance by the Savior.

3. *Journal of Discourses*, 18:170. See also Revelation 1:7.

## Physical Light Throughout Our Galaxy

The book of Abraham teaches us that all physical light found throughout our galaxy comes from Kolob, or the planet located "nearest unto the throne of God" (Abraham 3:2). As we might imagine, Kolob radiates a tremendous amount of light and glory. The Lord taught Abraham that from Kolob, this light is passed to the rest of our galaxy through a series of channels and mediums until it finally reaches our earth.[4] The Doctrine and Covenants reaffirms this process: "Which light proceedeth forth from the presence of God to fill the immensity of space" (Doctrine and Covenants 88:12).

Hyrum L. Andrus stated:

> Joseph Smith taught that there are various channels through which the glory and power of God are manifested. In other words, there is an organization of light in the cosmos. The sun, as the center of our solar system, is one of the basic channels through which the Spirit, or glory, of Christ is manifested to this earth. The sun does not derive its light and power directly from Christ, however, but through a series of spheres that go back to Kolob.[5]

The book of Abraham also teaches us that Kolob is geographically located right in the center of all of our Heavenly Father's creations.[6] This is one reason why many Latter-day Saint scholars believe Kolob to be located at the center of our Milky Way Galaxy.[7] What is interesting about this idea is that science has also verified that there is a massive amount of light coming from the center of our galaxy, and that there is also a very real veil, made up of dust and gas, which blocks the majority of this light from ever reaching the earth.

---

4. Abraham facsimile #2, explanation of figure 5.
5. Hyrum L. Andrus, *God, Man, and the Universe* (Bookcraft, 1968), 50.
6. Abraham facsimile #2, figure 1.
7. For a detailed discussion on this theory, including why the Milky Way Galaxy is believed to include all of our Heavenly Father's creations, see Lynn M. Hilton, *The Kolob Theorem* (Granite Publishing, 2006), 14–21; Eric N. Skousen, *Earth in the Beginning* (Verity Publishing, 1997), 226–34; Rodney Turner, *This Eternal Earth* (Granite Publishing, 2000), 14–15; W. Cleon Skousen, *Isaiah Speaks to Modern Times* (Ensign Publishing, 1984), 136–37.

Latter-day Saint scientist Eric Skousen stated, "At the very center of the Galaxy is one super-powerful object. It is estimated to be thousands of times larger than our sun. . . . If we back out several thousand light-years from this energetic center we come to a region consisting of huge clouds of interstellar dust and gas. This material so effectively blocks visible light from the galactic center that less than one trillionth of it ever reaches us."[8]

Of this veil, former Brigham Young University (BYU) professor Lynn Hilton stated, "The radiations of God's light, which proceed forth from His presence to fill the immensity of space (Doctrine and Covenants 88:12) are filtered through veils of interstellar dust, which block our mortal view of the celestial kingdom."[9]

Joseph Smith explained the reason for this veil when he said, "God has set the bounds of Light lest it pass over and consume the planets."[10]

By creating this veil, God has made it so that exactly the right amount of light reaches our earth and no more. In the words of Hyrum Andrus:

> Joseph [Smith] . . . indicates that God has established laws which regulate the emission of His glory so that "the right degree of light" cheers "the face of millions of planets." The Prophet thus anticipated the discovery of the ionosphere that shields the earth from harmful forms of radiation coming from outer space. . . .
>
> Some spheres cannot endure the full glory of God. Consequently the great Creator has set "a cloud round about the heavens," by which certain bounds and limits are given to light "lest it pass over and consume the planets."[11]

Lynn Hilton added, "Consider that nearly 150 years ago, long before science had any idea of the structure of the Universe, God's prophet said that there exists 'clouds round about in the heavens' . . . and that the purpose of these clouds is to keep the planets from being

8. Skousen, *Earth in the Beginning*, 232–33.

9. Hilton, *The Kolob Theorem*, 23.

10. Joseph Smith, *Egyptian Alphabet and Grammar* (Utah Lighthouse Ministry, 1966), under "Flos isis: Fifth degree."

11. Andrus, *God, Man, and the Universe*, 251.

consumed. What profound insight! We stand with awe and respect for Joseph's prophetic powers."[12]

## The Veil Which Hideth the Earth is Removed

What is interesting is that at the Second Coming, the Lord has said that "the veil . . . which hideth the earth, shall be taken off" (Doctrine and Covenants 101:23). Once this veil is removed, our earth will suddenly be exposed to much more light coming from the outside universe than we as mortals will be able to endure. The result? According to the prophet Malachi, the earth "shall burn as an oven" (Malachi 4:1).

## The Glory of the Lord

Furthermore, once this veil is removed, the entire world, either worthily or unworthily, will come into the presence of the Lord, who will appear in all His glory. The Lord tells us that this glory will be so bright that it will instantly consume the wicked. We read in the Doctrine and Covenants, "They that do wickedly shall be as stubble; *and I will burn them up*, saith the Lord of Hosts, that wickedness shall not be upon the earth. . . . For I will reveal myself from heaven with power and great glory" (Doctrine and Covenants 29:9–11; emphasis added).

And on another occasion, the Lord said, "I . . . will come down in heaven from the presence of my Father and consume the wicked with unquenchable fire" (Doctrine and Covenants 63:34).

How Christ's glory is able to consume the wicked at this time is best explained by the Prophet Joseph Smith. On more than one occasion, the Prophet described God as dwelling in "everlasting burnings,"[13] meaning that there is a tremendous amount of light and glory radiating from God's person. So much light, in fact, that if we were to come into His presence without first being transfigured, we are told that we would be consumed instantly (see Doctrine and Covenants 67:11–12). Joseph Smith said it this way: "God Almighty Himself

---

12. Hilton, *The Kolob Theorem*, 25.

13. *Teachings of the Prophet Joseph Smith*, sel. Joseph Fielding Smith (1976), 367; see also page 347. This phrase originated from Isaiah 33:14.

dwells in eternal fire; flesh and blood cannot go there, for all corruption is devoured by the fire. 'Our God is a consuming fire.'"[14]

Similarly, Elder Parley P. Pratt said that God is "filled and encircled with light unapproachable by those of the lower spheres."[15]

To give us an idea of just how much glory the resurrected Savior will bring with Him when He comes, consider that at the Second Coming, Christ's glory, according to Elder Orson Pratt, will "outshine the sun in his strength."[16] This information originated from the Doctrine and Covenants, which reads, "And the Lord shall be red in his apparel. . . . And so great shall be the glory of his presence that the sun shall hide his face in shame" (Doctrine and Covenants 133:48–49).

Amazingly, just as the stars in the night sky disappear when the sun rises in the morning, so too will the sun, according to this verse, "hide his face in shame" (Doctrine and Covenants 133:49) and refuse to give its light when compared to the Lord who will appear in the clouds of heaven in all His glory. Truly, "our God is a consuming fire" (Hebrews 12:29).

## The Light of Christ

Because of all this light radiating from the outside universe, as well as from the Lord's person, we are told that the only way we can be in His presence and not be consumed by this glory is for us to be filled with this Light of Christ ourselves. How do we do this? The Doctrine and Covenants teaches us that when we are obedient to the commandments of God, our bodies actually receive light: "He that keepeth his commandments receiveth truth and light" (Doctrine and Covenants 93:28).

The Lord has told us that this Light of Christ "quickeneth your understandings" (Doctrine and Covenants 88:11). In other words, this light is given to the obedient so that they may clearly see and understand what type of lives they should be living before God. Those who receive this light through their obedience are strengthened in

14. *Teachings of the Prophet Joseph Smith*, 367; see also Hebrews 12:29.

15. Parley P. Pratt, *Key to the Science of Theology* (Deseret Book, 1965), 41.

16. *Journal of Discourses*, 18:59.

their desire to keep the commandments, and as they continue to keep the commandments, they receive more light.

On the other hand, those who are disobedient to the commandments of God can actually lose portions of that Light of Christ that they previously gained through obedience. The Doctrine and Covenants states, "And that wicked one [Satan] cometh and taketh away light and truth, through disobedience" (Doctrine and Covenants 93:39). "And he that repents not, from him shall be taken even the light which he has received" (Doctrine and Covenants 1:33).

This life is a constant struggle to earn and keep this Light of Christ. However, if we continue faithful, the Lord taught, "He that receiveth light, and continueth in God, receiveth more light; and that light groweth brighter and brighter until the perfect day" (Doctrine and Covenants 50:24).

Those who receive this light can worthily stand in the presence of God and not be consumed, and this because they are filled with this light themselves. The Doctrine and Covenants reads, "And if your eye be single to my glory, *your whole bodies shall be filled with light*, and there shall be no darkness in you; and that body which is filled with light comprehendeth all things. Therefore, sanctify yourselves that your minds become single to God, and the days will come that you shall see him; for *he will unveil his face unto you*" (Doctrine and Covenants 88:67–68; emphasis added).

## Saints Caught Up

As "the curtain of heaven [is] unfolded . . . and the face of the Lord [is] unveiled" (Doctrine and Covenants 88:95), all celestial individuals whose bodies have been filled with this Light of Christ "shall be quickened and be caught up to meet him" (Doctrine and Covenants 88:96).

This means that all celestial-worthy Saints, including any who have not yet experienced it prior to this moment,[17] will undergo a translation process at the Second Coming so that they may stand in

17. It is likely that all the Saints who were previously sealed in their foreheads will have already experienced translation by the time the Lord makes His appearance (see chapter 9).

the presence of the Lord and not be consumed, for "no man has seen God at any time in the flesh, except quickened by the Spirit of God" (Doctrine and Covenants 67:11).

However, it is important to note that these "quickened" Saints will not be resurrected at this time, only translated. President Joseph Fielding Smith made this clear when he said, "When Christ comes the saints who are on the earth will be quickened and caught up to meet him. This does not mean that those who are living in mortality at that time will be changed and pass through the resurrection, for mortals must remain on the earth until after the thousand years are ended."[18]

And as it turns out, righteous mortals will not be the only ones caught up to meet Christ in the clouds. We read in the Doctrine and Covenants that at the Second Coming, "they who have slept in their graves shall come forth, for their graves shall be opened; and they also shall be caught up to meet him in the midst of the pillar of heaven" (Doctrine and Covenants 88:97).

In other words, all celestial spirits who have died prior to the Second Coming will be resurrected to celestial glory when Christ appears and will join Him, along with the translated mortal Saints, in the clouds of heaven.

## Telestial and Terrestrial Individuals

We should also note that it will only be celestial individuals who will be caught up to meet Christ in the clouds. Hyrum Andrus stated:

> Sometimes we entertain the idea that if Christ were to come today, we would be caught up to meet him in the cloud. But . . . only those who are prepared to see him in his glory and partake of that glory which will be so intense that the mountains will flow down at his presence and the wicked will be consumed; only such people will be prepared to meet him in the clouds. Only Zion will be caught up; not a Gentile-oriented church. Let me make this point clear;

18. Joseph Fielding Smith, *The Way to Perfection* (Zion's Publishing Company, 1940), 298–99.

> only Zion (or the church of the Firstborn) will be caught up to meet Christ in the cloud.[19]

The Lord Himself also stated as much when He said, "For ye are the church of the Firstborn, and [God] will take you up in a cloud" (Doctrine and Covenants 78:21). This means that all terrestrial and telestial individuals will remain on the earth at the Second Coming and will not meet Christ in the air.

However, those who remain on the earth who lived a terrestrial life, or, in the words of President Joseph Fielding Smith, "those who have lived virtuous lives, who have been honest in their dealings with their fellow man,"[20] will be able to endure Christ's presence from afar because they will have received enough of the Light of Christ to not be consumed by Christ's glory at the Second Coming. Those of a telestial nature, however, "shall not abide the day" (Doctrine and Covenants 38:8) and will be removed from the earth when Christ appears in all His glory.

President Joseph Fielding Smith taught, "When the reign of Jesus Christ comes during the millennium, only those who have lived the telestial law will be removed."[21] He also stated, "All who belong, by virtue of their good lives, to the terrestrial order, as well as those who have kept the celestial law, will remain upon the face of the earth during the millennium."[22]

## After the Second Coming

Once the earth has thus been cleansed and purified by fire, those who were caught up to meet Christ in the clouds, both translated mortals and resurrected Saints, will descend and again set foot upon the earth to join the terrestrial individuals who were worthy enough to survive the cleansing process.

---

19. Hyrum L. Andrus, *Joseph Smith Lecture Series: What is Zion?* (BYU Press, 1973), 41.
20. Joseph Fielding Smith, *Doctrines of Salvation*, comp. Bruce R. McConkie (Bookcraft, 1954–56), 3:62.
21. Joseph Fielding Smith, *Doctrines of Salvation*, 3:62.
22. Joseph Fielding Smith, *Doctrines of Salvation*, 1:86–87.

At this time, our earth will leave our present solar system and be relocated to another place in our galaxy. It will thus move closer in proximity to Kolob and partake of terrestrial glory. The Lord said in Isaiah, "Therefore I will shake the heavens, and *the earth shall remove out of her place*" (Isaiah 13:13; emphasis added).

Daniel H. Ludlow explained, "One of the predicted events associated with the second coming of Jesus Christ is that 'the stars shall fall from heaven.' . . . As the earth moves through the stars of its present heaven to its new position, these stars will appear to be falling in relationship to the movement of the earth."[23]

President Brigham Young taught us the reason why the earth will eventually be relocated: "When the earth was framed and brought into existence and man was placed upon it, it was near the throne of our Father in heaven . . . but when man fell, the earth fell into space, and took up its abode in this planetary system, and the sun became our light. . . . This is the glory the earth came from, and when it is glorified it will return again unto the presence of the Father, and it will dwell there."[24]

## The Millennium

After the earth has been relocated, we are told that Satan will be bound and will not have power to tempt man for a thousand years (see Doctrine and Covenants 88:110; 101:28). While there is much that could be said of this Millennium, suffice it to say that it will be a time of peace and happiness for all who dwell on the earth. Isaiah said:

> [The Lord] shall judge among the nations . . . and they shall beat their swords into plowshares, and their spears into pruninghooks: nation shall not lift up sword against nation, neither shall they learn war any more.
>
> The wolf also shall dwell with the lamb, and the leopard shall lie down with the kid; and the calf and the young lion and the fatling together; and a little child shall lead them. . . .

---

23. Daniel H. Ludlow, *A Companion to Your Study of the Doctrine and Covenants* (Deseret Book, 1978), 278–79 (appendix A).

24. *Journal of Discourses*, 17:143.

> And the sucking child shall play on the hole of the asp, and the weaned child shall put his hand on the cockatrice' den.
>
> They shall not hurt nor destroy in all my holy mountain: for the earth shall be full of the knowledge of the Lord, as the waters cover the sea. (Isaiah 2:4; 11:6, 8–9)

## Mortals and Immortals

As mentioned previously, according to Elder Bruce R. McConkie, "During the Millennium there will, of course, be two kinds of people on earth. There will be those who are mortal, and those who are immortal."[25] Those who are mortal during the Millennium will still be able to bear children and raise them to maturity. Elder Bruce R. McConkie added, "Millennial man will live in a state akin to translation. His body will be changed so that it is no longer subject to disease or death as we know it. . . . He will, however, have children, and mortal life of a millennial kind will continue."[26]

Those who are mortal during the Millennium will still grow old (see Doctrine and Covenants 63:51); however, the scriptures tell us that when they are ready to die, "they shall not sleep in the dust, but they shall be changed in the twinkling of an eye" (Doctrine and

---

25. Bruce R. McConkie, *The Millennial Messiah* (Deseret Book, 1982), 644. See also Bruce R. McConkie, *Mormon Doctrine*, 2nd ed. (Bookcraft, 1966), 496–97; *Doctrine and Covenants Student Manual* (2001), 204.

26. Bruce R. McConkie, *The Millennial Messiah*, 644. Similarly, concerning those who have lost children at a young age in this life, the Prophet Joseph Smith taught that during the Millennium, those children would be resurrected to the age they were when they died. These children would then grow and develop as normal until they reached the age of maturity, and this so that the parents would not be deprived of raising them in the flesh. This insight came to us from President Joseph F. Smith, who said, "Joseph Smith taught the doctrine that the infant child that was laid away in death would come up in the resurrection as a child; and, pointing to the mother of a lifeless child, he said to her: 'You will have the joy, the pleasure, and satisfaction of nurturing this child, after its resurrection, until it reaches the full stature of its spirit.' There is restitution, there is growth, there is development, after the resurrection from death. I love this truth. It speaks volumes of happiness, of joy and gratitude to my soul. Thank the Lord he has revealed these principles to us." Joseph F. Smith, *Gospel Doctrine* (Deseret Book, 1939), 455–56.

Covenants 63:51), which means that they will undergo death and resurrection instantly, at the same moment.

Resurrected persons, on the other hand, will not live exclusively on the earth during the Millennium but will come and go as needed. Joseph Smith said, "Christ and the resurrected Saints will reign over the earth during the thousand years. They will not probably dwell upon the earth, but will visit it when they please, or when it is necessary to govern it."[27]

## Concerning the Resurrection

It has been said that every individual who is resurrected to a celestial body—either at the Second Coming or when they are "changed in the twinkling of an eye" during the Millennium (Doctrine and Covenants 63:51)—will come forth in the morning of the First Resurrection,[28] while the afternoon of the First Resurrection is reserved for terrestrial individuals and occurs "after our Lord has ushered in the Millennium."[29]

Telestial spirits, however, will not be resurrected "until the thousand years are ended" (Doctrine and Covenants 88:101), during which time, we are told that they will be "thrust down to hell" (Doctrine and Covenants 76:84) and will have to suffer for their own sins, as Christ suffered, and this because they chose not to repent during their mortal probation. The Lord warned:

> Repent—repent, lest I smite you by the rod of my mouth, and by my wrath, and by my anger, and your sufferings be sore—how sore you know not, how exquisite you know not, yea, how hard to bear you know not.
>
> For behold, I, God, have suffered these things for all, that they might not suffer if they would repent;
>
> But if they would not repent they must suffer even as I;

27. *Teachings of the Prophet Joseph Smith,* 268. See also Revelation 5:10; Revelation 20:4.

28. See Mosiah 15:22–24; Doctrine and Covenants 88: 97–98; Bruce R. McConkie, *Mormon Doctrine,* 640.

29. Bruce R. McConkie, *Mormon Doctrine,* 640.

> Which suffering caused myself, even God, the greatest of all, to tremble because of pain, and to bleed at every pore, and to suffer both body and spirit—and would that I might not drink the bitter cup, and shrink. (Doctrine and Covenants 19:15–18)

Once these telestial spirits have finished drinking from their own bitter cups, they will gratefully bow the knee and confess with the tongue that Jesus is the Christ, for that is the only way they may be redeemed from this eternal torment (see Mosiah 27:31; see also Doctrine and Covenants 76:109–110; 88:104). At the end of the Millennium, and once these two conditions are met, these telestial spirits will be resurrected as well (see Doctrine and Covenants 88:100–101).

## The Close of the Millennium

As the Millennium comes to a close, Satan "shall be loosed for a little season" (Doctrine and Covenants 88:111). "Because men are still mortal," writes President Joseph Fielding Smith, "Satan will go out to deceive them. Men will again deny the Lord, but in doing so they will act with their eyes open and because they love darkness rather than light . . . they become sons of perdition."[30]

Once Satan has thus gathered together his armies of perdition, "even the hosts of hell" (Doctrine and Covenants 88:113), he will "come up to battle against Michael and his armies" (Doctrine and Covenants 88:113). John the Revelator described the ensuing battle that follows: "And [Satan and his angels] went up on the breadth of the earth, and compassed the camp of the saints about . . . and fire came down from God out of heaven, and devoured them. And the devil . . . was cast into the lake of fire and brimstone" (Revelation 20:9–10; see also Doctrine and Covenants 88:114; Jacob 5:77).

---

30. Joseph Fielding Smith, *Doctrines of Salvation*, 1:87. Similarly, Elder Orson Pratt said, "When the period called the Millennium has passed away, Satan will again be loosed . . . and will go forth and tempt [humankind], and overcome some of them, so that they will rebel against God; not rebel in ignorance or dwindle in unbelief, as the Lamanites did; but they will sin willfully against the law of heaven" (*Journal of Discourses*, 16:322).

## The Great White Throne

After Satan and his angels have been cast into the lake of fire and brimstone, John saw in vision "a great white throne, and him that sat on it" (Revelation 20:11). It will be at this time, and upon this throne, that Jesus Christ will issue His Final Judgment on Satan and the sons of perdition. After He finds them guilty, He will provide for them their gifts of resurrection and then cast them into outer darkness for eternity. The Lord said in the Doctrine and Covenants, "And they who remain [i.e., sons of perdition] shall also be quickened [i.e., resurrected]; nevertheless, they shall return again to their own place [i.e., outer darkness] . . . because they were not willing to enjoy that which they might have received" (Doctrine and Covenants 88:32).

## A New Heaven and a New Earth

After this occurs, the earth will once again be cleansed by fire. In the allegory of the olive tree, as recorded in the Book of Mormon, the Lord described this event as follows, "And then cometh the season and the end; and my vineyard will I cause to be burned with fire" (Jacob 5:77; see also Revelation 20:9).

When this occurs, the righteous will again be caught up into the celestial heavens. Elder Orson Pratt explains:

> All the Saints that are on the earth [at the end of the Millennium] . . . will be caught up, and [righteous mortals] who have not undergone their full change from mortality to immortality will be changed in the twinkling of an eye [i.e., resurrected]. . . . Where are they taken to? Up into the celestial heavens. . . . What will they be caught up for? That they may not pass away, when the earth passes away.[31]

At this time, as the righteous are being caught up, "the earth shall be consumed and pass away" (Doctrine and Covenants 29:23). The earth will then be resurrected, and once this occurs, "there shall be a new heaven and a new earth" (Doctrine and Covenants 29:23; see also Ether 13:9).

Once the earth has thus been resurrected, those with a terrestrial resurrected body will be reassigned to a terrestrial kingdom,

---

31. *Journal of Discourses*, 16:322–23.

while those with a celestial body will descend to "inherit the earth" (Matthew 5:5). John the Revelator said, "And I saw a new heaven and a new earth. . . . And I John saw the holy city, new Jerusalem, coming down from God out of heaven" (Revelation 21:1–2).

After the earth is thus resurrected, it will once again move closer in proximity to Kolob and partake of celestial glory. President Brigham Young said, "When [the earth] is glorified it will return again unto the presence of the Father, and it will dwell there."[32] Similarly, Joseph Smith said, "This earth will be rolled back into the presence of God, and crowned with celestial glory."[33]

Once our earth is thus celestialized, the Doctrine and Covenants tells us that it will be "like a sea of glass and fire, where all things . . . are manifest, past, present, and future" (Doctrine and Covenants 130:7; see also Revelation 4:6; Doctrine and Covenants 77:1). President Brigham Young explained, "This earth will become a celestial body—be like a sea of glass, or like a Urim and Thummim; and when you wish to know anything, you can look in this earth and see all the eternities of God."[34]

May each of us live our lives in a way that we may be found worthy to dwell on such an earth when the time comes.

---

32. *Journal of Discourses*, 17:143; see also Revelation 20:11.

33. *Teachings of the Prophet Joseph Smith*, 181. See also *Journal of Discourses*, 9:317; *Journal of Discourses*, 17:143.

34. *Journal of Discourses*, 8:200.

# Part II

## Understanding the Second Coming through Types and Shadows

# 13
# What Is a Type?

What is a type? Understanding the meaning of this important gospel term is fundamental to understanding the symbolism contained throughout Part II of this book. To state it plainly, a type is an event, an object, or a person that closely resembles another event, object, or person of greater significance.[1] Synonyms for *type* could include terms such as similitude, likeness, model, prototype, pattern, symbol, or shadow. An important characteristic common in most types is that they usually point forward to a future period of time, which can often make them prophetic in a sense.

## Types of Christ

Most of the types that are contained in the scriptures are what we call "types of Christ," meaning that they closely resemble Christ in one form or another. The Lord taught, "All things have their likeness, and all things are created and made to bear record of me" (Moses 6:63).

---

1. See similar definitions in Alonzo L. Gaskill, *The Lost Language of Symbolism: An Essential Guide for Recognizing and Interpreting Symbols of the Gospel* (Deseret Book, 2003), 12; Joseph Fielding McConkie, *Gospel Symbolism* (Bookcraft, 1985), 274.

The prophet Jonah, for example, was a type of Christ. Jonah's experience in the whale foreshadowed the Lord's experience in the grave. The Lord Himself stated as much when He said, "For as Jonas was three days and three nights in the whale's belly; so shall the Son of man be three days and three nights in the heart of the earth" (Matthew 12:40).

Similarly, John the Baptist made the connection that the Passover lamb was a type of Christ when he declared Jesus to be "the Lamb of God" (John 1:29).

The offering of Isaac by his father Abraham was an event that is considered a type of Christ. This offering was done, according to the Book of Mormon, in "similitude of God and his Only Begotten Son" (Jacob 4:5).

Types can also take on the form of an object. For example, the Lord declared that the brazen serpent that Moses raised in the wilderness was a type of Christ: "And as Moses lifted up the serpent in the wilderness, even so must the Son of man be lifted up: That whosoever believeth in him should not perish, but have eternal life" (John 3:14–15).

## Types of Christ's Second Coming

The types of Christ that we have highlighted above are just a few examples of literally hundreds that we could have chosen from to illustrate this concept. And as you may have noticed based on the examples cited above, the vast majority of the types of Christ found in the scriptures are types of Christ's first coming, meaning that they foreshadow Christ's birth, ministry, Atonement, death, or Resurrection in some form or another. As King Benjamin stated, "And many signs, and wonders, and types, and shadows showed [the Lord] unto [the children of men] concerning his coming" (Mosiah 3:15).

But as interesting as Christ's first coming types may be, the purpose of Part II of this book is to examine the types associated with Christ's Second Coming. While there may not be as many Second Coming types located in the scriptures, the types that we have been able to identify are, in each case, filled with rich symbolism and can teach us much about our Savior's return.

# 14
# The Betrothal at Sinai

In the scriptures, the Second Coming of Christ has often been compared to a wedding ceremony.[1] An example of this is found in the parable of the ten virgins: "Then shall the kingdom of heaven be likened unto ten virgins, which took their lamps, and went forth to meet the bridegroom" (Matthew 25:1).

The bridegroom in this parable represents Christ (see Mark 2:19–20),[2] and wherever there is a bridegroom to be found, you are also sure to find a bride and a wedding. The wedding, according to the Lord, represents the Second Coming: "And at that day, when I shall come in my glory, shall the parable be fulfilled which I spake concerning the ten virgins" (Doctrine and Covenants 45:56).

President Joseph Fielding Smith taught that "the marriage of the Lamb is a figure of speech, having reference to the second coming of

---

1. See, for example, the parable of the wedding garment, as recorded in Matthew 22:1–14.
2. President Joseph Fielding Smith said, "The Savior spoke of the Bridegroom when referring to himself." Joseph Fielding Smith, *Doctrines of Salvation*, comp. Bruce R. McConkie (Bookcraft, 1954–56), 3:61.

our Savior and the feast, or supper, that the righteous shall receive at his coming."[3]

Knowing that the wedding in this parable is the Second Coming, and knowing that the bridegroom is Christ, the next question is, Who is Christ's bride?

## The Identity of the Bride

While the identity of the bride is not revealed in this particular parable, she has fortunately been identified in several other passages of scripture. For example, John the Revelator wrote, "The marriage of the Lamb is come, and his wife hath made herself ready. And to her was granted that she should be arrayed in fine linen, clean and white: for the fine linen is the righteousness of saints. . . . Blessed are they which are called unto the marriage supper of the Lamb" (Revelation 19:7–9; see also Revelation 21:2).

According to John, the bride of Christ consists of individuals who are "called unto the marriage supper of the Lamb" (Revelation 19:9). They are the individuals who have been pronounced "clean and white" and who have been clothed in "righteousness" (Revelation 19:8).

Other prophets have also confirmed that the bride of Christ is identified with the righteous followers of Christ. For example, President Joseph Fielding Smith taught that "the bride of the Lamb is the organization of the righteous who have inheritance in the holy city."[4]

This was also confirmed by Joseph Smith, who, during the dedication of the Kirtland Temple, prayed that the Lord's Church would someday be "adorned as a bride for that day when thou shalt unveil the heavens" (Doctrine and Covenants 109:74). Similarly, the prophet Isaiah twice referred to the righteous as the Lord's "bride" (Isaiah 62:5; 61:10) while simultaneously referring to the Lord as Israel's "husband" (Isaiah 54:5).

## Husband and Wife

Now that we have discovered the true identity of Christ's bride, we must ask ourselves why the Lord chose to use the analogy of a

3. Joseph Fielding Smith, *Doctrines of Salvation*, 3:61.

4. Joseph Fielding Smith, *Doctrines of Salvation*, 3:62.

husband and wife to describe the relationship between Himself and His followers. As it turns out, there are many similarities between the two. For example, just as "a man . . . shall cleave unto his wife: and they shall be one flesh" (Genesis 2:24), so too has the Lord commanded us to become "one" with him (John 17:21). And just as we are meant to love our spouse, we have also been asked to "love the Lord thy God with all thine heart, and with all thy soul, and with all thy might" (Deuteronomy 6:5). The Apostle Paul taught us the following: "For the husband is the head of the wife, even as Christ is the head of the church. . . . Husbands, love your wives, even as Christ also loved the church, and gave himself for it" (Ephesians 5:23–25).

Donald Parry and Jay Parry added this insight:

> The marriage of the Lamb, who is Christ (Doctrine and Covenants 33:17–18), to his bride, who is the Church (Doctrine and Covenants 109:73–74) . . . is a metaphor for the union between the Lord and his people, made possible through the atonement of Christ. . . . The Lord uses marriage as a symbol to underscore the sweetness and blessing of that union. There is no sweeter or more meaningful relationship on earth than that between a holy husband and a holy wife; that is the kind of relationship (in depth of feeling and completeness of union) that the Lord is inviting us to participate in.[5]

It is also interesting to note that anciently, the Israelite men had to pay an expensive dowry for the bride of their choice, which made these women somewhat of a "purchased possession."[6] For example, before his marriage to Ruth, Boaz declared to the elders that "Ruth the Moabitess . . . have I *purchased* to be my wife" (Ruth 4:10; emphasis added). In a similar way, the Apostle Paul referred to the Saints of his day as "the church of God, which [Christ] hath *purchased* with his own blood" (Acts 20:28; emphasis added).

One additional similarity worth mentioning is how each party is joined together. Just as the husband and wife are to be sealed together for eternity in the Lord's temple, so too must each and every one of us

---

5. Donald W. Parry and Jay A. Parry, *Understanding the Signs of the Times* (Deseret Book, 1999), 430.

6. Donna B. Nielsen, *Beloved Bridegroom: Finding Christ in Ancient Jewish Marriage and Family Customs* (Onyx Press, 1999), 108.

enter into sacred covenants with the Lord in His temple if we are to be bound to Him in the eternities.

## The Engagement

As we have just learned from the parable of the ten virgins and from other scriptures, we are symbolically married to the Lord *at* His Second Coming. However, just as a man and woman do not get married until after they become engaged, so too must we be engaged to the Lord *before* His Second Coming.

As we shall soon see, this symbolic engagement occurs when we receive our endowments in the Lord's holy temple. As we enter into these temple covenants with the Lord, it is as if we are agreeing *to be* married to Him at His Second Coming. However, just like an actual engagement, our symbolic marriage to Christ at the Second Coming will only occur if we remain true and faithful from the time of our engagement until the time of the wedding.

## The Hebrew Betrothal

In the Hebrew culture, engagements were known as *betrothals*. And while the Hebrew betrothal was very similar in many respects to our modern-day engagement, it is worth pointing out a few minor differences between the two. According to Donna Nielsen, "Betrothal in Jewish mind was a serious covenant, with a much greater idea of commitment than an engagement has today. . . . Betrothal was so legally binding that one could not break the contract without a divorce. . . . During betrothal, a couple was considered legally married, even though the marriage was not yet consummated."[7]

Similarly, according to Reed Durham, "The betrothal was considered to be more than the promise of marriage. . . . Engagements could be broken off, a promise might be set aside, but the betrothal was considered binding because it was entered into by a sacred oath and covenant."[8]

---

7. Nielsen, *Beloved Bridegroom*, 24.
8. Reed C. Durham, "Mary Was Espoused to Joseph," *Instructor,* July 1967, 265, as quoted in Richard K. Hart, "The Marriage Metaphor," *Ensign*, Jan. 1995, 22.

This oath and covenant that the Hebrew couple entered into at the time of betrothal was considered the first of two ceremonies in connection with their marriage, the second being the wedding ceremony itself. According to Richard Hart, "First there was a betrothal—an engagement ceremony at which covenants between the bride and groom were formalized. . . . Following the year of betrothal, the solemnization of the wedding vows took place."[9]

In addition to covenants being made, "the betrothal," according to Marvin Wilson, also included "an act of sanctification or consecration," where the future bride was "set apart" and made "holy."[10] There is even some evidence that suggests that the bride was washed, anointed, and clothed as part of her betrothal.[11] Knowing that the Hebrew betrothal included making sacred covenants, washings, anointings, and the act of being clothed, is it any wonder that the temple endowment should be viewed as a betrothal ceremony between the participant and the Lord?

This means that once we are betrothed to the Lord in His temple, we should consider ourselves legally married to Him, just as the Israelites of old considered themselves legally married to each other after exchanging their betrothal vows. And similar to the Israelites of old, we too are expected to remain faithful to the Lord from the time of our symbolic betrothal to the time of our symbolic marriage at the Second Coming. Parry and Parry put it this way, "Though we are to prepare for the marriage all our lives (Matt. 25:1–13; Doctrine and Covenants 45:56–57), it will be brought to its culmination, with the body of the Church, when Christ returns in glory."[12]

---

9. Hart, "The Marriage Metaphor," 22.

10. Marvin R. Wilson, *Our Father Abraham: Jewish Roots of the Christian Faith* (Eerdmans, 1989), 205.

11. Joseph Benson, "Ezekiel 16:8–12," *Commentary of the Old and New Testaments* (T. Carlton & J. Porter, 1857). See also Matthew Brown, *The Gate of Heaven: Insights on the Doctrines and Symbols of the Temple* (Covenant Communications, 1999), 135.

12. Parry and Parry, *Understanding the Signs of the Times*, 430–31.

## The House of Israel's Betrothal

Just as we are symbolically betrothed to the Lord today by entering into sacred covenants in our modern-day temples, so too was the house of Israel given the opportunity to be betrothed to the Lord at Mount Sinai. After the house of Israel fled Egypt, and after they crossed the Red Sea, the Lord led them safely to His holy mountain, where He proceeded to offer to them the same betrothal terms that He offers us in our day. According to Hart, "The symbolic betrothal of the bride (the house of Israel) to the Bridegroom (Jehovah) took place in the Sinai wilderness after the Exodus. There, characteristic of Hebraic betrothal, the Lord entered into a covenant relationship with Jacob's descendants."[13]

According to the Old Testament, this symbolic betrothal occurred when the Lord called out unto Moses from Mount Sinai and said to him, "Thus shalt thou say to . . . the children of Israel . . . if ye will obey my voice indeed, and keep my covenant, then ye shall be a peculiar treasure unto me above all people. . . . And ye shall be unto me a kingdom of priests, and an holy nation" (Exodus 19:3–6).

And thus a proposal—or rather a betrothal covenant—was offered by the Lord to the Israelites. The Israelites responded to the Lord's proposal by saying, "All that the Lord hath spoken we will do" (Exodus 19:8).

With both parties in agreement, the betrothal ceremony would soon be underway. As part of this betrothal ceremony, the Lord offered to reveal Himself to the Israelites upon Mount Sinai and gave them three days to sanctify themselves in preparation for this sacred event. This preparation was to include being washed, anointed, and clothed (see Ezekiel 16:8–12; Exodus 19:10), which was not unlike the customs of the traditional Jewish betrothal.[14] According to the text, here is what happened next:

---

13. Hart, "The Marriage Metaphor," 22. See also Brown, *The Gate of Heaven*, 138.

14. Of these verses in Ezekiel (Ezekiel 16:8–12), Joseph Benson noted, "*Yea, I entered into covenant with thee* — This was done in mount Sinai, when the covenant between God and Israel was sealed and ratified. . . . *Then I washed thee with water* — It was a very ancient custom among the eastern people to purify virgins who were to be espoused. *And I anointed thee with oil* — Thus

> And it came to pass on the third day in the morning, that there were thunders and lightnings, and a thick cloud upon the mount, and the voice of the trumpet exceeding loud; so that all the people that was in the camp trembled.
>
> And Moses brought forth the people out of the camp to meet with God; and they stood at the nether part of the mount.
>
> And mount Sinai was altogether on a smoke, because the Lord descended upon it in fire: and the smoke thereof ascended as the smoke of a furnace, and the whole mount quaked greatly. (Exodus 19:16–18)

According to Donna Nielsen, while this mountain was no doubt a frightening sight for many of the Israelites, there were nevertheless many manifestations of God's love being shown here, which one might expect from a formal betrothal ceremony:

> The Semitic root word for "love" is *haw* or *hav*. It means "to warm," "to kindle," "to set on fire." To the Hebrews, a "burning in the bosom" could be a manifestation of *love*. It is interesting that at Mt. Sinai (which the Jews think of as the place where God chose Israel as a covenant marriage partner), the mountain appeared to be on fire. This dramatic event naturally terrified the Israelites. But it is a sweet thought that perhaps the fire represents a level of love that we mortals cannot even comprehend. The truths that "God is love" (1 John 4:8) and that "He dwells in everlasting burnings" (Isaiah 33:14–15) are semantically related.[15]

## Broken Covenants

Unfortunately for the Israelites, soon after their betrothal to the Lord, they were unable to obey the voice of the Lord in all things as they had previously covenanted to do, and they failed to live up to the higher law which was offered to them. We read, "Moses plainly taught to the children of Israel in the wilderness, and sought diligently to sanctify his people that they might behold the face of God; But they

---

also were women, on some occasions, prepared for their nuptials" (Benson, "Ezekiel 16:8–12," *Commentary of the Old and New Testaments*). See also Nielsen, *Beloved Bridegroom*, 125.

15. Nielsen, *Beloved Bridegroom*, 13.

hardened their hearts and could not endure his presence" (Doctrine and Covenants 84:23–24).

Knowing that the Israelites would have a hard time living up to the terms of their betrothal covenants, the Lord warned the Israelites that "thou shalt have no other gods before me . . . for I the Lord thy God am a jealous God" (Exodus 20:3, 5). As noted previously, in ancient Judaism the man and woman who were betrothed were "considered legally married, even though [their] marriage was not yet consummated."[16] Because the Lord considered Himself to be a jealous God, and because He considered the covenants that the house of Israel entered into at Mount Sinai to be as serious as marriage covenants, He often referred to the house of Israel as adulterers and fornicators when they later broke their end of the covenant by serving other gods throughout their history. For example, "[Jerusalem is] as a wife that committeth adultery, which taketh strangers instead of her husband" (Ezekiel 16:32).

And again: "I have a few things against thee, because thou hast [allowed] . . . the children of Israel, to eat things sacrificed unto idols, and to *commit fornication*" (Revelation 2:14; emphasis added).

And again: "For the land hath *committed great whoredom*, departing from the Lord" (Hosea 1:2; emphasis added).

And again: "Though thou, *Israel, play the harlot* . . ." (Hosea 4:15; emphasis added).

And finally: "Turn, O backsliding children, saith the Lord; *for I am married unto you*. . . . Surely as a wife treacherously departeth from her husband, so have ye dealt treacherously with me, O house of Israel" (Jeremiah 3:14, 20, emphasis added; see also Exodus 34:15–16; Jeremiah 3:6–8; Ezekiel 16; Ezekiel 23).

Interestingly enough, even the very word for *adultery* in Hebrew implies apostasy.[17]

## A New Covenant

Because the house of Israel constantly broke their betrothal covenants, the Lord chose to scatter them throughout various times of

16. Nielsen, *Beloved Bridegroom*, 24.

17. Nielsen, *Beloved Bridegroom*, 120.

their history. However, "thus saith the Lord [to the house of Israel]: Have I put thee away, or have I cast thee off forever? . . . Where is the bill of your mother's divorcement?" (2 Nephi 7:1).

Although the house of Israel rejected the Lord several times throughout their history, rather than calling off the marriage entirely, the Lord in His mercy has offered to renew this betrothal covenant to latter-day Israel. This was prophesied of by the prophet Jeremiah: "Behold, the days come, saith the Lord, that I will make a new covenant with the house of Israel, and with the house of Judah: Not according to the covenant that I made with their fathers in the day that I took them by the hand to bring them out of the land of Egypt; which my covenant they brake, although I was an husband unto them" (Jeremiah 31:31–32).

We have been invited to enter into this "new covenant" with the Lord in our day through the ordinances of His holy temple. By doing so, we are symbolically betrothed to the Lord, which makes us eligible to one day enter into a symbolic marriage with Him at His Second Coming if we remain faithful. John the Revelator prophesied of this future event, saying, "The marriage of the Lamb is come, and his wife hath made herself ready. . . . Blessed are they which are called unto the marriage supper of the Lamb" (Revelation 19:7, 9).

# 15
# The Veiled Bride

As we have just seen, the Lord often used the imagery of a marriage to teach us certain truths concerning our relationship to Him, particularly when it comes to His Second Coming. As we shall see, the Lord also used this same symbolic imagery behind the scenes in the famous story of Abraham and Isaac.

## Isaac as a Type of Christ

According to the Book of Mormon, the offering of Isaac by his father Abraham was done in "similitude of God and his Only Begotten Son" (Jacob 4:5). This famous Old Testament story is perhaps one of the most commonly cited examples of a type of Christ in all of scripture. Abraham, whose name literally means "father of a multitude"[1] and represents our Heavenly Father, willingly offered his son Isaac, a type for the Savior. But the symbolism in this story does not end here.

For example, God sent a heavenly messenger to earth to announce each of their respective births (see Genesis 17; Luke 1). Furthermore, the birth of each individual involved a miracle: Mary miraculously

1. Joseph Fielding McConkie and Donald W. Parry, *Guide to Scriptural Symbols* (Deseret Book, 1990), 12.

conceived Christ as a virgin (see Matthew 1:23) and Sarah miraculously conceived Isaac in her old age (see Genesis 17:17).

Furthermore, according to Jewish tradition, Isaac, like Christ, was in his thirties at the time of his offering.[2] If this proves to be true, it means that Isaac could have easily withstood his aged father and chosen not to participate in the sacrifice. As Jewish scholar Kenneth Seeskin wrote, "Isaac did not protest when his father strapped him to an altar. Instead of an innocent victim, [Isaac] not only understands but participates in his father's action."[3] The same can be said of Christ.

## The Offering

Prior to the offering, Abraham and Isaac journeyed three full days before arriving at the place of Isaac's sacrifice (see Genesis 22:4). These three days could represent the three years of Christ's mortal ministry before His Crucifixion. It is also worth noting that these two sacrifices took place on the same mountain range and were located very closely to one another. Isaac was offered on Mount Moriah, just a few hundred yards away from Golgotha.[4]

When Abraham and Isaac arrived at the mount, the record states that "Abraham took the wood of the burnt offering, and laid it upon Isaac his son" (Genesis 22:6), which Isaac then carried to the site of the sacrifice. After reading this account, one cannot help but recall the heavy wooden crossbar that was laid upon the Savior's back: "And they took Jesus, and led him away. And he bearing his cross went forth into a place called the place of a skull, which is called in the Hebrew Golgotha" (John 19:16–17).

---

2. A common misconception is that Isaac was a young child when he was offered up by his father. However, we know that Sarah was ninety years old when Isaac was born (see Genesis 17:17) and that she died at the age of 127 not long after Isaac was offered (see Genesis 23:1). This would mean that Isaac could have been as old as thirty-seven at the time of the offering. Kenneth Seeskin wrote, "The Isaac of rabbinic commentators is a man in his thirties." Kenneth Seeskin, *Jewish Philosophy in a Secular Age* (State University of New York Press, 1990), 135.
3. Seeskin, *Jewish Philosophy in a Secular* Age, 135.
4. Artel Ricks, "Mount Moriah: Some Personal Reflections," *Ensign*, Sept. 1980, 59–65.

Isaac, like Christ, was bound to the altar in preparation of the sacrifice (see Genesis 22:9; Matthew 27:35). Unlike the Crucifixion, however, the offering of Isaac was stopped by an angel before it was able to take place (see Genesis 22:10–12).[5]

According to the Old Testament, Abraham then "went and took the ram, and offered him up for a burnt offering in the stead of his son" (Genesis 22:13). It is at this point that our story takes an interesting turn. Isaac is treated as if he died on the mount! We read, "So Abraham returned [from the mount] unto his young men [who were at the base of the mount], and they rose up and went together to Beersheba" (Genesis 22:19).

Biblical scholar Chuck Missler said of this verse:

> Notice that in the list of who came down from the mountain to return home, only Abraham and the two young men at the bottom of the hill are listed. Where is Isaac? Naturally, we infer that Isaac also joined them and that there were four who traveled back to Beersheba. But that's *not* what the text says! It seems that Isaac has disappeared; the person of Isaac has been *edited out of the record*, from the time that he is offered on the mount *until he is united with his bride [Rebekah]*, two chapters later![6]

How does this small omission in the biblical record relate to Christ after His sacrifice? Since His death, Christ has chosen to go unrevealed to the world at large. With few exceptions, no longer has Christ physically ministered on the earth to humankind. What is more, Christ will continue to go unrevealed to the world at large until His Second Coming, during which time He will return to marry

---

5. It is also interesting to note that in connection with these two sacrifices, thorns appear in both accounts. After the angel appeared, Abraham "lifted up his eyes, and looked, and behold behind him a ram caught in a thicket [of thorns]" (Genesis 22:13). Similarly, it was a crown of thorns that was placed upon Christ's brow prior to His Crucifixion (see Matthew 27:29). Scripturally, thorns can be said to represent sin. For example, after Adam's transgression, sin was introduced into the world, and as a result, the earth began to produce thorns and thistles naturally (Moses 4:24). In other words, both sin and thorns are produced naturally in a fallen world. No doubt the crown of thorns upon Christ's brow represented the sins of all of us that He bore alone on that day.

6. Chuck Missler, *Cosmic Codes: Hidden Messages from the Edge of Eternity* (Koinonia House, 1999), 195; emphasis in original.

His bride, whom we already identified in the previous chapter as the Church (see Doctrine and Covenants 109:73–74).

If Isaac is a type of Christ, then his bride Rebekah is a type for Christ's Church. And as we shall see, the marriage between these two individuals will prove to be extremely symbolic because it represents our future marriage ceremony at Christ's Second Coming.

However, before we discuss the details of this marriage, we must first return to the text to find out how Rebekah was chosen to be Isaac's bride in the first place.

## Finding a Wife for Isaac

After Abraham returns home from the mount, he immediately sets out to find a wife for his son Isaac by sending his unnamed servant[7] to Mesopotamia with this very objective in mind (see Genesis 24:2–10). If Abraham is a type for our Heavenly Father in this story, then his unnamed servant represents the unnamed Holy Ghost, whose entire purpose is to seek out those who are willing to be united in a symbolic marriage covenant with the Lord.[8]

After Abraham's unnamed servant arrives in Mesopotamia, he came up with a plan for finding an honorable woman worthy of Isaac. He led his ten camels to a well outside the city (see Genesis 24:10–11) and there offered a prayer to the Lord: "And he said, O Lord God . . . let it come to pass, that the damsel to whom . . . shall say [to me], Drink, and I will give thy camels drink also: let the same be she that thou hast appointed for thy servant Isaac" (Genesis 24:12–14).

It goes without saying that someone who would voluntarily draw water for a stranger and his ten thirsty camels is a person with a great deal of charity.[9] Nevertheless, this was the very thing that Rebekah of-

7. Chuck Missler, *Hidden Treasures in the Biblical Text* (Koinonia House, 2000), 60. Although the name of Abraham's servant is not mentioned in this chapter of Genesis, it is assumed that this person is Abraham's servant Eliezer, who is named in Genesis 15:2.

8. Missler, *Hidden Treasures in the Biblical Text*, 60–61.

9. According to Nielsen, "The task of watering ten camels *until they had their fill* was difficult enough, but we are told in Genesis 24:16, 20 that she had to go down into the well (often several dozen steps), draw the water, come up, empty the pitcher into the trough, and return again many times. Camels after a long

fered to do for Abraham's servant (see Genesis 24:15–20). In addition, Rebekah also offered him lodging in her father's house and food for his camels (see Genesis 24:25). No doubt a woman of this nature was truly a woman worthy of being Isaac's bride.

When Abraham's servant reached Rebekah's home, he explained to her family the reason why he had traveled all the way to Mesopotamia. He said to them, "I am Abraham's servant. And the Lord hath blessed my master greatly; and he is become great: and he hath given him flocks, and herds, and silver, and gold, and menservants, and maidservants, and camels, and asses. And Sarah my master's wife bare a son to my master when she was old: *and unto him hath he given all that he hath*" (Genesis 24:34–36; emphasis added).

Returning to our analogy, Abraham (representing our Heavenly Father), sent his servant (representing the Holy Ghost) to seek out Rebekah (representing the Church) and invite her to enter into a marriage covenant (representing the Second Coming) with Isaac (representing Christ), with the promise that upon marriage, all that Abraham owned would be given to her through her relationship with Isaac. Interestingly enough, the same offer has also been extended to us by the Lord: "For he that receiveth my servants receiveth me; And he that receiveth me receiveth . . . my Father's kingdom; *therefore all that my Father hath shall be given unto him*" (Doctrine and Covenants 84:36–38; emphasis added).

There is a catch to this offer, however. Rebekah had never met Isaac and therefore had to act on faith that what Abraham's servant was offering to her was in fact true.[10] So too is it with us. If we are to receive "all that [the] Father hath" (Doctrine and Covenants 84:38), we too must learn to listen to the promptings of the Holy Ghost and act on those promptings in faith. Ultimately, we must agree to enter into a marriage covenant with someone we have not yet come in contact with.

---

journey are quite naturally depleted, and each camel can drink from ten to thirty gallons of water." Donna B. Nielsen, *Beloved Bridegroom: Finding Christ in Ancient Jewish Marriage and Family Customs* (Onyx Press, 1999), 16.

10. Missler, *Hidden Treasures in the Biblical Text*, 60.

We have much to learn from the faithful example of Rebekah, for when Rebekah was asked by her family, "Wilt thou go with this man?" she responded quickly by saying, "I will go" (Genesis 24:58).

## Rebekah's Veil

As Rebekah approached Isaac's residence, Isaac went out to greet her. When Rebekah saw Isaac approaching, "she took a veil, and covered herself" (Genesis 24:65). This veil, which was worn by Rebekah "as a sign of her virtue, modesty, respect, and readiness for a covenant marriage,"[11] was most likely worn until the actual marriage ceremony had taken place between her and Isaac sometime later (see Genesis 24:65–67). According to traditional Jewish weddings, a veil was worn by the bride until she and her husband entered "the marriage chamber, [where] the bride and groom were alone. When she removed her veil in his presence, they could then see and be seen as they really were."[12]

If the wedding between Isaac and Rebekah represents the Second Coming, then Rebekah's veil represents the veil that is currently covering our earth and separating us from the Lord. We are told that this veil will be removed from the earth at the Second Coming: "The veil . . . which hideth the earth, shall be taken off, and all flesh shall see me together" (Doctrine and Covenants 101:23)

And again: "The curtain of heaven [shall] be unfolded, as a scroll is unfolded after it is rolled up, and the face of the Lord shall be unveiled; And the saints that are upon the earth, who are alive, shall be quickened and be caught up to meet him" (Doctrine and Covenants 88:95–96).

Being worthy of this Second Coming marriage ceremony is what we should all be striving for and is what the story of Abraham, Isaac, and Rebekah should remind us of. Remember, we as a Church are to be "adorned as a bride for that day when [the Lord] shalt unveil the heavens" (Doctrine and Covenants 109:74). Until that day comes, however, we are to faithfully wear a veil that separates us from the Lord's presence and go forward with faith, knowing that if we do, we

---

11. "She Shall Be Called Woman: Women of the Old Testament," *Ensign*, Sept. 2006, 42.

12. Nielsen, *Beloved Bridegroom*, 138.

too can receive "all that [the] Father hath" (Doctrine and Covenants 84:38).

## Ruth and Boaz

As it turns out, the marriage between Isaac and Rebekah was not the only Old Testament marriage symbolic of Christ's Second Coming. One could argue that the marriage between Ruth and Boaz followed a similar pattern, with the husband, Boaz, representing Christ and the bride, Ruth, representing Christ's Church.[13]

As the story goes, Ruth, a Gentile woman, moved to Bethlehem with her mother-in-law Naomi from the land of Moab (see Ruth 1). After arriving in Bethlehem, Ruth, in want of food, went to a nearby wheat field to glean the unwanted wheat that the reapers had left behind for the poor (see Ruth 2:3). Little did Ruth know that the field belonged to her future husband, a wealthy man named Boaz.

Boaz, after noticing Ruth gleaning wheat in his field, inquired about her through his unnamed servant, and the two of them were soon after introduced (see Ruth 2:5–6). Much like the unnamed servant of Abraham who introduced Rebekah to Isaac, the unnamed servant of Boaz is yet another type for the Holy Ghost, whose job it is to bring us to Christ.

Once Ruth and Boaz were introduced, we read that Ruth "found grace" in the eyes of Boaz (Ruth 2:10). As a result, Boaz offered to provide Ruth with more food than she could otherwise gather from gleaning the fields alone (see Ruth 2:7–18). Ruth's newly found grace offered to her by Boaz closely parallels the grace that is freely given to us from Christ (see Ephesians 2:8), the "bread of life" (John 6:35).

Once Ruth returned home, she was eager to tell her mother-in-law, Naomi, of her new relationship. Naomi, sensing an opportunity, instructed Ruth to "wash thyself therefore, and anoint thee, and put thy raiment upon thee" (Ruth 3:3) and meet Boaz that night "in the threshingfloor" (Ruth 3:2).

---

13. Unless otherwise noted, the following types come from Chuck Missler, *Romance of Redemption: Gleanings from the Book of Ruth* (Seksok, 2016). See also Chuck Missler, *Ruth & Ester: An Expositional Commentary* (Koinonia House, 2001), 3–41.

## Threshing Floors

Anciently, threshing floors consisted of a hard, flat surface, usually located on top of a tall hill or mountain, where wheat was threshed and winnowed.[14] But more than this, threshing floors anciently had strong symbolic ties to the temple. In the words of Old Testament scholar Jamie Waters, "In ancient Israel threshing floors were not only agricultural spaces but were regarded as sacred spaces."[15]

Because wheat was one of the main food sources of the Israelites, and because the Israelites recognized that all of their food came from the hand of God, many of them considered their threshing floors sacred and would even go so far as to put their threshing floors under the Lord's divine control.[16]

For example, in 2 Samuel, the Lord commanded David to build an altar and offer sacrifices unto him. However, the Lord did not want this altar built just anywhere. Instead, He commanded David to purchase the threshing floor of a man named Ornan[17] and build the altar in the center of this threshing floor (see 2 Samuel 24:18–24). This location famously became known as the threshing floor of Ornan and shows us that even the Lord considered threshing floors to be sacred spaces. In fact, this particular threshing floor of Ornan was so sacred that the Lord eventually commanded David's son Solomon to build the temple of Solomon upon this very spot: "Then Solomon began to build the house of the Lord at Jerusalem in mount Moriah . . . in the place that David had prepared in the threshingfloor of Ornan" (2 Chronicles 3:1).

## Ruth Meets Boaz at the Threshing Floor

Thus, when Naomi tells Ruth to "wash thyself therefore, and anoint thee, and put thy raiment upon thee" (Ruth 3:3) and meet Boaz that night "in the threshingfloor" (Ruth 3:2), it is safe to assume

---

14. More of this process will be discussed in chapter 22.

15. Jaime L. Waters, *Threshing Floors in Ancient Israel:Their Ritual and Symbolic Significance* (Fortress Press, 2015), 1.

16. Waters, *Threshing Floors in Ancient Israel*, 1–2.

17. Also referred to as Araunah.

this will be more than just a casual meeting. And since Ruth in our analogy represents Christ's Church, it is no surprise to learn that similar instructions have also been given to us in our day. According to Degn and Christensen:

> Naomi outlined a four-step process of preparation for Ruth to meet her potential bridegroom. The same pattern must be employed by every individual who desires the rest that can come only through the Lord. To prepare for the meeting with Boaz, Naomi instructed Ruth, "*Wash* thyself therefore, and *anoint* thee, and put thy *raiment* upon thee, and get thee down to the *floor*" (Ruth 3:3; emphasis added). Before we can approach the presence of our own Bridegroom, we must [do the same].[18]

During Ruth and Boaz's meeting at the threshing floor, a marriage proposal was offered (see Ruth 3:9).[19] This threshing floor marriage proposal is not unlike Israel's symbolic betrothal at Mount Sinai, nor is it not unlike our symbolic betrothal to the Lord through the endowment.

It is also interesting to note that as part of her ceremonial clothing, Ruth also wore a "veil" on her person during her meeting with Boaz at the threshing floor (see Ruth 3:15). While this veil was somewhat different from the veil that Rebekah wore over her face,[20] it nevertheless represents the same veil that is currently covering our earth and separating us from the Lord's presence (see Doctrine and Covenants 88:95; 101:23).

After the marriage proposal at the threshing floor, arrangements were made for Boaz to purchase Ruth (see Ruth 4:9–10), which is not unlike the process the Lord went through when He "purchased [us]

---

18. Patrick D. Degn and David S. Christensen, *Types and Shadows of the Old Testament: Jesus Christ and the Great Plan of Happiness* (Deseret Book, 2018), 102.

19. According to *Matthew Poole's Commentary,* the phrase "spread thy skirt over thine hand-maid" (Ruth 3:9) meant "take me to be thy wife, and perform the duty of an husband to me." Matthew Poole, *Matthew Poole's Commentary on the Holy Bible* (Hendrickson Publishers, 1985), under Ruth 3:9.

20. According to *Matthew Poole's Commentary,* Ruth's veil was more of an "apron, such as women ordinarily wear." *Matthew Poole's Commentary,* under Ruth 3:15.

with his own blood" (Acts 20:28). When the day of the wedding finally came, we read that "Boaz took Ruth, and she [became] his wife" (Ruth 4:13).

Thus, in the story of Ruth and Boaz, we find yet another marriage ceremony that symbolizes the future day when Christ and His Church will be reunited and symbolically wed at His Second Coming.

# 16
# The Veiled Mountain

In the previous chapter, we saw that the heavenly veil—the veil that is currently covering our earth and separating us from the presence of the Lord—was represented by two veils worn by Ruth and Rebekah prior to their marriages. In this chapter, we will examine how the Red Sea also came to represent this same heavenly veil and show how it symbolically shielded the Israelites from the presence of the Lord at Mount Sinai. This analogy begins with the Exodus story.

## The Exodus Pattern

It is well known that the story of the Exodus is not exclusively the story of the ancient Israelites. It is also a type and shadow of our journey through mortality. In the Exodus story, Egypt represents our earth life, or the telestial world in which we live. Just like the Israelites, who considered themselves "strangers in the land of Egypt" (Exodus 23:9), we do not belong here; we journeyed here from a celestial home, and it is a celestial home which we long to return to.

After living in Egypt comfortably for many years, the Israelites suddenly found themselves in bondage under the reign of a pharaoh who "knew not Joseph" and feared his posterity (Exodus 1:8–9). This

Israelite bondage is a type and shadow for the prophesied bondage that the Saints of this generation will face prior to building up Zion. We read in the Doctrine and Covenants, "And ye must needs be led out of bondage by power, and with a stretched-out arm. And as your fathers were led at the first, even so shall the redemption of Zion be" (Doctrine and Covenants 103:17–18).

Commenting on this prophecy, Elder Orson Pratt said, "This indicates that there may be bondage ahead, and that the Latter-day Saints may see severe times, and that unless we keep the commandments of God, we may be brought into circumstances that will cause our hearts to tremble within us."[1]

On a second occasion, Elder Pratt continued this thought:

> I do not know what the purposes of the Lord are in relation to this particular thing. It may be that we shall have our rights completely taken from us; it may be, if we do not live sufficiently faithful before the Lord, that he will yet bring us into still greater tribulation than that which we have hitherto had. It may be that we shall yet be in bondage like the Israelites in the land of Egypt; for the Lord has said that . . . he would redeem his people by power out of bondage, and they should be led as their fathers were led at the first.[2]

Thankfully for the Israelites, the Lord sent Moses to deliver them from Egyptian bondage. In our day, the Lord will raise up a man like unto Moses to fulfill a similar role:

> Behold, I say unto you, the redemption of Zion must needs come by power;
>
> Therefore, I will raise up unto my people a man, who shall lead them like as Moses led the children of Israel.
>
> For ye are the children of Israel, and of the seed of Abraham, and ye must needs be led out of bondage by power, and with a stretched-out arm.
>
> And as your fathers were led at the first, even so shall the redemption of Zion be. (Doctrine and Covenants 103:15–18)

---

1. *Journal of Discourses*, 15:362.
2. *Journal of Discourses*, 17:303.

## The Ten Plagues

Moses delivered his people with a fantastic display of power given to him of the Lord, which included calling for ten plagues to torment Egypt. These ten plagues served a dual purpose, the first of which was to soften the heart of Pharaoh (see Doctrine and Covenants 105:27) and the second to show both the Israelites and Egyptians that the God of Israel was superior in every way to the gods of Egypt.

In fact, you could say that each of the ten plagues was a direct attack on one or more of Egypt's gods. For example, one of the most important Egyptian gods was Osiris, the god of the Nile. So when Moses turned the Nile into blood, it would have been viewed by both the Israelites and the Egyptians as a declaration of war issued by the God of Israel on the Nile god Osiris.[3] And when the Lord sent frogs and beetles[4] to cover the land (see Exodus 8:6, 24), it directly challenged the Egyptian goddess Hekt, depicted with the head of a frog,[5] and the Egyptian god Amon-Ra, depicted with the head of a beetle.[6] The Lord also declared war on the bull god Apis by sending a plague that killed "all the cattle of Egypt" (Exodus 9:6).[7] And when the Lord sent lice to Egypt (see Exodus 8:16), it would have surely been an embarrassment to Egyptian priests thus affected because having lice would have prohibited them from officiating in their Egyptian temples.[8]

Other Egyptian gods that were challenged were Thoth, the god who presided over medical learning yet was unable to provide a cure for the boils and blains sent by the Lord (see Exodus 9:9),[9] and Serapia, who failed to accomplish her one and only purpose of protecting

---

3. Harold L. Willmington, *Willmington's Guide to the Bible* (Tyndale House Publishers, 2011), 66–67.
4. This was incorrectly translated as flies in the King James Version.
5. *Willmington's Guide to the Bible*, 66–67.
6. Chuck Missler, "Against the Gods of Egypt: The Invisible War," Koinonia House, July 1, 2000, https://www.khouse.org/personal_update/articles/2000/against-gods-egypt.
7. *Willmington's Guide to the Bible*, 66–67.
8. Missler, "Against the Gods of Egypt."
9. Missler, "Against the Gods of Egypt."

Egypt from the plague of locusts (see Exodus 10:14).[10] And when the Lord sent fire mingled with hail (see Exodus 9:23–24) followed by thick darkness (see Exodus 10:21), Shu, the god of the atmosphere, and Ra, the god of the sun, were nowhere to be found.[11] Lastly, the Egyptian god Taweret, the protector of children, was also rendered helpless when the Lord sent His destroying angel to kill the firstborn of every family in Egypt (see Exodus 12:29).[12]

As bad as these plagues were for the Egyptians, the Lord has promised us that if the inhabitants of the earth in these latter days do not repent prior to the Second Coming, He will pour out even more devastating plagues among the wicked in our generation. In the book of Revelation, for example, the Apostle John saw "angels" sent from heaven to "the four corners of the earth," with the power and authority "to hurt the earth and the sea" (Revelation 7:1–2), meaning that they will be authorized to pour out plagues and destructions of all kinds upon the inhabitants of the earth.[13]

Thankfully, similar to the ten plagues in Egypt, the majority of the plagues that will be poured out on the earth by these heavenly angels are not intended to destroy people, only their surroundings in an attempt to encourage repentance.[14] And just as the majority of the ten plagues did not affect the Israelites,[15] the Saints of the latter days will also be unaffected by these plagues if they remain faithful.[16]

For example, Elder Orson Pratt stated that in the latter days, the Lord will bless many of His servants with a seal of protection, which seal will "prepare them to go forth in the days of tribulation and

---

10. *Willmington's Guide to the Bible*, 66–67. See also D. James Kennedy, "The Last Four Plagues," Coral Ridge Ministries, Apr. 20, 2017, https://www.djameskennedy.org/devotional-detail/20170420-the-last-four-plagues.

11. *Willmington's Guide to the Bible*, 66–67.

12. "The Goddess Taweret: Protector of Mothers and Children" *Glencairn Museum News*, Sept. 30, 2014, https://www.glencairnmuseum.org/newsletter/september-2014-the-goddess-taweret-protector-of-mothers-and.html.

13. For more information on these angels and the destruction they will bring, see chapter 10.

14. See, for example, Revelation 8:7–12.

15. See, for example, Exodus 8:22; 9:4–6; 9:25–26; 10:22–23; 12:12–13.

16. For more information, see chapters 9–10.

vengeance upon the nations of the wicked, when God will smite them with pestilence, plague and earthquake, such as former generations never knew. Then the servants of God will need to be armed with the power of God, they will need to have that sealing blessing pronounced upon their foreheads that they can stand forth in the midst of these desolations and plagues and not be overcome by them."[17]

This latter-day protective seal is not unlike the seal of protection offered to the Israelites just prior to the time that the Lord sent His angel of death to Egypt on the night of the Passover. Prior to this event, the Israelites were instructed to place the blood from the Passover lamb on "the two side posts and on the upper door post of the houses" (Exodus 12:7), which ultimately saved the lives of their firstborn children on that fateful night.

## The Parting of the Red Sea

Having survived the Lord's judgments, the Israelites were now prepared for the next stage of their journey. Following their prophet Moses, they fled Egypt, and in doing so, they symbolically left the telestial world behind. In their journey to the Red Sea, they were led by "a pillar of fire" (Exodus 13:21), which is not unlike the pillar of fire that will go before the Saints prior to the redemption of Zion.[18]

Once the Israelites arrived at the Red Sea, Moses parted the Red Sea, and the Israelites were allowed to cross over safely to the other side.

This event, the parting of the Red Sea, represents the moment in time when the righteous will, at the Second Coming, pass through the veil that is currently covering our earth and thereafter enter into the Lord's presence. We read in the Doctrine and Covenants that at the Second Coming, "the veil . . . which hideth the earth, shall be taken off, and all flesh shall see me together" (Doctrine and Covenants 101:23; see also Doctrine and Covenants 88:95).

---

17. *Journal of Discourses*, 15:366.

18. Regarding this latter-day pillar of fire, Elder Orson Pratt said, "There will be a very large organization consisting of thousands, and tens of thousands, and they will march forward [to Jackson County, Missouri], the glory of God overshadowing their camp by day in the form of a cloud, and a pillar of flaming fire by night." *Journal of Discourses*: 15:364.

And just as the Israelites survived this event by crossing safely to the other side, we read that the Lord "overthrew the Egyptians in the midst of the sea. And the waters returned, and covered [their] chariots" (Exodus 14:27–28). By way of comparison, when the veil of the earth is removed at the Lord's Second Coming, the entire world, either worthily or unworthily, will come into the presence of the Lord, who will appear in all His glory. We are told that this event will bring the righteous safely into the Lord's presence (see Doctrine and Covenants 88:95–96) while at the same time "consume the wicked with unquenchable fire" (Doctrine and Covenants 63:34).

Once the Israelites passed through the symbolic veil of the Red Sea, they were brought safely into the Lord's presence at Mount Sinai: "And Moses brought forth the people out of the camp to meet with God; and they stood at the nether part of the mount. And mount Sinai was altogether on a smoke, because the Lord descended upon it in fire: and the smoke thereof ascended as the smoke of a furnace, and the whole mount quaked greatly" (Exodus 19:16–18).

The Lord's descent upon Mount Sinai was a type and shadow of His Second Coming. We learn this from the Doctrine and Covenants, which states that at the Second Coming, "a trump shall sound both long and loud, even as [the trump that sounded] upon Mount Sinai" (Doctrine and Covenants 29:13).

The reasons that the events on Mount Sinai are considered a type of Christ's Second Coming are partly because of the many similarities between the two events. For example, as Degn and Christensen noted, "While the scriptures record many instances of trumpets being blown, there are only two instances when the Lord Himself blows a trumpet. The first was at Mt. Sinai when the Lord revealed Himself to Israel and proclaimed them as His peculiar treasure in Exodus 19. The second instance is when the Lord returns in glory at His second coming."[19]

In addition to the trumpet blasts, there are other similarities between these two events as well. For example, we read in Exodus that

---

19. Patrick D. Degn and David S. Christensen, *Types and Shadows of the Old Testament: Jesus Christ and the Great Plan of Happiness* (Deseret Book, 2018), 102.

"the Lord descended upon [Mount Sinai] in fire" (Exodus 19:18), which closely matches the Lord's description at His Second Coming: "And the Lord shall be red in his apparel . . . And so great shall be the glory of his presence that the sun shall hide his face in shame" (Doctrine and Covenants 133:48–49).

What is more, prior to the Lord's Second Coming, we find references to thunder, lightning, fire, smoke, and earthquakes throughout the world (see Doctrine and Covenants 88:89–90; 45:41), which were all conditions present at Mount Sinai (see Exodus 19:16–18). Parry and Parry observed, "The event at Sinai is a type and shadow of similar events that will occur when Christ comes. Again there will be a trumpet blast, and earthquake, and a sanctified people, and once again the Lord will descend to meet with his Saints."[20]

Thus, not only do the events on Mount Sinai represent the Lord's *betrothal* to the house of Israel (as discussed in chapter 14), but they also represent the Lord's future *marriage* to the house of Israel at His Second Coming.

## The Millennium

To take this analogy one step further, after the symbolic Second Coming interaction at Mount Sinai, the Israelites spent the next forty years in the wilderness, which, in our story, is a type for Christ's millennial reign.

To illustrate, consider that during His ministry, Jesus declared Himself to be "the bread of life" (John 6:35) and even declared Himself to be the very manna that fell from heaven which fed the Israelites during their wilderness journey (see John 6:32–33). During the Millennium, the world will again enjoy this manna from heaven, but this time it will take the form of the physical presence of Christ, who "will reign personally upon the earth" during the thousand years (Articles of Faith 1:10).

Furthermore, during the forty years in the wilderness, the Israelites built a tabernacle and carried it with them on their journey. When the tabernacle was set up, the Lord had the tribe of Judah camp on the

---

20. Donald W. Parry and Jay A. Parry, *Understanding the Signs of the Times* (Deseret Book, 1999), 426.

east side of the tabernacle (see Numbers 2:3) and the tribe of Ephraim camp on the west side (see Numbers 2:18), which nicely corresponds to where on the globe each tribe will be located during Christ's millennial reign.[21] According to Elder Bruce R. McConkie, "Before the Second Coming, gathered Judah . . . shall build up anew the Old Jerusalem [in the East] and prepare therein a holy temple: and gathered Ephraim . . . shall build a New Jerusalem [in the West] in an American Zion and prepare therein a holy temple."[22]

It is also interesting to note that the rebellious Israelites all died off during their forty-year journey in the wilderness. We read, "And the Lord's anger was kindled against Israel, and he made them wander in the wilderness forty years, until all the generation, that had done evil in the sight of the Lord, was consumed" (Numbers 32:13).

In a similar way, telestial persons will not be allowed to live on the earth during the Millennium but will instead be removed if they are not willing to obey a terrestrial law. Joseph Smith taught, "There will be wicked men on the earth during the thousand years. The heathen nations who will not come up to worship will be visited with the judgments of God, and must eventually be destroyed from the earth."[23]

More of how the Israelites' forty-year journey represented the Millennium will be discussed hereafter in chapter 18.

---

21. Robert Norman, "Exodus and Exaltation (Sacred Sites Part 12)," Contemplations, Mar. 11, 2009, https://rjnorman.blogspot.com/2009/03/exodus-and-exaltation-sacred-sites-part.html.

22. Bruce R. McConkie, *A New Witness of the Articles of Faith* (Deseret Book, 1985), 586–87.

23. *Teachings of the Prophet Joseph Smith*, sel. Joseph Fielding Smith (1976), 268–69. See also Isaiah 65:20; Zechariah 14:16–19. Joseph Fielding Smith clarified, "The saying that there will be wicked men on the earth during the millennium has been misunderstood by many, because the Lord declared that the wicked shall not stand, but shall be consumed. In using this term wicked it should be interpreted in the language of the Lord as recorded in [Doctrine and Covenants 84:49–53]. Here the Lord speaks of those who have not received the gospel as being wicked as they are still under the bondage of sin, having not been baptized. The inhabitants of the terrestrial order will remain on the earth during the millennium, and this class is without the gospel ordinances." Joseph Fielding Smith, *Doctrines of Salvation*, 3:63–64.

## The Celestial Kingdom

After the forty years in the wilderness had ended, the Israelites were finally allowed to cross the Jordan River and enter the promised land. We read, "And the priests that bare the ark of the covenant of the Lord stood firm on dry ground in the midst of Jordan, and all the Israelites passed over on dry ground, until all the people were passed clean over Jordan" (Joshua 3:17).

Thus, after a long and difficult journey, the Israelites were finally allowed to enter into their promised land, which is a representation of our final destination: the celestial kingdom. Just as the parting of the Red Sea represented the first veil that we must cross before entering into a terrestrial state and coming into the presence of Jesus Christ (see Doctrine and Covenants 88:95; Doctrine and Covenants 101:23), so too did the parting of the Jordan River represent the second veil that we all must cross before entering into our Heavenly Father's presence in the celestial kingdom.

Joseph Smith described this second veil as follows: "The heavens were opened upon us, and I beheld the celestial kingdom of God, and the glory thereof. . . . I saw the transcendent beauty of the gate through which the heirs of that kingdom will enter, which was like unto circling flames of fire; Also the blazing throne of God, whereon was seated the Father and the Son" (Doctrine and Covenants 137:1–3).

Clearly, the story of the Exodus is not exclusively the story of the Exodus. It is our story as well.

# 17
# Prophetic Spring Feasts

Before the Israelites left Mount Sinai, the Lord, as recorded in Leviticus 23, introduced to Moses seven religious feasts that He wanted the children of Israel to observe every year at their appointed times. When describing these seven feasts to Moses, the Lord was very specific in many of the details, even noting on which day of the year each feast should be celebrated. These seven "feasts of the Lord" (Leviticus 23:4) are listed in Leviticus 23 as follows:

- Passover
- Feast of Unleavened Bread
- Feast of Firstfruits
- Feast of Weeks (Pentecost)
- Feast of Trumpets (Rosh Hashanah)
- Day of Atonement (Yom Kippur)
- Feast of Tabernacles (Sukkot)

What is amazing about these seven feasts is that they were each prophetic of various roles of Jesus Christ. Kevin Howard explains, "Israel's four springtime holidays (Passover, Unleavened Bread, Firstfruits, and the Feast of Weeks) were fulfilled in connection with the Messiah's first coming. Israel's three autumn holidays (Feast of

Trumpets, Yom Kippur, and Tabernacles) will be fulfilled at His second coming."[1]

As already stated, the purpose of Part II of this book is to bring to light the various types associated with Christ's Second Coming, which in this case includes Israel's three fall feasts. However, before we can understand how Israel's fall feasts were prophetic of Christ's Second Coming, it will first be necessary to discuss how Israel's spring feasts were fulfilled at Jesus's first coming. We begin with the Passover.

## Passover

On the original Passover, the Israelites were instructed to slaughter a lamb "in the evening" on "the fourteenth day" of the Hebrew month called Nisan (Exodus 12:6). As we shall see, this date of Passover—the fourteenth day of Nisan—will turn out to be very significant later in our story.

Once the lamb had been slain, the Israelites were commanded to apply its blood "on the two side posts and on the upper door post of the houses" (Exodus 12:7). The Israelites were promised that if they did this, the Lord would "pass over the door, and will not suffer the destroyer to come in unto your houses to smite you" (Exodus 12:23). The Israelites were also instructed to "eat the flesh [of the lamb] in that night, roast with fire, and unleavened bread; and with bitter herbs they shall eat it" (Exodus 12:8).

According to the Lord, this first Passover in Egypt was to "be unto you for a memorial; and ye shall keep it a feast to the Lord throughout your generations" (Exodus 12:14). The Passover has been celebrated annually in the springtime by millions of Jews ever since this commandment was first given by the Lord.

The Feast of the Passover was laced with similitudes of Jesus Christ's first coming. The blood on the doorposts, for example, was a symbol for the saving blood that Christ would shed for humankind. Moreover, the Lord commanded that the Passover lamb "be without blemish" (Exodus 12:5), which was an obvious foreshadowing of the

---

1. Kevin Howard and Marvin Rosenthal, *The Feasts of the Lord: God's Prophetic Calendar From Calvary to the Kingdom* (Thomas Nelson Inc., 1997), 112. Yom Kippur is Hebrew for the Day of Atonement.

Savior, whom Peter described as "a lamb without blemish and without spot" (1 Peter 1:19).

To ensure that every Passover lamb was "without blemish," each family had to select a lamb and bring it into their house for examination three days prior to it being sacrificed on Passover (see Exodus 12:3–6). The same thing happened to Christ prior to His Crucifixion. Sam Nadler explains:

> In Exodus 12 the lamb to be sacrificed was to be selected on the tenth day of the month and kept until the fourteenth day of the month. Why? During that time the lamb had to be inspected to certify that it was without blemish. . . . [At his triumphal entry, Jesus] entered Jerusalem on the tenth of the month, [the same day that] a Passover lamb was being selected for each family. During this time, [Jesus] was inspected, questioned, interrogated, and then . . . on the fourteenth of the month the head of the Roman government declared, "I find no fault in Him" (Luke 23:4).[2]

Once Christ was found "without blemish" (1 Peter 1:19) by the Roman governor, he was sentenced and led away to be crucified.

After Christ had been on the cross for several hours, we read, "When [the soldiers] came to Jesus, and saw that he was dead already, they brake not his legs: But one of the soldiers with a spear pierced his side, and forthwith came there out blood and water . . . these things were done, that the scripture should be fulfilled, A bone of him shall not be broken" (John 19:33–34, 36).

This event was extremely prophetic because when the time came for the Passover lamb to be killed, the Israelites were instructed to handle the lamb with caution, so as not to "break a bone thereof" (Exodus 12:46). No doubt these instructions were given to foreshadow the manner of Christ's death.

## The Fourteenth Day of Nisan

While there are several other similarities we could point to, perhaps the most striking evidence that the Passover was prophetic of Christ's death is that Christ died *on* Passover, which fell on the "fourteenth

---

2. Sam Nadler, *Messiah in the Feasts of Israel, Revised Edition* (Word of Messiah Ministries, 2006), 35.

day" of the Hebrew month Nisan (Exodus 12:6). On the thirteenth day of that month—the night before the Passover lamb was to be killed—Jesus gathered His Apostles together in the Upper Room for the Last Supper. In other words, the Last Supper was not the Passover meal, because it took place on the evening *prior* to the Passover.

## The Last Supper Was Not Passover

Most scholars believe that the New Testament contains either some mistranslations or perhaps even some contradictions as to what day Jesus was crucified in relation to Passover. For example, John clearly states that the Last Supper took place one night "*before* the feast of the passover" (John 13:1; emphasis added). John also states that on the following morning, the morning Jesus was crucified, the Jewish hierarchy in Jerusalem had not yet eaten their Passover meals (see John 18:28). All this seems to indicate that Jesus was crucified on Passover, or the day following the Last Supper.

Conversely, Matthew, Mark, and Luke indicate that on the day of the Last Supper, the Apostles "made ready the passover" (Mark 14:16; see also Matthew 26:19; Luke 22:12), implying that the Last Supper itself was the Passover meal. This interpretation would place the Crucifixion on the day *following* Passover.

However, when Matthew, Mark, and Luke state that Jesus's disciples "made ready the passover" on the day of the Last Supper (Mark 14:16), research indicates that they were simply beginning their preparations for the Passover meal a full day in advance. Biblical scholar T. Alex Tennent observes that preparing for the Passover meal a full day in advance would allow the Apostles enough time to adequately "prepare a location that was ritually pure by having all leaven removed,"[3] which legally had to be done before noon on Passover, or the fourteenth day of Nisan.

Tennent further explains that while the Gospels of Matthew, Mark, and Luke each mention that this Passover meal preparation was done on "the first day of unleavened bread" (Mark 14:12; see also Matthew 26:17; Luke 22:7)—a day often associated with the

---

3. Alex T. Tennent, *The Messianic Feast: Moving Beyond the Ritual* (Messianic Publishing LLC, 2014), 385.

beginning of Passover—a more accurate translation from the original Greek should read, "And [in reference to] the first day of unleavened bread, when they killed the passover, his disciples said unto him, Where wilt thou that we go and prepare that thou mayest eat the passover?" (Mark 14:12).[4]

When translated in this light, Matthew, Mark, and Luke's accounts do *not* state that the Apostles made ready the Passover on the first day of unleavened bread but that they were making preparations for the Passover, *in anticipation of* the first day of unleavened bread, which suggests that this holiday may have occurred a full day later than their texts imply. When read in this light, the Matthew, Mark, and Luke accounts do not contradict John's record, leading us to believe that the Last Supper took place the night *before* Passover.

In fact, in the NKJV translation of the New Testament, Christ prophesied that He would be "delivered up to be crucified" (NKJV Matthew 26:2) on "the feast of the passover" (Matthew 26:2). This translation from the original Greek has Matthew agreeing with John's record and is a better fit than the KJV translation of this same verse, thus allowing the Passover and the Crucifixion to occur on the same day.

Other evidence concurs with this conclusion as well. For example, the Last Supper could not have been the Passover meal simply because Christ served leavened bread to His Apostles at the Last Supper as opposed to unleavened bread. This is significant because, as Tennent noted, "When referring to what was eaten at the Last Supper, the scriptures all use the Greek word *arton* for daily leavened bread. . . . Had it actually been the Passover, serving such 'bread' would have been illegal according to the law of Moses. . . . [However, it] was perfectly acceptable to eat regular, leavened bread (*arton* in Greek) instead of unleavened (*azumos* in Greek) only because the Last Supper took place the evening *before* the Passover sacrifice."[5]

---

4. See Tennent, *The Messianic Feast*, 377–82. In addition to Mark 14:12, this Greek translation, which conveys the added phrase "in reference to" in the text, can also be applied to Matthew 26:17 and Luke 22:7.

5. Tennent, *The Messianic Feast*, 75, 71.

In addition, Tennent also referenced several Jewish and Christian documents dating back to the first and second centuries AD, which show that according to their earliest oral and written traditions, "Jesus was crucified on the fourteenth of Nisan and therefore could not have eaten the Jewish Passover at the Last Supper."[6]

It is important to remember, however, that the setting of the sun on the night of the Last Supper (on the thirteenth day of the month) did technically mark the very beginning of Passover, for in Judaism, days began at sundown, not at midnight like they do in our culture.[7] However, while Passover officially began at sunset on the night of the Last Supper, it was illegal according to the law of Moses to eat the Passover meal that night. The law of Moses clearly stated that the Passover lamb was not to be slain until the following day, on the fourteenth of the month (see Exodus 12:6).[8] Furthermore, after the Passover lamb was slain on the fourteenth, the Israelites then had to wait several more hours for the sun to set before they could legally eat the Passover meal (see Exodus 12:8).

## The Crucifixion

As we know, there was much that happened to the Savior during this important twenty-four-hour period. Once the sun set on the thirteenth day of Nisan, Jesus partook of the Last Supper with His Apostles and then suffered in Gethsemane for "some three or four hours,"[9] at which time He was arrested by an angry Jewish mob. He was tried late into the evening by the Jewish leaders Annas and Caiaphas and tried a second time by Caiaphas very early the following

---

6. Tennent, *The Messianic Feast,* 10.

7. This reckoning stems from how the Lord originally determined the beginning of a day during the seven days of Earth's creation: "And the evening and the morning were the first day" (Genesis 1:5).

8. In other words, Passover began at the setting of the sun on the thirteenth day of Nisan and ended at the setting of the sun on the fourteenth day of Nisan. According to Perdue, "Nisan 14 begins at sunset [between 6:00–6:30 p.m.] on Nisan 13, and ends on Nisan 14 [at sunset]." Thomas H. Perdue, *Passover & Sukkot* (AuthorHouse, 2011), 82.

9. Bruce R. McConkie, "The Purifying Power of Gethsemane," *Ensign*, May 1985, 9.

morning. Following this morning trial, Jesus was bound and taken to Pilate, then to Herod, and eventually back to Pilate. At this point, Jesus was scourged and finally crucified at about 9:00 that morning (see Mark 15:25).[10] Clearly, the Jewish leaders were trying to get Jesus sentenced to death and on the cross before His followers could awaken and put up resistance.

The majority of these events, including the scourging and Crucifixion, all occurred on the morning of the fourteenth day of Nisan, which, as we have already established, coincided with the day of Passover. Knowing that Christ was on the cross for six hours, from 9 a.m. to 3 p.m. (see Mark 15:25, 33),[11] we can therefore pinpoint the timing of Christ's death to have occurred on Passover, the fourteenth day of Nisan, at, or very near, 3 p.m.

This means that as Christ was on the cross, the Passover meal was just a few hours away (eaten at sunset). During these important hours leading up to sunset, the Israelites, in preparation for this meal, were instructed to kill a lamb "at the going down of the sun" (Deuteronomy 16:6), which according to Jewish tradition, did *not* mean at sunset but rather any time after *noon*, or the time when the sun began to fall in the sky.[12]

If Christ died at 3 p.m. (see Matthew 27:45), then the timing of His death would certainly qualify as having occurred "at the going

---

10. It should be noted that John places the Crucifixion at noon (see John 19:14), which differs somewhat from the Matthew, Mark, and Luke accounts (compare Matthew 27:45; Mark 15:25; Luke 23:44).

11. It should be noted that John places the death of Christ at 6 p.m. (see John 19:14). Matthew, Mark, and Luke all put the death of Christ at 3 p.m. (compare Mark 15:25, 33; Matthew 27:45; Luke 23:44).

12. Similarly, we read in Exodus that the Passover lamb was to be slain "in the evening" (Exodus 12:6), which in Hebrew was also translated to mean in the afternoon. According to Tennent, the phrases "at the going down of the sun" (Deuteronomy 16:6) and "in the evening" (Exodus 12:6) simply meant anytime "between noon and sunset" (Tennent, *The Messianic Feast*, 451). Research shows that this was the traditional time frame that the Jews at the time of Jesus killed their Passover lambs. For example, the famous Jewish historian Josephus, who was born shortly after the Crucifixion, noted that the Passover lamb was typically slain (in his time) between the hours of 2 p.m. to 5 p.m. See Flavius Josephus, "The Wars of the Jews," in *The Complete Works of Josephus*, trans. William Whiston (Thomas Nelson Publishers, 1998), 6:9:3.

down of the sun" (Deuteronomy 16:6). It is incredible to think that the death of Christ occurred during the very window of time that the Passover lambs were being slain in Jerusalem. Thomas Perdue noted, "The Passover lamb would have been sacrificed at [approximately] 3:00 p.m. on Nisan 14, and would have been eaten after sunset. . . . Thus the death of our Lord at the ninth hour (*3 p.m. . . . Matthew 27:45*) agrees with the time of the offering of the Passover lamb."[13]

Truly, as the Apostle Paul stated, "Christ our passover [was] sacrificed for us" (1 Corinthians 5:7). Stated differently, Christ fulfilled the Passover not only in theme but also on the very day and hour it was meant to be observed.

Incredibly, as it was with Passover, so too will it be with the remaining six feasts of Israel. Chuck Missler wrote, "It is provocative to note that not only are [all seven] feasts prophetic, *but each gets fulfilled at its appointed time on the very day it is observed*."[14] Degn and Christensen agree, stating, "The [seven] feasts are stunning in that their typological fulfillment occurs *on the exact days and times* that they foreshadow."[15]

With that, we turn our attention to the second prophetic feast of spring, the Feast of Unleavened Bread.

## The Feast of Unleavened Bread

The Feast of Unleavened Bread began at the same time as the Passover meal itself, or as soon as the sun set on the fourteenth day of Nisan.[16] But rather than lasting only one day like Passover, the Feast of Unleavened Bread lasted seven days, from the fifteenth day of Nisan

---

13. Perdue, *Passover & Sukkot*, 82; emphasis in original.

14. Chuck Missler, *The Feasts of Israel* (Koinonia House, 2016), 21–22; emphasis added.

15. Patrick D. Degn and David S. Christensen, *Types and Shadows of the Old Testament: Jesus Christ and the Great Plan of Happiness* (Deseret Book, 2018), 78–79; emphasis added.

16. "The Feast of Unleavened Bread is the Feast which begins at about 6:15 p.m. [at sunset on Nisan 14]. . . . And on the same evening after the sacrifice, the paschal meal was eaten, and the Jewish day changed from Nisan 14 to Nisan 15. This was the First day of the Feast of Unleavened Bread." Perdue, *Passover & Sukkot*, 82.

to the twenty-first day of Nisan (see Leviticus 23:5–6). According to Howard, "Because the Feast of Unleavened Bread (a seven-day holiday) begins the day after Passover (a one-day holiday), often the two holidays are blurred together and collectively referred to as 'the eight days of Passover.' In the days of the Second Temple (in Jesus' time), it was also common to call all eight days the Feast of Unleavened Bread (Luke 22:1, 7)."[17]

It should be noted that the setting of the sun on the fourteenth day of the month not only marked the beginning of the Feast of Unleavened Bread, but it also marked the beginning of an *annual* Sabbath day as well. This annual Sabbath day (the first day of unleavened bread) was somewhat different from the weekly Sabbath (Saturday), but the same rules of no work performed thereon still applied (see Leviticus 23:7). Knowing that work was not permitted on this first day of unleavened bread, and knowing that the first day of unleavened bread began at sunset shortly after Jesus died on the cross (Passover), the Jewish leaders made every effort possible to get Christ's body down from the cross before sunset so as not to break this important commandment.

We read, "The Jews therefore, because it was the preparation, that the bodies should not remain upon the cross on the Sabbath day, (*for that Sabbath day was an high day,*) besought Pilate that their legs might be broken, and that they might be taken away" (John 19:31; emphasis added).

Many have interpreted this scripture as meaning the *weekly* Sabbath (or Saturday) and have therefore assumed that the Crucifixion of Christ took place on a Friday. However, knowing that Christ was resurrected on a Sunday morning (see John 20:1), and knowing that Christ was in the tomb for three days *and three nights* (see Matthew 12:40), a Thursday Crucifixion seems to fit much better in this context. If the Sabbath day spoken of by John was in fact the first day of unleavened bread as opposed to the weekly Sabbath, then a Thursday

---

17. Howard and Rosenthal, *The Feasts of the Lord*, 112.

Crucifixion would allow for Christ to be resurrected on a Sunday morning and still be in the tomb for three days and three nights.[18]

In fact, if the Sabbath day spoken of by John was the first day of unleavened bread, then technically there would have been *two* Sabbath days (one weekly and one annual) that fell in between the Crucifixion and the Resurrection. As it turns out, this two-Sabbath-day theory is confirmed in Matthew 28:1, which, when translated from the original Greek, reads, "In the end of the *Sabbaths* [plural] came Mary Magdalene and the other Mary to see the sepulchre" (Matthew 28:1).[19]

Now that we have an understanding of when the Feast of Unleavened Bread was to be celebrated, we can now turn our attention to what was required from the Israelites during this feast and how it was fulfilled in Christ.

Before the Feast of Unleavened Bread began, the Israelites were commanded to completely remove all leavened bread from their homes (see Exodus 12:15; Leviticus 23:6). Leaven (or yeast) was symbolic of the sin of pride because it caused bread to rise by puffing. As described by one author, leaven "puffs up the bread to make it seem greater than it is."[20] It was for this reason that Jesus warned his dis-

---

18. Jesus was resurrected on a Sunday, which was referred to in the scriptures as "the first day of the week" (Luke 24:1). According to Luke, Jesus was resurrected on "the third day since" the Crucifixion (see Luke 24:19–21). A Thursday crucifixion is the only day of the week that would fulfil this important requirement. According to this model, Christ would have been dead for three days (Thursday, Friday, and Saturday) and three nights (Thursday, Friday, and Saturday), thus fulfilling the requirement of "three days and three nights in the heart of the earth" (Matthew 12:40; emphasis added). It should be noted that this Thursday model counts Thursday as day one in the grave, even though Christ did not die until 3 p.m. on that day. However nowhere does it state that the Lord spent three full days and three full nights in the tomb, which means that a partial day on Thursday could have very well been included as one of Christ's three days in the grave. A Friday crucifixion only contains two nights before a Sunday morning resurrection, and a Wednesday crucifixion would mean Jesus was resurrected the "fourth day since" the Crucifixion rather than the "third day since," as required by Luke 24:19–21. See Tennent, The Messianic Feast, 394.

19. See Missler, *The Feasts of Israel*, 34; Tennent, *The Messianic Feast*, 375.

20. Nadler, *Messiah in the Feasts of Israel*, 25.

ciples to "beware of the leaven of the Pharisees" (Matthew 16:6). By ridding their houses of any and all leavened bread, the Israelites were symbolically cleansing their homes of sin.

However, because the Israelites were to refrain from working on the first day of unleavened bread (see Leviticus 23:7), this leaven, legally, had to be completely removed well before the sun set on Passover.[21]

As it was with Passover, Christ also fulfilled the Feast of Unleavened Bread in his death. Christ, who is referred to in the scriptures as "the bread of life" (John 6:35) is typically referred to in this context as our *unleavened* bread because of His sinless nature. However, in Gethsemane and again on the cross, Christ willingly took upon Him the sins of the world, symbolically transforming Himself from unleavened bread to leavened bread: "For [Christ] hath made him to be sin for us, who knew no sin" (2 Corinthians 5:21). In this context, Christ can also affectionately be referred to as our *leavened* "bread of life" (John 6:35).

After Christ had been leavened with our sins through the Atonement, both in Gethsemane and upon the cross, He "bowed his head, and gave up the ghost" (John 19:30). Once this occurred, His leavened spirit left His body and He was taken from the earth in death just hours before the Feast of Unleavened Bread officially began. In other words, at the same time the Israelites were removing leaven from their homes, Christ was removing leaven from the earth, and by the time this feast officially arrived at sunset, the leavened Christ was dead.

Furthermore, just as the Israelites were commanded to keep their homes free from this leavened bread during this entire *seven-day* feast, so too will the Atonement *completely and perfectly* free us from our sins if we apply it in our lives, for in the Hebrew culture, the number seven represented completion and perfection.[22]

---

21. Specifically, before noon on Passover. See Tennent, *The Messianic Feast*, 385.

22. Alonzo L. Gaskill, *The Lost Language of Symbolism: An Essential Guide for Recognizing and Interpreting Symbols of the Gospel* (Deseret Book, 2003), 124.

## The Feast of Firstfruits

The third feast of the spring, celebrated on the first Sunday after the Passover, was called the Feast of Firstfruits, and as we shall soon see, it was filled with rich symbolism of Christ's Resurrection. As Keven Howard noted, "Passover pictures the substitutionary *death* of the Messiah as the Passover Lamb, the Feast of Unleavened Bread pictures the *burial* of the Messiah, and Firstfruits pictures the *resurrection* of the Messiah."[23]

The Feast of Firstfruits was celebrated annually in connection with the spring harvest. The purpose of this feast was to give thanks to the Lord for new life after the long, cold winter. According to Rosenthal, "The barley harvest—the first crop planted in the winter—is now, in the spring, beginning to ripen. The first sheaf (Firstfruits) of the harvest is cut and, in a carefully prescribed and meticulous ceremony, presented to the Lord."[24]

In connection with this ceremony, the priest, on behalf of the house of Israel, was commanded to "wave the sheaf before the Lord" (Leviticus 23:11), which would then be accepted and blessed by the Lord (see Leviticus 23:11). This gesture was as if the Lord was blessing Israel's entire harvest, which would soon be at hand.

This sheaf, or firstfruits, was meant to represent the resurrected Christ. The cold hard ground from which this sheaf was produced represented the grave, for just like a grave, the winter ground is truly dead with no signs of agricultural life. No doubt, the first sight of sprouting barley crops in the early spring must have seemed like a miracle to Israelite farmers each year. This barley sheaf, the first crop to be harvested each spring, was a type of Christ because Christ was the first of us to be resurrected. As the prophet Abinadi taught, "But behold, the bands of death shall be broken, and the Son reigneth, and hath power over the dead; therefore, he bringeth to pass the resurrection of the dead" (Mosiah 15:20).

As one might expect, not only was the Feast of Firstfruits a type and shadow of Christ's Resurrection, but Christ was resurrected *on*

---

23. Howard and Rosenthal, *The Feasts of the Lord*, 69.

24. Howard and Rosenthal, *The Feasts of the Lord*, 19–20.

the Feast of Firstfruits as well. According to Leviticus, the Feast of Firstfruits was to always be celebrated on the Sunday following the Passover (see Leviticus 23:10–11), which coincided exactly with the day of Christ's Resurrection, or on "the first day of the week" (Luke 24:1). In the words of Sam Nadler, "[Three days after the death of Christ], early that Sunday morning, the priests were in the Temple offering up the firstfruits of the harvest. At this very time, our Messiah and High Priest was raised from the dead, offering up Himself as our atonement. In so doing, He became the Firstfruits of the rest of the harvest of believers in Him."[25]

It was for this reason that the Apostle Paul stated, "But now is Christ risen from the dead, and become the firstfruits of them that slept" (1 Corinthians 15:20).

By referring to Christ as "the firstfruits of them that slept," Paul was no doubt helping the Saints of his day make the connection that the Feast of Firstfruits was instituted by the Lord with the sole purpose of testifying of the Resurrection of Jesus Christ, a Resurrection that miraculously occurred on the very day that the Feast of Firstfruits was being celebrated.

## The Feast of Weeks (Pentecost)

Fifty days after the Feast of Firstfruits, the Israelites were to celebrate the fourth feast of the year, the Feast of Weeks (see Leviticus 23:15–16). The Greek word for fifty is *pentecost*, which is why you will sometimes hear this particular feast, especially during New Testament times, referred to as the day of Pentecost as opposed to the Feast of Weeks (see Acts 2).

Because the Feast of Weeks was to be observed fifty days after Firstfruits, and because of some similarities found between these two feasts, the Feast of Weeks was widely considered to be the *conclusion* of the Feast of Firstfruits. The Feast of Firstfruits marked the beginning of the barley harvest in Israel, whereas the Feast of Weeks marked the beginning of the wheat harvest in Israel (see Exodus 34:22).

During the Feast of Weeks, the Israelites were commanded to make several offerings to the Lord, including an offering of two

---

25. Nadler, *Messiah in the Feasts of Israel*, 64.

loaves of wheat bread, which were to "be of fine flour . . . [and baked] with leaven" (Leviticus 23:17). Wheat has always been a symbol for the righteous followers of Christ (see Doctrine and Covenants 4:4; Matthew 13:24–30); therefore, if the barley sheaf offered on the Feast of Firstfruits represented Christ, then these two loaves of wheat bread offered on the Feast of Weeks represented God's harvested souls as a result of Christ.

This feast saw its fulfillment fifty days after Christ's Resurrection, on the day of Pentecost spoken of in Acts 2. On this day, Jews from all around the region, as required by the law of Moses (see Deuteronomy 16:16), were gathering at Jerusalem to celebrate and observe the Feast of Weeks. Also gathered at Jerusalem on this day in a house nearby were Jesus's Apostles (see Acts 2:1–2). The New Testament states, "And when the day of Pentecost was fully come, [Jesus's Apostles] were all with one accord in one place. And suddenly there came a sound from heaven as of a rushing mighty wind, and it filled all the house where they were sitting. And there appeared unto them cloven tongues like as of fire, and it sat upon each of them" (Acts 2:1–3).

Amazingly, many Jews who had gathered for this feast at the nearby Jewish temple saw the "cloven tongues like as of fire" (Acts 2:3) and heard the sound of "rushing mighty wind" (Acts 2:2) that was radiating from this house. As they made their way toward this house to investigate, the Apostles began to address the crowd: "And [the Apostles] were all filled with the Holy Ghost, and began to speak with other tongues, as the Spirit gave them utterance" (Acts 2:1–4).

As this occurred, the Jews who were gathering around this house each heard and understood the words spoken by the Apostles, even though many of them spoke very different languages (see Acts 2:5–11). Seeing that they had been "pricked in their heart" (Acts 2:37), Peter invited them to "repent, and be baptized every one of you in the name of Jesus Christ for the remission of sins, and ye shall receive the gift of the Holy Ghost" (Acts 2:38).

Because the Lord poured out His Spirit with such magnitude and to so many people on this day, this particular day of Pentecost is often referred to by Christians as "the birth of the Church." Interestingly enough, Jewish tradition also has it that the nation of Israel was also born on this day several hundred years earlier at Mount Sinai.[26] Degn and Christensen explain, "The giving of the law at Mount Sinai is traditionally understood to have been at the time of [Pentecost]. The children of Israel celebrated the Passover the night before leaving Egypt; they received the law fifty days after leaving Egypt, thus becoming the nation of Israel" (Exodus 19).[27]

Because the day of Pentecost is said to have occurred on the anniversary that the Lord appeared on Mount Sinai, the latter has often been considered a type for the former. Lancaster noted, "Before it was a New Testament event . . . Pentecost [was] the anniversary of the day God spoke the Torah at Mount Sinai . . . Before tongues of fire ever fell upon the believers in Jerusalem, there was fire falling on Mount Sinai."[28]

Furthermore, just as the events on Mount Sinai represented the betrothal (or endowment) of the house of Israel, so too did the manifestations of God's glory at this particular house on the day of Pentecost typify of the endowment, for it was on this day that the restoration of the endowment occurred in the meridian of time and was first made available to the Apostles.

This was made clear by the Lord who instructed His Apostles after His Resurrection to "tarry ye in the city of Jerusalem, *until ye be endued with power from on high*" (Luke 24:49, emphasis added; see also Acts 1:4; Doctrine and Covenants 95:8–9; 109:35–37). That the fulfillment of this promise came on the day of Pentecost was made clear by Joseph Smith, who said, "God obtained a house where Peter washed and anointed [the Apostles] on the day of Pentecost."[29]

---

26. Grant R. Jeffery, *Armageddon: Appointment With Destiny* (WaterBrook Press, 1997), 63–64.

27. Degn and Christensen, *Types and Shadows of the Old Testament*, 95.

28. Thomas D. Lancaster, *Restoration: Returning the Torah of God to the Disciples of Jesus* (First Fruits of Zion, 2005), 93. See also Nadler, *Messiah in the Feasts of Israel*, 25; Howard and Rosenthal, *The Feasts of the Lord*, 94–95; Degn and Christensen, *Types and Shadows of the Old Testament*, 95.

29. Andrew F. Ehat and Lyndon W. Cook, *The Words of Joseph Smith* (Bookcraft, 1980), 211; spelling and grammar corrected. Similarly, Andrew Ehat wrote, "The scriptures reveal that the disciples' endowment took place in a house (probably an upper room) and was interrupted by a multitude of curious men (see Acts 2:1–6)." "'Who Shall Ascend into the Hill of the Lord?,'

Elder Orson Pratt added, "On the Day of Pentecost, a great feast which had been observed by the Jewish nation for many generations, there were gathered . . . the Seventies as well as the Twelve. They were gathered together in one place, in an upper room of [a house set apart as] the Temple; and they were engaged in fervent prayer and supplication before the Lord. What for? For the endowments and qualifications necessary to assist them in the work of the ministry."[30]

The Lord anticipated the importance of this endowment on the day of Pentecost and therefore spent "forty days" (Acts 1:3) ministering to His Apostles prior to this event, all the while teaching them the importance of these sacred temple ordinances that were to come.[31] After this forty-day temple preparation class had ended, the Lord "was taken up; and a cloud received him out of their sight" (Acts 1:9). The Apostles were now sufficiently prepared to receive their endowment on the day of Pentecost.

It is important to note that one of the main purposes of the Lord's endowment, both past and present, is to prepare the recipient for a season of missionary work. Elder Bruce R. McConkie explained, "The apostles—or missionaries in any age—are not fully qualified to go forth, preach the gospel, and build up the kingdom, unless they have the gift of the Holy Ghost and also are endowed with power from on high, meaning have received certain knowledge, powers, and special blessings, normally given only in the Lord's Temple."[32]

In our day, missionaries are required to receive their endowment prior to their missionary service, and it appears that it was no different for the Lord's ancient Apostles. The Lord commanded His Apostles to

---

Sesquicentennial Reflections of a Sacred Day: 4 May 1842," in *Temples of the Ancient World* (Deseret Book and FARMS, 1994), 56.

30. *Journal of Discourses*, 14:174. Similarly, George Q. Cannon stated, "Prior to the completion of the [Nauvoo] Temple, [Joseph Smith] took the Twelve and certain other men, who were chosen, and bestowed upon them a holy anointing, similar to that which was received on the day of Pentecost by the Twelve, who had been told to tarry at Jerusalem." Ehat and Cook, *Words of Joseph Smith*, 306.

31. See Hugh Nibley, *Temple and Cosmos*, ed. Don E. Norton (Deseret Book and FARMS, 1992), 295–317.

32. Bruce R. McConkie, *Doctrinal New Testament Commentary* (Bookcraft, 1973), 1:859.

"go ye therefore, and teach all nations" (Matthew 28:19), which could not be accomplished until they had been endowed with this power from on high. This point was made clear by President Joseph Fielding Smith, who said, "The apostles were awaiting the endowment that came on the day of Pentecost before commencing their ministry."[33]

Once endowed, the Apostles were ready to preach the gospel with power and authority. And that is exactly what happened. As a result of their endowment, and in connection with their preaching, nearly 3,000 converts joined the Church on the day of Pentecost (see Acts 2:41).

We read that these 3,000 souls traveled to Jerusalem "out of every nation under heaven" (see Acts 2:5). Thus, while these new converts consisted mainly of Jews, in many ways they represented people from all nations of the earth, both Jew and Gentile, who would be given the opportunity to hear the gospel and join Christ's Church. Soon after this event, Peter was instructed in vision to take the gospel to the Gentiles (see Acts 10), which would not have been possible had the Apostles not first been "endued with power from on high" on the day of Pentecost (Luke 24:49).

Thus, the two loaves of wheat bread, which were to be offered at the temple during the Feast of Weeks (Pentecost), were symbolic of the harvested souls that would come into the Church as a result of the events that occurred on this important day of Pentecost. Elder Orson Pratt noted:

> Peter informs the inquiring believers on the Day of Pentecost that if they would repent and be baptized they should not only receive the remission of their sins, but they should also receive the Holy Ghost. Was this promise only to the people then present? No, for if we read the next verse we find that "the promise is to you and to your children, *and to all that are afar off,* even to as many as the Lord our God shall call" [Acts 2:39]. Is not that promise universal—to every people, nation, kindred and tongue, Jew and Gentile, bond and free? Yes.[34]

---

33. Joseph Fielding Smith, *Doctrines of Salvation,* comp. Bruce R. McConkie (Bookcraft, 1954–56), 1:239.

34. *Journal of Discourses,* 14:178; emphasis added.

Perhaps this was also the reason why leaven was sanctioned in the wheat bread offering on the Feast of Weeks (Pentecost) when it was otherwise forbidden in temple offerings (see Leviticus 2:11). Perhaps this combination of wheat and leaven represented both Jew and Gentile, who would later become one in Christ as a result of the harvest of souls that began on the day of Pentecost.[35]

The conclusion of the Feast of Weeks (Pentecost) marked the end of the four spring feasts of Israel. However, during the several months that followed the Feast of Weeks, the Israelites were to anxiously look forward and prepare themselves for the three remaining fall feasts of the Lord. The following chapter will discuss these three fall feasts, illustrating how each of them will be fulfilled in connection with Christ's Second Coming. Rosenthal wrote, "Each major event of the Messiah's first coming occurred *on the precise date* of the appropriate Jewish holiday. Each of the three major events associated with His second coming will, likewise, fall on the appropriate Jewish holiday."[36]

Grant R. Jeffery added, "Four of the seven feasts . . . have already been prophetically fulfilled, each one on the same day of the month on which God commanded that the feast should be commemorated. Because of this documented phenomenon, we can expect, therefore, that those prophecies that are still in our future will also be fulfilled on the exact calendar day on which these feasts are celebrated."[37]

It is to these three fall feasts we now turn our attention.

---

35. Degn and Christensen, *Types and Shadows of the Old Testament*, 96; Howard and Rosenthal, *The Feasts of the Lord*, 22; Tennent, *The Messianic Feast*, 231.

36. Howard and Rosenthal, *The Feasts of the Lord*, 23; emphasis added.

37. Jeffery, *Armageddon: Appointment With Destiny*, 44.

# 18
# Prophetic Fall Feasts

Shortly after being endowed on the Day of Pentecost, the Apostles took the gospel to as many Gentile nations as they could in an attempt to "teach all nations" (Matthew 28:19). However, sometime after the Apostles were killed, the priesthood keys were taken from the earth and the Great Apostasy officially began. If the four spring feasts represented Christ's first coming, and if the three fall feasts represent Christ's Second Coming, then the interval of time between the spring and fall feasts corresponds to this period of apostasy.

## The Feast of Trumpets (Rosh Hashanah)

The Feast of Trumpets, the first feast celebrated in the fall, marked the ending of this so-called apostasy period by ushering in a feast that had a theme of, among other things, revelation sent from heaven. This feast allowed the Israelites to once again turn their minds to the Lord in the form of religious ceremonies.

It was named the Feast of Trumpets because one of the major rituals during this feast was the blowing of actual trumpets (see Leviticus 23:24; Numbers 29:1). The trumpet traditionally used during this feast was called a *shofar,* or ram's horn. According to a recent article published in the *Ensign*, the primary purpose for sounding the shofar anciently was to "signal a gathering of the people."[1] It therefore should come as no surprise that the Feasts of Trumpets also carried with it a theme of gathering.

In fact, the Feast of Trumpets was always celebrated in connection with the fall harvest, or that time of year when the Israelites gathered their final crops of the season. In other words, the Feasts of Trumpets was a type for Israel's latter-day gathering. We read in the Doctrine and Covenants, "For behold the field is white already to harvest; and lo, he that thrusteth in his sickle with his might, the same layeth up in store that he perisheth not, but bringeth salvation to his soul" (Doctrine and Covenants 4:4).

During the Feast of Trumpets, "the trumpet blasts were the clarion call to the harvesters to gather the harvested fields together before they were burned for the season."[2] One could say that the trumpet blasts during this particular feast were types for the angelic latter-day trumpet blasts that have been sounded in our day, sending the call for modern-day Israel to gather: "And angels shall fly through the midst of heaven, crying with a loud voice, *sounding the trump of God*, saying: Prepare ye, prepare ye, O inhabitants of the earth; for the judgment of our God is come. Behold, and lo, the Bridegroom cometh; go ye out to meet him" (Doctrine and Covenants 88:92; emphasis added).

One such angel to sound his trump in these latter days was the angel Moroni, who appeared to Joseph Smith several times in connection with the Restoration. During one of these visitations, on September 22, 1827, the angel Moroni gave Joseph Smith the gold plates. This date is extremely significant because, according to Lenet Hadley Read, "On 22 September 1827, *the very day Israel celebrated the Feast of Trumpets*, Moroni gave the golden plates to the Prophet Joseph Smith. Since this feast was ripe with meaning for the theme of the regathering of Israel, it is unlikely this timing was accidental.

1. "Hear the Sound of the Trumpet," *Ensign*, July 2018, 63.
2. Patrick D. Degn and David S. Christensen, *Types and Shadows of the Old Testament: Jesus Christ and the Great Plan of Happiness* (Deseret Book, 2018), 102.

Indeed, young Joseph was asked to meet Moroni for four years in preparation for that significant day in 1827."[3]

Thus, not only did the coming forth of the Book of Mormon mark the beginning of Israel's final gathering, but its record was given to Joseph Smith *on the exact day* the Feast of Trumpets was being observed by millions of Jews around the world.

No doubt this is one of the reasons why there is a statue of Moroni holding a trumpet on top of nearly every Latter-day Saint temple, for it was Moroni who gave the gold plates to Joseph Smith on this symbolic Feast of Trumpets. Moroni's trumpet on top of our temples should remind us all of our call to gather. As one non-Latter-day Saint author observed, "For disciples of the Messiah, the Feast of Trumpets is a reminder of that appointed time yet to come when the Master 'will send forth His angels with a great trumpet and they will gather together His elect from the four winds, from one end of the sky to the other' (Matthew 24:31)."[4]

How spot-on this comment is! Many Jews and Christians around the world are anxiously waiting on the Lord to send heaven's angels to sound the call for Israel to gather. It is our responsibility to inform the world that the Lord has already sent His angel, that He has already blown His trumpet, and that He has already extended this invitation for Israel to gather in preparation for His Second Coming.

It is also worth noting that the Feast of Trumpets also carried with it a heavy theme of repentance. According to Samuele Bacchiocchi, "The blowing of the trumpets was understood to be a call to repent and prepare oneself to stand trial before God who would execute His judgment ten days later on the Day of Atonement."[5]

---

3. Lenet Hadley Read, "The Golden Plates and the Feast of Trumpets," *Ensign*, Jan. 2000, 26; emphasis added.
4. Thomas D. Lancaster, *Restoration: Returning the Torah of God to the Disciples of Jesus* (First Fruits of Zion, 2005), 94.
5. Samuele Bacchiocchi, *God's Festivals in Scripture and History Volume II: The Fall Festivals* (Biblical Perspectives, 1996), 53.

## The Day of Atonement (Yom Kippur)

As just stated by Bacchiocchi, the Day of Atonement was the next feast of the year for the Israelites, which was observed ten days after the Feast of Trumpets. According to Read, "The [ten days] between the Feast of Trumpets and the Day of Atonement can signify the time one has left to repent. Thus the trumpet of the Feast of Trumpets sounds a final warning: time is crucial for returning to God and to righteousness."[6]

The reason the Israelites considered the Day of Atonement to be a day of judgment was because it was the one and only day of the year that the high priest was allowed to pass through the veil of the temple and enter into the Holy of Holies, an event symbolic of the entire house of Israel coming into the presence of the Lord.

This sacred event on the Day of Atonement was a symbol for the actual day when the righteous will pass through the heavenly veil and enter into the Lord's presence at His Second Coming: "Prepare for the revelation which is to come, when the veil of the covering of my temple, in my tabernacle, which hideth the earth, shall be taken off, and all flesh shall see me together" (Doctrine and Covenants 101:23).

For those of us who live in this time period between the Restoration of the gospel and the Lord's Second Coming, we are symbolically living in this ten-day waiting period that falls between the Feast of Tabernacles and the Day of Atonement. How we spend our time is up to us, but if we are to be found worthy to enter into the Lord's presence at His Second Coming, we must prepare ourselves for this sacred event in ways similar to how the Israelites prepared themselves for the Day of Atonement: through constant repentance.

## The Feast of Tabernacles (Sukkot)

The seventh and final feast of Israel was called the Feast of Tabernacles. After the children of Israel were freed from bondage in Egypt, they wandered in the wilderness for forty years, all the while dwelling in tabernacles, or tents. Thus, the Feast of Tabernacles was

---

6. Read, "The Golden Plates," 28.

instituted to remind the Israelites of their forty-year journey in the wilderness.

During this feast, for one week, the Israelites were to eat outside in tents to remind them of the journeys made by their ancestors, "that your generations may know that I made the children of Israel to dwell in booths, when I brought them out of the land of Egypt" (Leviticus 23:43).

Interestingly enough, the purpose of this feast was not only to point Israel's minds to the past but also to the future. According to Lenet Hadley Read, "The feast of Tabernacles signifies a completed harvest, Christ's millennial reign."[7] And according to Grant R. Jeffery, "This great Feast of Tabernacles will see its prophetic fulfillment in that glorious day when the Lord of hosts will usher in the long-awaited Millennium of peace."[8]

Before we can fully understand how this feast is a type of Christ's millennial reign, we need to remind ourselves that the story of the Exodus is also the story of humankind's journey through this earth life. In other words, after the symbolic parting of the Red Sea (or veil), and after the Israelites came into the presence of the Lord at Mount Sinai (the Second Coming), the Israelites would spend the next forty years in the wilderness, which, as we discussed in chapter 16, is a type for the Millennium.

Because the Israelites dwelled in tabernacles during this time, the Feast of Tabernacles has much to teach us about the future Millennium. In the words of Rosenthal, "The Feast of Tabernacles speaks of the day when the Messiah Himself will tabernacle among men."[9] Lancaster explained it this way: "The Apostle John uses a verb form of the same Greek word that is used to translate booth (*sukkah*) when he wrote, 'And the Word became flesh, and dwelt [tabernacle]

---

7. Read, "The Golden Plates," 28.

8. Grant R. Jeffery, *Armageddon: Appointment With Destiny* (WaterBrook Press, 1997), 91.

9. Kevin Howard and Marvin Rosenthal, *The Feasts of the Lord: God's Prophetic Calendar From Calvary to the Kingdom* (Thomas Nelson Inc., 1997), 23.

among us' (John 1:14). He tabernacled among us then, and He will tabernacle among us again in the Messianic age."[10]

The prophet Zechariah even made the connection that the Feast of Tabernacles was to be associated with Christ's millennial reign. He said that this feast would, at some future day, be reinstated by the Lord and observed by "all the families of the earth" during the Millennium (Zechariah 14:17).

Moreover, while the Feast of Tabernacles was to last for seven days (see Leviticus 23:34), the main day of celebration, known as the Great Hosanna,[11] fell on the seventh and final day of this feast. Perhaps the first six feast days represented the first six thousand years of the earth's temporal existence, and this seventh and final day of celebration, known as the Great Hosanna, represented the seventh and final thousand-year period corresponding to the Millennium.[12]

Also of note is the fact that the Feast of Tabernacles always began on "the fifteenth day of [the] seventh month" (Leviticus 23:34). What makes this significant is that since these feast days were kept using the lunar calendar, the fifteenth day of the month always marked the full moon and, subsequently, the time of the month when the moon was the brightest in the sky. Not surprisingly, both the moon and the Millennium are often associated with a terrestrial state (see Doctrine and Covenants 76:78; Articles of Faith 1:10).

The full moon on the Feast of Tabernacles symbolizes that during the Millennium, the earth will be free from darkness, both figuratively and literally. The prophet Isaiah said that during Christ's millennial reign, "thy sun shall no more go down; neither shall thy moon withdraw itself: for the Lord shall be thine everlasting light" (Isaiah 60:20), and President John Taylor said that the Millennium will be a

---

10. Lancaster, *Restoration*, 97.

11. Howard and Rosenthal, *The Feasts of the Lord*, 141–42.

12. The scriptures teach us that "one day is with the Lord as a thousand years, and a thousand years as one day" (2 Peter 3:8). Furthermore, "As God made the world in six days, and on the seventh day he finished his work, and sanctified it . . . even so, in the beginning of the seventh thousand years will the Lord God sanctify the earth, and complete the salvation of man" (Doctrine and Covenants 77:12).

time when "the mists of darkness [shall] be swept away by the light of eternal truth."[13]

No doubt that Jesus had this very theme of light in mind when He proclaimed during the Feast of Tabernacles,[14] "I am the light of the world: he that followeth me shall not walk in darkness, but shall have the light of life" (John 8:12), and when, on this same day, He gave sight (or light) to a man who was born blind (see John 9).

It is in these ways that the Feast of Tabernacles represents Christ's millennial reign.

---

13. *Journal of Discourses,* 11:94; see also Isaiah 11:9.

14. See John 7:37.

# 19

# First and Second Coming Parallels

One may say that the first and second comings of Jesus Christ are polar opposites of one another, and in many ways they are. Elder Parley P. Pratt expressed this contrast beautifully in the form of a poem:

> Jesus, once of humble birth,
> Now in glory comes to earth.
> Once he suffered grief and pain;
> Now he comes on earth to reign.
>
> Once a meek and lowly Lamb,
> Now the Lord, the great I Am.
> Once upon the cross he bowed;
> Now his chariot is the cloud.
>
> Once he groaned in blood and tears;
> Now in glory he appears.
> Once rejected by his own,
> Now their King he shall be known.

Once forsaken, left alone,
Now exalted to a throne.
Once all things he meekly bore,
But he now will bear no more.[1]

As this poem suggests, there are many differences between Christ's humble birth in a stable and His return to earth in power. However, the more one studies Christ's first and second comings, the more similarities one begins to notice as well. For example, many of the signs associated with Christ's birth and death are also prophesied signs of His Second Coming.

## Signs of the Times

To illustrate, when Christ was born, there appeared a new "star in the east" (Matthew 2:2). Similarly, according to Joseph Smith, prior to Christ's Second Coming, the world will be shown yet another "grand sign of the Son of Man in heaven . . . which will be as the light of the morning cometh out of the east."[2]

Furthermore, God sent an angel to a group of shepherds to announce the birth of Christ (see Luke 2:9), which will not be unlike the angels sent in our day to announce the Lord's return: "And angels shall fly through the midst of heaven, crying . . . Behold, and lo, the Bridegroom cometh; go ye out to meet him" (Doctrine and Covenants 88:92).

There were also several calamities that fell upon Jerusalem after the death of Christ, including an earthquake (see Matthew 27:51) and a "darkness over all the land" (Matthew 27:45). By way of comparison, in the last days, "before the day of the Lord shall come, the sun shall be darkened" (Doctrine and Covenants 45:42), and there will be "earthquakes, in divers places" (Matthew 24:7).

---

1. This poem would later be included in the hymnal as "Jesus, Once of Humble Birth," *Hymns*, no. 196.

2. *History of the Church*, 5:337.

## The Battle of Armageddon

One of the more well-known signs of the times is the famous battle of Armageddon. As discussed in chapter 11, Gog and his army will one day attempt to come up "against Jerusalem to battle" (Zechariah 14:2).

During this battle, "half of the city shall go forth into captivity" (Zechariah 14:2). However, just as it appears that Gog and his army will be victorious, the Lord will descend from heaven and set foot upon the Mount of Olives, causing a massive earthquake and splitting the Mount of Olives in two (see Zechariah 14:4).

When this occurs, the Jews will "flee" to this newly formed "valley of the mountains" for safety (Zechariah 14:5), at which time the Lord will send down fire from heaven to destroy the army of Gog (see Ezekiel 39:6; 38:22).

As the Jews gather around their Messiah in safety, the Lord revealed:

> And then shall the Jews look upon me and say: What are these wounds in thine hands and in thy feet?
>
> Then shall they know that I am the Lord; for I will say unto them: These wounds are the wounds with which I was wounded in the house of my friends. I am he who was lifted up. I am Jesus that was crucified. I am the Son of God.
>
> And then shall they weep because of their iniquities; then shall they lament because they persecuted their king. (Doctrine and Covenants 45:51–53; see also Zechariah 12:10–11; 13:6)

The prophet Ezekiel tells us that once this occurs, the Jews will proceed to carry Christ from the Mount of Olives, through the eastern gate of the Temple Mount, to the newly rebuilt Jewish temple at Jerusalem, where they will honor Him as their rightful king (see Ezekiel 44:1–2). As Sam Nadler stated, "The day is coming when [Christ] will return and make what will truly be His triumphal entry. . . . We will forever glorify Him as the Lamb of Glory, even as we wave palm branches to signify His eternal majesty."[3]

---

3. Sam Nadler, *Messiah in the Feasts of Israel, Revised Edition* (Word of Messiah Ministries, 2006), 55.

In other words, this future triumphal entry will, in many ways, be patterned after Christ's first triumphal entry. In each case, Christ descends from the Mount of Olives (see Luke 19:29; Doctrine and Covenants 45:48), travels through the Kidron Valley, and enters into the Jerusalem temple through the gate of the eastern temple wall (see Luke 19:45; Ezekiel 44:1–2). Furthermore, Christ rode on a colt during His first triumphal entry (see Matthew 21:7), which may very well be a type for the white horse that He will ride during His Second Coming when He will come in power (see Revelation 19:7–11).

During Christ's first triumphal entry, His followers welcomed him with "branches of palm trees" (John 12:13), while singing, "Blessed be the King that cometh in the name of the Lord" (Luke 19:38). During his second triumphal entry, the newly converted Jews who were just saved from the army of Gog will no doubt be counted among those with "palms in their hands" (Revelation 7:9) and among those crying with a loud voice, saying "salvation to our God . . . and unto the Lamb" (Revelation 7:9–10).

During His first triumphal entry, Christ, notwithstanding receiving a king's welcome by many of his followers, "wept" over the city of Jerusalem because of their wickedness (Luke 19:41). During Christ's second triumphal entry, it will be the Jews who will "weep . . . because they persecuted their king" (Doctrine and Covenants 45:53).

## Cleansing the Temple of Moneychangers

Immediately after His first triumphal entry, we read that Jesus "went into the temple, and began to cast out" the moneychangers (Luke 19:45). This cleansing of the temple is a type for the Lord's Second Coming in the clouds of heaven, which will occur sometime after His second triumphal entry. During this final Second Coming appearance, we read that the Lord will "come down in heaven from the presence of my Father and consume the wicked with unquenchable fire" (Doctrine and Covenants 63:34).

The reason why the cleansing of the Jerusalem temple is a type for this event is that the Jerusalem temple was made up of three sections—the outer courtyard, the holy place, and the Holy of Holies—and these three sections represented the telestial, terrestrial, and celestial states, respectively. Thus, when Christ cleansed the temple's outer courtyard, it was a type for the future day when He will cleanse the earth of telestial individuals. Joseph Fielding Smith taught, "When the reign of Jesus Christ comes during the millennium, only those who have lived the telestial law will be removed. The earth will be cleansed of all its corruption and wickedness."[4]

Furthermore, just as Jesus cast out moneychangers "that sold therein, and them that bought" during this temple cleansing (Luke 19:45), so too will He destroy all those who have received Satan's mark when He comes in power, a mark given to the followers of Satan which would ensure "that no man might buy or sell, save he that had the mark" (Revelation 13:17).

## Red in His Apparel

Not long after Christ cleansed the temple of the moneychangers, He took upon Himself our sins in the Garden of Gethsemane. "And being in an agony . . . he sweat as it were great drops of blood" (Joseph Smith Translation, Luke 22:44 [in Luke 22:44, footnote *b*]). The Lord described this agony in the Doctrine and Covenants: "Which suffering caused myself, even God, the greatest of all, to tremble because of pain, and to bleed at every pore" (Doctrine and Covenants 19:18).

No doubt the effects of this intense suffering stained Christ's garments red with blood, and this so that we "may be found spotless, pure, fair, and white, having been cleansed by the blood of the Lamb, at that great and last day" (Mormon 9:6). Interestingly, this same theme will be repeated at the Second Coming:

> And the Lord shall be red in his apparel, and his garments like him that treadeth in the wine-vat. . . .
>
> And his voice shall be heard: I have trodden the wine-press alone, and have brought judgment upon all people. . . .
>
> And I have trampled them in my fury, and I did tread upon them in mine anger, and their blood have I sprinkled upon my garments, and stained all my raiment. (Doctrine and Covenants 133:48, 50–51)

---

4. Joseph Fielding Smith, *Doctrines of Salvation*, comp. Bruce R. McConkie (Bookcraft, 1954–56), 3:62.

## The Torn Veil of the Temple

As Christ appears in all His glory and "red in his apparel" (Doctrine and Covenants 133:48), we are told that "the veil . . . which hideth the earth, shall be taken off, and all flesh shall see me together" (Doctrine and Covenants 101:23). When this occurs, all humankind will come into the presence of the Lord. It is interesting to note that a similar thing occurred in connection with Christ's death. We read, "And Jesus cried with a loud voice, and gave up the ghost. And the veil of the temple was rent in twain from the top to the bottom" (Mark 15:37–38).

Julie Smith explains:

> The veil was the barrier between the main area of the temple and the Holy of Holies (see Exodus 26:33), which was the sacred space that could be entered only once per year and only by the high priest. . . . Its rending signifies that this most sacred of spaces is now accessible to all people because of Jesus's death. The barrier between God and humans has been torn asunder. Access to the divine is no longer limited to one person and to one day of the year, but is now available to all as a direct result of the death of Jesus.[5]

Thus, the rending of the temple veil and the rending of the heavenly veil at the Second Coming each, in their own way, allows for humankind to come into the presence of the Lord.

## Resurrection of the Righteous

Shortly after the veil of the temple was rent, and after Christ's Resurrection, we read that "the graves were opened; and many bodies of the saints which slept arose . . . and appeared unto many" (Matthew 27:52–53). Remarkably, at the Second Coming, we are told that a similar thing will occur to the righteous Saints who have died prior to this event: "And the graves of the saints shall be opened; and they shall come forth and stand on the right hand of the Lamb" (Doctrine and Covenants 133:56).

---

5. Julie M. Smith, "Narrative Atonement Theology in the Gospel of Mark," *BYU Studies Quarterly* 54, no. 1 (2015): 30–31.

## Clouds of Heaven

As we have just shown, much can be said about the many similarities, or types, between Christ's first and second comings. We can therefore, along with the two angels who appeared to the Apostles on the mount after Jesus's ascension into heaven, testify that "this same Jesus, which is taken up . . . into heaven, shall so come in like manner" (Acts 1:11). As Orson Pratt stated, Jesus "was received into a cloud, taken up in a cloud, and when he comes the second time he will come in a cloud,"[6] which echoes what the Lord said in modern-day revelation: "Behold, I will come; and they shall see me in the clouds of heaven, clothed with power and great glory" (Doctrine and Covenants 45:44).

---

6. *Journal of Discourses*, 18:170.

# 20
# The Book of Mormon as a Type

The Second Coming types that we have examined up to this point have mainly been examples from the Old and New Testaments. But what does the Book of Mormon have to say on the subject? As it turns out, quite a bit. In fact, not only does the Book of Mormon contain several Second Coming types throughout its pages, but the entire Nephite history, in and of itself, can be considered a type for the latter days, ranging all the way from the discovery of America to Christ's Second Coming and Millennial reign. As Jeffery Marsh noted, "[The] recorded history in the Nephite record is a type of our day—our modern history echoes Book of Mormon history."[1]

This massive "Nephite-history type" begins with the ocean journey that Nephi and Lehi made from the Old World to the New World. This ocean journey was a model, or pattern, which would later

1. W. Jeffrey Marsh, "The Second Coming of Jesus," in *The Book of Mormon and the Message of the Four Gospels,* ed. Ray L. Huntington and Terry B. Ball (BYU Religious Studies Center, 2001), 91.

be replicated by other groups in the latter days, most notably by the Pilgrims.

The similarities between the Pilgrims' story and that of Lehi are striking. For example, Lehi's group fled the Old World to avoid being "carried away captive" (1 Nephi 1:13), and the Pilgrims fled the Old World, according to the Book of Mormon, to escape "captivity" (1 Nephi 13:13). Furthermore, once in the New World, the Book of Mormon states that the Pilgrims "did prosper and obtain the land for their inheritance" (1 Nephi 13:15), which can also be said of the Nephites (see 2 Nephi 3:2).

When the prophet Nephi saw the latter-day colonization of America in vision, he was also shown "a book, and it was carried forth among them" (1 Nephi 13:20). Nephi was told that this book—the Bible—would contain "a record of the Jews" (1 Nephi 13:23) and would be "of great worth unto the Gentiles" in America (1 Nephi 13:23). By way of comparison, Nephi and Lehi also brought with them a book to the New World, even Laban's brass plates, which too contained "a record of the Jews" (1 Nephi 5:12) and also proved to be "of great worth" (1 Nephi 5:21) unto Lehi's seed.

Remarkably, the events that followed each of these two groups in the coming years would continue to mirror one another, some in striking detail. For example, after several hundred years in the New World, the Nephites, under King Mosiah, decided to reform their system of government. Rather than electing to be ruled by kings, the Nephites chose instead to "appoint judges to rule over them, or to judge them according to the law" (Mosiah 29:41). This reformation of the Nephite government shifted the balance of power from that of kings "to the voice of the people" (Mosiah 29:29). As a result, the Nephites were blessed to live in what they referred to as "a land of liberty" (Mosiah 29:32). By way of comparison, after the Revolutionary War, a Constitutional Republic was put in place in America, which produced a similar favorable result for all Americans.[2] The Lord de-

---

2. It should be noted that while the Nephite society shared some similarities with the United States' Constitutional Republic, the two governments operated much differently. According to Ryan Davis, "Mosiah's new regime is not a democracy as the term is understood in contemporary society." Ryan W. Davis, "For the Peace of the People: War and Democracy in the Book of Mormon,"

clared, "And for this purpose have I established the Constitution of this land, by the hands of wise men whom I raised up unto this very purpose" (Doctrine and Covenants 101:80).

Furthermore, it was also around this time that a "church of Christ" (Mosiah 18:17) was organized among the Nephites. This Church of Christ was formed by Alma the Elder at the Waters of Mormon and later relocated to the land of Zarahemla during the reign of King Mosiah (see Mosiah 25:19). As Brant Gardner explained, "Zarahemla did not have churches prior to Alma's arrival."[3]

This Church of Christ, established by Alma the Elder, was a type for The Church of Jesus Christ of Latter-day Saints, restored to the earth in our day through the Prophet Joseph Smith. In the Doctrine and Covenants, the Lord described this restored Church in a very interesting way. He said, "And verily, verily, I say unto you, that this church have I established and called forth *out of the wilderness*" (Doctrine and Covenants 33:5, emphasis added; see also Doctrine and Covenants 109:73).

Our Church is described as coming forth out of the wilderness because it was symbolically driven "into the wilderness" (Revelation 12:6; Doctrine and Covenants 86:3) by Satan during the Great Apostasy. Interestingly enough, this symbolic wilderness was mirrored by an actual wilderness in the case of Alma's Church, for, after Alma established the Church of Christ at the Waters of Mormon, and after escaping persecution from the hand of Amulon, we read that Alma and his followers "departed . . . and took their journey into the wilderness. And after they had been in the wilderness twelve days they arrived in the land of Zarahemla" (Mosiah 24:24–25). Thus, both

*Journal of Book of Mormon Studies* 16, no.1 (2007): 44. And according to John Sorenson, "Such modern political concepts as republican representation, the use of an apparatus of public employees or bureaucrats, public record keeping, the notion of factions or parties formally competing in elections, and other rights such as one might expect from Joseph Smith's familiarity with the political institutions and thought of Jacksonian America were all absent, or virtually so, from Book of Mormon societies." John L. Sorenson, *Mormon's Codex: An Ancient American Book* (Deseret Book, 2013), 258.

3. Brant A. Gardner, *Traditions of the Fathers: The Book of Mormon as History* (Greg Kofford Books, 2015), 241.

churches, whether literally or figuratively, are described as emerging from a wilderness setting.

It is also interesting to note that each of these two churches were forced to relocate several times in the early stages of their histories due to government persecution. Alma's Church relocated twice before arriving in Zarahemla (see Mosiah 18:34; Mosiah 24:8–25), and the Latter-day Church was driven from several states throughout its history, including Missouri and Illinois.

As Alma's Church was being established in the land of Zarahemla, King Mosiah, through the means of the Jaredite interpreters, translated the Jaredite record that was discovered by the Limhi expedition. We read, "Now king Mosiah . . . translated and caused to be written the records which were on the plates of gold which had been found by the people of Limhi, which were delivered to him by the hand of Limhi. . . . And now he translated them by the means of those two stones which were fastened into the two rims of a bow" (Mosiah 28:10–13).

Several hundred years later, Joseph Smith would be given these same Nephite interpreters[4] and also used them to translate an ancient record, which was also inscribed on plates of gold. Amazingly, once translated, each record told a similar tale of a once righteous civilization destroyed due to their wickedness. Each record no doubt served as a warning to the reader "that whoso should possess this land of promise . . . should serve him, the true and only God, or they should be swept off when the fulness of his wrath should come upon them" (Ether 2:8).

Sometime after Mosiah translated the Jaredite record, a contention broke out between the Nephites and a group of Mulekites who called themselves Amlicites (see Alma 2:11). Amlici, the leader of the Amlicites, "commanded them that they should take up arms

4. Mosiah's interpreters were handed down among the Nephites from generation to generation until they were given to Moroni, who buried them with the gold plates. Interestingly enough, as we learn from the Lord in the Doctrine and Covenants, the interpreters that Moroni gave to Joseph Smith were the same ones given to the brother of Jared (see Doctrine and Covenants 17:1). This tells us that there was only one set of interpreters used between the brother of Jared, Mosiah, Moroni, Joseph Smith, and everyone in between.

against their brethren; and this he did that he might subject them to him" (Alma 2:10). This rebellion resulted in a civil war between the Nephites and the Amlicites in which thousands of soldiers on both sides were slain (see Alma 2:16–19). By way of comparison, starting in 1861, the United States was engulfed in its own Civil War, which resulted in the deaths of over 600,000 soldiers.

Some years after the Civil War had ended, the United States found themselves involved in two major world wars, World War I and World War II. In some ways, these two world wars could be comparable to the two wars that the Nephites and the Lamanites fought in several years after the Nephite civil war had ended (see Alma 43–44; 46–62). Thanks to righteous military leaders such as Captain Moroni and Helaman, the Nephites walked away from each of these two major Nephite-Lamanite wars as victors.

After the two major wars with the Lamanites had ended, we read that the Nephites continued to have lesser battles with the Lamanites over the next several years (see Alma 63:15; Helaman 1:14–33). By way of comparison, after World War II, the United States also found themselves involved in several lesser wars, including the Cold War, the Korean War, and the Vietnam War.

After these wars had ended, the United States enjoyed a period of peace and prosperity. During this period of peace, The Church of Jesus Christ of Latter-day Saints experienced a tremendous amount of growth thanks in part to dedicated missionary work.[5] In a similar way, after their period of warfare with the Lamanites had ended, we read that the Nephites experienced "exceedingly great prosperity in the church, insomuch that there were thousands who did join themselves unto the church and were baptized unto repentance" (Helaman 3:24).

The above examples are just some of the many similarities between the history of the Nephites and the history of the United States of America. According to Hugh Nibley, there is a reason for this: "It is into our hands that the Book of Mormon has been placed. . . . Plainly it is meant for us, as it reminds us many times; it is the story of what

5. See, for example, William Edwin Berrett, *The Restored Church* (Deseret Book, 1973), 345–84.

happened to the Nephites—*and we are the Nephites*: 'It must needs be that the riches of the earth are mine to give; but beware of pride, lest ye become as the Nephites of old' (Doctrine and Covenants 38:39)."[6]

If "we are the Nephites," as Hugh Nibley has suggested, then it would be wise for us to pay close attention to the remaining portions of the Nephite record because, as President Ezra Taft Benson noted, their story may end up mirroring the final chapters of our story: "The record of the Nephite history just prior to the Savior's visit reveals many parallels to our own day as we anticipate the Savior's Second Coming."[7]

With this in mind, it is to the remaining portion of the Nephite record that we now turn.

---

6. Hugh Nibley, *Since Cumorah*, ed. John W. Welch (Deseret Book and FARMS, 1988), 354; emphasis added.
7. Ezra Taft Benson, *A Witness and a Warning* (Deseret Book, 1988), 37.

# 21
# The Book of Mormon as a Type for the Last Days

As we have just discovered, the history of the Nephites is a type for the history of America. But the types that we have analyzed so far do not end with America's past. Indeed, the remaining portion of Nephite history is also a type for the last days, including the Second Coming of Christ and His millennial reign.[1] In the words of President Ezra Taft Benson, it is in the Book of Mormon that we find "a pattern for preparing for the Second Coming."[2]

Over the last several decades, our Church, similar to that of the Nephites after their wars ended (see Helaman 3:24), has experienced a

1. The many parallels contained in this chapter were taken from *Book of Mormon Student Manual: Religion 121–122* (1979), 395; W. Jeffrey Marsh, "The Second Coming of Jesus," in *The Book of Mormon and the Message of the Four Gospels,* ed. Ray L. Huntington and Terry B. Ball (BYU Religious Studies Center, 2001); Donald W. Parry and Jay A. Parry, *Understanding the Signs of the Times* (Deseret Book, 1999), 448–456; John Welch, "Chart 51: The Coming of Christ to the Nephites: A Pattern for His Second Coming" *Charting the Book of Mormon,* https://byustudies.byu.edu/online-book/charting-the-book-of-mormon.

2. Conference Report, Oct. 1986, 5.

tremendous amount of growth. In fact, Joseph Smith prophesied that our Church will continue to grow in numbers "till it has penetrated every continent, visited every clime, swept every country, and sounded in every ear."[3] No doubt this prophecy is coming true right before our very eyes.

In Nephi's vision of the tree of life, Nephi not only saw this time period described by Joseph Smith (see 1 Nephi 14:12), but he also got to see some the events that are to follow, which he described as a period of persecution that the Saints will experience at the hands of "that great and abominable church" (1 Nephi 14:9–13). Elder Heber C Kimball spoke of this future time period: "Persecution comes next and all true Latter-day Saints will be tested to the limit. Many will apostatize and others will be still not knowing what to do. . . . the Saints will be put to tests that will try the integrity of the best of them."[4]

Amazingly, a similar thing happened to the Nephites. After they had experienced a period of rapid growth among the Church (see Helaman 3:24), the Nephite Saints began to experience some persecution. We read, "And they were lifted up in pride, even to the persecution of many of their brethren" (Helaman 3:34).

As a result of this persecution, we read that many of the Nephite Saints "did wax stronger and stronger in their humility, and firmer and firmer in the faith" (Helaman 3:35). However, while many the Nephite Saints were waxing stronger and stronger in their faith, Mormon also tells us that more and more Nephites around them were becoming increasingly wicked, even to the point where "they who chose evil were more numerous than they who chose good" (Helaman 5:2). Eventually the Nephites became so wicked that they were actually building up and supporting the Gadianton robbers "until they had overspread all the land of the Nephites" (Helaman 6:38).

Similarly, we have been warned by the prophet Nephi that there would also be "secret combinations" found among us, "even as in times of old, according to the combinations of the devil" (2 Nephi 26:22). Ezra Taft Benson taught, "Secret combinations lusting for power,

---

3. *History of the Church*, 4:540.

4. *Deseret News*, May 23, 1931.

gain, and glory are flourishing. A secret combination that seeks to overthrow the freedom of all lands, nations, and countries is increasing its evil influence and control over America and the entire world."[5]

Eventually the Gadianton robbers, the secret combination among the Nephites, completely infiltrated the government by "filling the judgment-seats" (Helaman 7:4). As a result, the government that once produced "a land of liberty" (Mosiah 29:32) was now virtually "destroyed, because of the secret combination" (3 Nephi 7:6).

By way of comparison, Joseph Smith prophesied that there will come a time "when the Constitution of the United States" will hang, "as it were, upon a single thread."[6]

When this occurs, we have been told that "the Latter-day Saints—the Elders of Israel—will step forward to rescue and save it."[7] No doubt this rescuing of our Constitution will occur as we Latter-day Saints raise "an ensign to the nations" (Isaiah 5:26) and build up the Lord's Zion. As we do this, we are told that one group in particular, those of Lamanite descent, will become converted to the gospel of Jesus Christ en masse and will play a major role in helping us build the New Jerusalem (see Doctrine and Covenants 49:24–25).

Interestingly enough, this future event will not be unlike the massive Lamanite conversion that helped to strengthen the Nephite Church before the coming of Christ:

> And it came to pass that . . . the Lamanites had become, the more part of them, a righteous people, insomuch that their righteousness did exceed that of the Nephites. . . .
>
> And it came to pass that many of the Lamanites did come down into the land of Zarahemla, and did declare unto the people of the Nephites the manner of their conversion, and did exhort them to faith and repentance. (Helaman 6:1, 4)

Furthermore, just as the headquarters of the Restored Church will one day be relocated from Salt Lake City, Utah, to Jackson County,

---

5. Conference Report, Oct. 1988, 103.

6. *Journal of Discourses*, 2:182.

7. *Journal History of the Church*, Church History Library, MSF 143 #28, July 24, 1871.

Missouri,[8] so too were the headquarters of the Nephite Church relocated from Zarahemla to Bountiful around this time of their history (see Helaman 4:4–6). Joseph and Blake Allen explained, "The fact that the Savior appeared to the Nephites at Bountiful rather than at Zarahemla . . . suggests that the Church had moved its headquarters from Zarahemla to Bountiful sometime before the visit of Christ."[9]

Once at Bountiful, the Nephites wasted no time building a new temple, which would one day welcome the resurrected Christ. Similarly, we are told that our Church will one day build a temple at "the New Jerusalem . . . that my covenant people may be gathered in one in that day when I shall come to my temple" (Doctrine and Covenants 42:35–36).

Before the Savior appears at His temple in the New Jerusalem, however, we are told that several destructions must first be poured out among the wicked nations of the earth. We read in the scriptures of "earthquakes also in divers places, and many desolations" (Doctrine and Covenants 45:33). We also read that the Lord will attempt to bring the wicked to repentance with "the voice of thunderings, and the voice of lightnings, and the voice of tempests, and the voice of the waves of the sea heaving themselves beyond their bounds" (Doctrine and Covenants 88:90).

In many ways, these future destructions could be compared to the destructions that the Nephites experienced at the time of Christ's Crucifixion. We read in the Nephite record of "a great storm" that included "a great and terrible tempest; and . . . terrible thunder. . . . And there were exceedingly sharp lightnings, such as never had been known in all the land" (3 Nephi 8:5–7). In addition to this great storm, the Nephites also experienced an earthquake so terrible "that it did shake the whole earth as if it was about to divide asunder" (3 Nephi 8:6).

---

8. Brigham Young asked, "Are we going back to Jackson County? Yes. When? As soon as the way opens up." *Journal of Discourses*, 18:355.

9. Joseph L. Allen and Blake J. Allen, *Exploring the Lands of the Book of Mormon (Revised Edition)* (Covenant Communications, 2011), 613. Allen and Allen also noted, "At 36 BC, or seventy years before Christ visited the Nephites, the Church moved its headquarters from Zarahemla to Bountiful (Helaman 4:6)." Allen and Allen, *Exploring the Lands of the Book of Mormon*, 759.

After these destructions had passed, we read of "thick darkness upon all the face of the land" (3 Nephi 8:20), which darkness lasted "for the space of three days" (3 Nephi 8:23). By way of comparison, in the last days, we read that "before the day of the Lord shall come, the sun shall be darkened" (Doctrine and Covenants 45:42).

It is interesting to note that in reference to the Nephite destruction, "it was the more righteous part of the people who were saved" (3 Nephi 10:12). Thankfully, we have been given a similar promise regarding our safety in the latter days if we remain faithful: "For behold, and lo, vengeance cometh speedily upon the ungodly as the whirlwind. . . . Nevertheless, Zion shall escape if she observe to do all things whatsoever I have commanded her" (Doctrine and Covenants 97:22–25).

After the three days of darkness had ended, the Nephites had to turn their attention to the rebuilding of their cities. Interestingly enough, the Lord tells us that in connection with the building up of Zion, we will also "return to the lands of [our] inheritances, and shall *build up the waste places of Zion*" (Doctrine and Covenants 103:11; emphasis added).

This phrase, "waste places," is often used in the scriptures to describe the setting in Zion just before its redemption. Because of the destruction in America that will have occurred just prior to this time, much of the land will have been left desolate and destroyed. It will be necessary, therefore, for the Saints to "build up the waste places of Zion" when they return (Doctrine and Covenants 103:11).

Similar to the Nephites, who had to turn their attention to rebuilding their temple at Bountiful, we are told that we Latter-day Saints, as we attempt to "build up the waste places of Zion" (Doctrine and Covenants 103:11), will endeavor to construct a temple at New Jerusalem, at the center stake of Zion in Jackson County, Missouri (see Doctrine and Covenants 57:1–3; 84:2–5). Once this New Jerusalem temple has been built, we are told that the righteous will gather to it from around the world in preparation for the Lord's return (see Doctrine and Covenants 42:35–36).

Similarly, we read in the Book of Mormon that just prior to the Lord's appearance, there was "a great multitude gathered together, of the people of Nephi, round about the temple which was in the land Bountiful" (3 Nephi 11:1).

As the Nephites were gathering, "they heard a voice as if it came out of heaven . . . [which] did pierce them to the very soul, and did cause their hearts to burn" (3 Nephi 11:3). In a like manner, we are told that in the last days, "the Lord shall utter his voice [from heaven], and all the ends of the earth shall hear it" (Doctrine and Covenants 45:49).

Once the Lord revealed Himself to the Nephites, His first invitation to them was to have them "arise and come forth unto me, that ye may thrust your hands into my side, and also that ye may feel the prints of the nails in my hands and in my feet, that ye may know that I am the God of Israel" (3 Nephi 11:14). A similar event will occur in the last days, as Christ descends in glory upon the Mount of Olives next to the newly rebuilt Jewish temple in Jerusalem.[10] Speaking of this event, the Lord said, "And then shall the Jews look upon me and say: What are these wounds in thine hands and in thy feet? Then shall they know that I am the Lord; for I will say unto them: These wounds are the wounds with which I was wounded in the house of my friends. I am he who was lifted up. I am Jesus that was crucified. I am the Son of God" (Doctrine and Covenants 45:51–52).

Sometime after this event, Christ will make His final appearance in the clouds of heaven, and when this occurs, it will be for the entire earth to see (see Doctrine and Covenants 101:23). This sacred event will commence a resurrection of righteous Saints who had previously died: "And the saints that are upon the earth, who are alive, shall be quickened and be caught up to meet him. And they who have slept in their graves shall come forth" (Doctrine and Covenants 88:96–97).

Interestingly enough, the Book of Mormon tells us that a similar thing also occurred after Christ's appearance to the Nephites: "Many saints did arise [from the grave] and appear unto many and did minister unto them" (3 Nephi 23:11).

---

10. That the Jewish temple will be built before Christ descends upon the Mount of Olives was made clear by Joseph Smith, who said, "Judah must return, Jerusalem must be rebuilt, *and the temple* . . . and all this must be done *before* the Son of Man will make His appearance." *Teachings of the Prophet Joseph Smith*, sel. Joseph Fielding Smith (1976), 286; emphasis added.

Christ, as part of His ministry among the Nephites, also implemented a new form of government among them. Under this new form of government, no longer would the Nephites be subject to the law of Moses. Instead, Christ declared unto them, "I am the [new] law" (3 Nephi 15:9).

This new form of government, with Christ at the center and implemented by a righteous Nephite nation, brought with it a fantastic period of "peace in the land" (4 Nephi 1:4). The Nephites even began practicing the law of consecration by having "all things common among them" (4 Nephi 1:3). Of this time period, Mormon wrote, "And there were no envyings, nor strifes, nor tumults, nor whoredoms, nor lyings, nor murders, nor any manner of lasciviousness; and surely there could not be a happier people among all the people who had been created by the hand of God" (4 Nephi 1:16).

This period of peace enjoyed by the Nephites was a type and shadow of Christ's millennial reign,[11] for during the Millennium, "Satan shall be bound . . . and shall not be loosed for the space of a thousand years" (Doctrine and Covenants 88:110).

During these thousand years, the Lord revealed that the inhabitants of the earth—similar to the Nephites— "shall have no laws but my laws when I come, for I am your lawgiver" (Doctrine and Covenants 38:21–22). The result will be a period of peace rivaled only by the Nephites. Isaiah tells us that during the Millennium, Christ "shall judge among the nations . . . and they shall beat their swords into plowshares, and their spears into pruninghooks: nation shall not lift up sword against nation, neither shall they learn war any more" (Isaiah 2:4).

As this thousand-year period comes to an end, we are told that Satan "shall be loosed for a little season" and "shall gather together his armies; even the hosts of hell, and shall come up to battle against Michael and his armies" (Doctrine and Covenants 88:111–113). John the Revelator described the ensuing battle as follows: "And [Satan and his angels] went up on the breadth of the earth, and compassed the

---

11. Parry and Parry wrote, "This specific, historic group of people [in 4 Nephi] is a model of a larger assembly who will live in joy during the Millennium, after Jesus' second coming." Parry and Parry, *Understanding the Signs of the Times*, 452.

camp of the saints about . . . and fire came down from God out of heaven, and devoured them. And the devil . . . was cast into the lake of fire and brimstone" (Revelation 20:9–10).

While some differences do exist, it is interesting to note that the Nephites, after falling into apostasy several hundred years after the visitation from Christ, also found themselves involved in one final battle with their brethren the Lamanites (see Mormon 6). This final battle between the Nephites and Lamanites at the Hill Cumorah turned out to be the eventual downfall of the Nephite nation. Thankfully, our last battle with Satan at the end of the Millennium will prove to be his eventual downfall.

With so many parallels between our story and that of the Nephites, is it any wonder that the Book of Mormon was written with us in mind? In the words of Dale LeBaron, "Truly the Lord showed [the Nephite prophets] the last days and told them what to record."[12]

---

12. Dale E. LeBaron, "The Book of Mormon: The Pattern in Preparing a People to Meet the Savior," in *Doctrines of the Book of Mormon: 1991 Sperry Symposium*, ed. Bruce A. Van Orden and Brent L. Top (Deseret Book, 1992), 72.

# 22
# Wheat and Tares

In addition to types, the Lord has also used several parables to teach us about His Second Coming. One such parable worth mentioning here is the parable of the wheat and tares (see Matthew 13:24–30).

Section 4 of the Doctrine and Covenants gives us an introduction to this parable. Here, the Lord refers to the people of the world who are waiting to hear the gospel as a field of wheat: "For behold the field is white already to harvest; and lo, he that thrusteth in his sickle with his might, the same layeth up in store that he perisheth not, but bringeth salvation to his soul" (Doctrine and Covenants 4:4).[1]

If the wheat field in this scripture represents the people of the world who are ready and waiting for the gospel message, then the harvesters represent the Lord's missionaries who have been "called to the work" (Doctrine and Covenants 4:3).

However, as anyone who has ever done missionary work in the past knows, not everyone in the field is ready for the gospel message.

1. We know this scripture is describing a wheat field because while wheat is normally gold in color, unharvested wheat stalks can often have the appearance of pure white when the light of the sun reflects upon them.

In fact, there are many people in the world who want nothing to do with the Lord's gospel and, in some cases, will do anything they can to thwart God's efforts. In the parable of the wheat and tares, the Lord described such individuals as tares: "The kingdom of heaven is likened unto a man which sowed good seed in his field: But while men slept, his enemy came and sowed tares among the wheat, and went his way. But when the blade was sprung up, and brought forth fruit, then appeared the tares also" (Matthew 13:24–26).

This means that the field that we as missionaries are asked to harvest is not simply a field of pure wheat but a field mixed with wheat and tares, which is a much more difficult field to harvest.

Surprisingly, one of the more challenging aspects of harvesting such a field is telling the two crops apart. As the wheat and tares mature, it becomes much easier to identify which crop is which; however, when the wheat and tares are still in their infancy, it is nearly impossible to tell the difference between the two. According to *Smith's Bible Dictionary*, "The [tare] before it comes into ear is very similar in appearance to wheat."[2]

In our analogy, we could say that it is very difficult to judge a person's heart based on their looks alone. As Richard Skousen wrote, "Unfortunately, the tares often look and act deceptively like wheat."[3] In fact there is only one true test that we can use to determine the wheat from the tares. In the Sermon on the Mount, the Lord taught, "A good tree cannot bring forth evil fruit, neither can a corrupt tree bring forth good fruit . . . Wherefore by their fruits ye shall know them" (Matthew 7:18–20).

As one might expect, the fruit produced by wheat is much different from the fruit produced by tares. According to nutritionist Kiran Patil, "Wheat is rich in catalytic elements, mineral salts, calcium, magnesium, potassium, sulfur, chlorine, arsenic, silicon, manganese, zinc, iodine, copper, vitamin B, and vitamin E."[4] By way of com-

---

2. William Smith, *Smith's Bible Dictionary* (Hendrickson Publishers, 1990), entry for "Tares."
3. Richard N. Skousen, *His Return* (Verity Publishing, 2007), 66
4. Kiran Patil, "18 Incredible Wheat Benefits," OrganicFacts, last modified Apr. 15, 2024, www.organicfacts.net/health-benefits/cereal/wheat.html.

parison, "The grains of the L. temulentum [tares], if eaten, produce convulsions, and even death."[5]

It comes as no surprise then to learn of the devastation that was felt by both the sower and the servants of the parable when they learned that the seeds of wheat they had planted were now growing next to dangerous tares: "So the servants of the householder came and said unto him, Sir, didst not thou sow good seed in thy field? from whence then hath it tares? He said unto them, An enemy hath done this" (Matthew 13:27–28).

The servant's reaction to this travesty was to ask the sower if they should go to the field and pluck out the tares from among the wheat: "Wilt thou then that we go and gather them up?" (Matthew 13:28). Although this seems like the natural thing to do under these circumstances, the sower responded otherwise by saying, "Nay; lest while ye gather up the tares, ye root up also the wheat with them" (Matthew 13:29).

The danger in removing the tares from among the wheat prematurely lies in the fact that the roots of the tares often intertwine with those of the wheat. This makes it extremely difficult to extract only the tares without damaging the wheat during the early stages of maturation. For this reason, "God has held the angels of destruction for many years, lest they should reap down the wheat with the tares."[6]

In our world today, some individuals embody the role of tares by spiritually choking those around them, hindering others from receiving the essential nutrients needed for spiritual growth. Thankfully, while some may succumb to these negative influences, many others choose to remain steadfast. Like the stalks of wheat in our parable, they find ways to grow and flourish despite the presence of tares.

In fact, there is a unique benefit for wheat growing alongside tares. When the roots of the tares wrap around those of the wheat, they compel the wheat roots to dig deeper into the soil to access water. As a result, the wheat often grows taller and stronger than it would have otherwise had it not been surrounded by tares. This principle was illustrated in the Book of Mormon when the Lord told Nephi that

---

5. *Smith's Bible Dictionary*, entry for "Tares."

6. *Young Woman's Journal*, Aug. 1894, 511–12.

the Lamanites would "be a scourge unto thy seed, to stir them up in remembrance of me" (2 Nephi 5:25).

But the wheat is not to grow among the tares forever. The Lord said that they are only to "grow together until the harvest" (Matthew 13:30).

According to the Joseph Smith Translation, the harvest will come to a culmination at the "end of the world" (Joseph Smith Translation, Matthew 13:39 [in Matthew 13:39, footnote *a*]); however, we read in Doctrine and Covenants 4 that the preparations for this harvest have already begun: "For behold the field is white *already to harvest*" (Doctrine and Covenants 4:4; emphasis added).

This means that the time is not far distant when the Lord will start separating the wheat from the tares. Soon the wheat of the world will come to maturity and its roots will be strong enough to allow the sowers to separate it from the tares without causing harm to the wheat.

This event—when the wheat is separated from the tares—is one of the prophesied events of the last days. Eventually, humankind will be unable to remain neutral in the war between good and evil. The Lord stated that "the day speedily cometh . . . when peace shall be taken from the earth, and the devil shall have power over his own dominion. And also the Lord shall have power over his saints" (Doctrine and Covenants 1:35–36). When this day comes, "an entire separation of the righteous and the wicked" will occur (Doctrine and Covenants 63:54).

Once this day arrives, it will be very easy for the sower to harvest the wheat of the world and remove it from a field of tares. In section 4 of the Doctrine and Covenants, this stage of missionary work is described by cutting the wheat at the base of the stalk with a sickle and removing it from the field: "And lo, he that thrusteth in his sickle with his might, the same layeth up in store that he perisheth not, but bringeth salvation to his soul" (Doctrine and Covenants 4:4).

At this point in our story, the wheat is separated from the tares, and the tares are "bound in bundles to be burned" (Joseph Smith Translation, Matthew 13:29 [in Matthew 13:30, footnote *b*]).

## Threshing of Wheat

Once the wheat has been cut down, the next step is to remove the wheat kernels from the stalk. But how? As you can imagine, removing each kernel of wheat by hand for an entire wheat field would take a very long time. To solve this problem, anciently, the Israelites took the wheat through a process called threshing.

There were several different ways to thresh wheat. One way was to pound the wheat with a hammer, which caused the wheat kernels to separate themselves from the husks. And since the wheat kernels were strong, this could be done without damaging the wheat kernels themselves. Once the wheat kernels had been separated from the stalks, the stalks were discarded.

Another method of threshing wheat anciently (especially when done in larger quantities) was to have an animal such as an ox trample the grain (see Deuteronomy 25:4). The ox would often be yoked to a sleigh, which would be weighed down by rocks or weights. Attached to the underneath of the sleigh would be teeth of stones that did the actual threshing of the wheat. When the ox pulled the sleigh over the wheat, the stone teeth under the sleigh would cut the wheat and separate its kernels from the stalks.

If we compare this threshing of wheat with section 4 of the Doctrine and Covenants, we learn that being harvested is just the beginning for those who are converted to the gospel of Jesus Christ. In other words, all individuals harvested into the Lord's Church will eventually be threshed by the Lord. And from what we can gather based on the above methods of threshing, being pounded with a hammer, or being trampled by oxen, does not sound like a very pleasant process for anyone.

Why then would the Lord put the members of His Church through this threshing process? The answer is simple. That is the only way to get to the wheat: "Therefore, [ye] must needs be chastened and tried, even as Abraham. . . . For all those who will not endure chastening . . . cannot be sanctified" (Doctrine and Covenants 101:4–5).

According to this scripture, we are threshed when we are "tried, even as Abraham," but as a result of this process, we can become "sanctified." Joseph Smith said it this way: "God will feel after you, he will take hold of you and wrench your very heartstrings, and if you cannot stand it you will not be fit for an inheritance in the Kingdom of God."[7]

The purpose of being threshed spiritually is explained in the *History of the Church*, which reads:

> The wheat and tares must grow together till the harvest, at the harvest the wheat is gathered together into the threshing floor; so with the Saints. . . . Here they will be threshed with all sorts of difficulties, trials, afflictions and everything to mar their peace which they can imagine . . . but he that endures the threshing till all the chaff, superstition, folly and unbelief are pounded out of him, and does not suffer himself to be blown away as chaff but endures faithfully to the end, shall be saved.[8]

## Winnowing

After the wheat has been threshed, there is still one last step that the sower needs to go through before they can retrieve the wheat, which includes a process called winnowing. While the hammer or oxen can remove the wheat kernels from the stalk, threshing also has a tendency to leave behind unwanted chaff alongside the wheat. To solve this problem anciently, wheat farmers would toss the remaining pile of wheat and chaff high up into the air using instruments such as a winnowing fork or shovel. Because wheat kernels are heavier than chaff, the wind would blow away the unwanted chaff while the wheat fell safely back to the ground.

Scripturally, the wheat belongs to the Lord and the chaff belongs to Satan. The Lord warned us in the Doctrine and Covenants to "beware, for Satan desireth to sift [us] as chaff" (Doctrine and Covenants 52:12). Similarly, Mormon noted, "For behold, the Spirit of the Lord hath already ceased to strive with their fathers; and they are without Christ and God in the world; and *they are driven about as chaff before the wind*" (Mormon 5:16, emphasis added; see also Psalms 1:4).

---

7. *Journal of Discourses*, 24:197.

8. *History of the Church*, 4:451–52.

Unfortunately, both chaff and wheat can be found within the Church today. While some members are producing wheat, others may be described as "lukewarm" (Revelation 3:16). And just as the Lord allowed the tares to grow alongside the wheat during the earlier stages of harvest, He will also permit the chaff to temporarily remain among the wheat in His Church. However, the time will come when this chaff must be removed to make way for the building up of Zion.

This will be done in several different ways. One way is through persecution from the outside world. Elder McConkie explains, "Persecution is the tool of Satan to harass, hinder, and destroy, if possible, the cause of righteousness. The spiritually weak, the lukewarm disciples, those who have not given themselves wholly to the Cause of Christ are purged from the Church by persecution."[9]

As it turns out, this is exactly what has been prophesied to happen to the Church in the last days. Heber C. Kimball prophesied, "Persecution comes next and all true Latter-day Saints will be tested to the limit. Many will apostatize and others will be still not knowing what to do."[10]

The second way the Lord plans to remove the chaff from among His harvested wheat is through the destructions that will soon be poured out upon the wicked. These destructions will begin "first among those among you, saith the Lord, who have professed to know my name and have not known me, and have blasphemed against me in the midst of my house" (Doctrine and Covenants 112:26).

In the New Testament, John the Baptist described these future events as follows: "[The Lord will] gather his wheat into the garner; but he will [first] burn up the chaff with unquenchable fire" (Matthew 3:12).

As a result of these two events—persecution and destruction at the hand of the Lord—the chaff inside the Church will be removed and the Lord will be left only with pure wheat.

---

9. Bruce R. McConkie, *Doctrinal New Testament Commentary* (Bookcraft, 1973), 2:63.

10. *Deseret News*, May 23, 1931.

## Gathering the Wheat into the Barn

According to the Lord, once the wheat had been separated from the chaff, it will then be time to gather it safely in the barn: "In the time of harvest I will say to the reapers, Gather ye together first the wheat into my barn" (Joseph Smith Translation, Matthew 13:30 [in Matthew 13:30, footnote *b*]).

In many ways, this barn represents the city Zion, and perhaps more specifically, the temple that will be built in Jackson County, Missouri, prior to the Second Coming (see Doctrine and Covenants 57:1–5). It will be here where the Saints will be safely gathered prior to the burning of the tares at the Second Coming.

According to the Lord, "the reapers" who gather the wheat into the barn "are the angels" (Matthew 13:39) sent to the earth by the Lord to bring the righteous to Zion. Elder Orson Pratt explained, "All the elect of God, of whatever nation, tongue, and people, will be gathered out year after year [to the New Jerusalem]; and by-and-by, the great and last gathering will be done through instrumentality of angels."[11]

Then, referring to a statement made by the Savior in Matthew 24:40–41, Elder Pratt continued: "There will be two, as it were, grinding at a mill; the faithful one will be taken, and the other will be left: there will be two, as it were, sleeping in one bed; one will be picked up by the angels, and the other will be left; and the remnant of the children of God scattered abroad on all the face of the earth will receive their last gathering by the angels."[12]

## Burned with Fire

With the wheat safely in the barn, "the tares are gathered and burned in the fire" (Matthew 13:40). So shall it be at the end of this world: "I . . . will come down in heaven from the presence of my Father and consume the wicked with unquenchable fire" (Doctrine and Covenants 63:34). "They that do wickedly shall be as stubble;

11. *Journal of Discourses*, 7:187–88.

12. *Journal of Discourses*, 7:187–88.

and I will burn them up, saith the Lord of Hosts" (Doctrine and Covenants 29:9).

## We Shall Be Like Him

While the earth is thus being burned with fire, we are told that the Saints "shall be caught up together . . . in the clouds, to meet the Lord in the air" (1 Thessalonians 4:17; see also Doctrine and Covenants 88:95–97).

Of course, the main purpose of harvesting wheat anciently was to make bread. This is significant because it will be at this time—when we are "caught up . . . in the clouds" (1 Thessalonians 4:17)—that we will be reunited with Christ, who is "the bread of life" (John 6:35). And according to John, "When [Christ] shall appear, we shall be like him; for we shall see him as he is" (1 John 3:2).

In other words, it is only after this process of being harvested (through conversion), threshed (through trials), winnowed (through sanctification), and gathered into the barn (in Zion) that we too can be transformed into bread and become like Jesus Christ, preparatory to meeting Him at His Second Coming.

# Acknowledgments

I WISH TO EXPRESS APPRECIATION TO MANY PEOPLE FOR THEIR contribution to this work. Gina Swapp, Daniel Hogan, Julie Heaps, and Liz Kazandzhy for editing, Shawnda Craig for cover design, John McNaughton for allowing me to use his incredible painting "Parting the Veil" on my book cover, and Dick Heath for giving a young missionary the framework of events pertaining to the last days that led to this study. Finally, I wish to thank my family for their support and encouragement in this process.

# About the Author

Richard Brunson's passion for studying and teaching the gospel was ignited during his mission in Washington, DC, in 2002–2004. It was here that he engaged in enriching discussions with a fellow Church member who was interested in the signs of the times. These conversations sparked a curiosity in Richard that blossomed into a lifelong passion. Upon returning home from his mission, Richard began reading every book and article he could find on the subject, and before long, he had amassed a valuable collection of insights that he felt needed to be organized and shared with the world. Ultimately, this twenty-year endeavor eventually led to the publication of a book on the Second Coming.

In addition to learning about the signs of the times, Richard also enjoys studying other gospel topics, including Book of Mormon geography, the Creation and Fall, and other ancient scriptures. He shares his research and insights on these subjects and more at his blog found at www.LDSTheology.com.

In his professional career, Richard studied accounting and earned his bachelor's degree from the University of Utah in 2008 and completed his master's degree in 2011. Richard currently works as an accountant and is the owner of a successful bookkeeping firm that provides tailored financial services to over 300 small businesses across the United States. Richard is also an avid chess player and enjoys dedicating his free time to volunteering as a chess coach for youth. He currently resides in Utah with his wife and three daughters.

Scan to visit

www.LDSTheology.com.